PLANKTON AND FISHERIES

PLANKTON AND FISHERIES

Edited by

Dr. Vishwas Balasaheb Sakhare
Associate Professor and Head
Post Graduate
Department of Zoology
Yogeshwari Mahavidyalaya
Ambajogai - 431 517
Maharashtra (INDIA)

Dr. Hansraj Kashinath Jadhav
Assistant Professor and Head
Post Graduate
Department of Zoology
Arts, Science and Commerce College
Naldurg - 413 602
Maharashtra (INDIA)

&

Dr. Shyam Sampatrao Jadhav
Associate Professor and Head
Department of Zoology
Vasant Mahavidyalaya
Kaij - 431 123
Maharashtra (INDIA)

DPH

DISCOVERY PUBLISHING HOUSE PVT. LTD.
INDIA

Published by:

Namit Wasan

DISCOVERY PUBLISHING HOUSE PVT. LTD.

4383/4B, Ansari Road, Darya Ganj
New Delhi-110 002 (India)
Phone : +91-11-23279245, 43596064-65
Fax : +91-11-23253475
E-mail : discoverypublishinghouse@gmail.com
namitwasan9@gmail.com
sales@discoverypublishinggroup.com

website: www.discoverypublishinggroup.com

***First Edition:* 2017**

ISBN: 978-93-5056-811-8

Plankton and Fisheries

Printed at:
Infinity Imaging Systems
Delhi

Acknowleldgements

This volume is the compilation of eleven research and review articles contributed by senior faculty members of Indian universities and scientific institutions. With its application oriented and inter-disciplinary approach, we hope that the students, teachers, researchers, scientists, policy-makers and environmental lawyers will find this volume much more useful.

Editors are grateful to the following under mentioned distinguished scientists and other fellow colleagues for their constant encouragements, suggestions, valuable guidelines and necessary help. These distinguished, beloved scientists and well wishers are Dr. Indranil Ghosh of West Bengal University of Animal and Fishery Sciences, Kolkata (West Bengal), Dr. Satyendranath Maitra of Acharya Prafulla Chanadra College, New Barrackpore (West Bengal), Dr. Bidhan Chandra Patra of Vidyasagar University, Paschim Mednipur, (West Bengal), Dr. Tapas Kumar Dutta of Bankura Sammilani College, Bankura (West Bengal), Dr. R.K. Sadawarte and Dr. S.L. Bhandkoli of College of Fisheries, Shirgaon, Ratnagiri (Maharashtra), Dr. V.R. Sadawarte of Marine Biological Station, Zadgaon, Ranagiri (Maharashtra), Dr. A.C. Kumbhar and P.H. Agarwal of Shankarrao Mohite Mahavidyalaya, Akluj (Maharashtra), Dr. S.V. Khandke and Dr. P.R. Kanthale of Nutan Mahavidyalaya, Selu (Maharashtra) and Dr. S.G. Jetithor of Arts, Science and Commerce College, Naldurg (Maharashtra).

We thank to publisher Shri Tilak Wasan of Discovery Publishing House Pvt. Ltd., New Delhi for taking pains in bringing out the book.

We are grateful to our family members for helping us by several ways and encouraging us for publication of this volume.

– Editors

Contents

PLANKTON AND FISHERIES
Edited by: **V.B. Sakhare; H.K. Jadhav** and **S.S. Jadhav**
Edition: **2017**
ISBN : 978-93-5056-811-8
Published by: **Discovery Publishing House Pvt. Ltd., New Delhi (India)**

1

Food and Feeding Habits of Marine Fishes
A Review

Vishwas Balasaheb Sakhare
Post Graduate Department of Zoology
Yogeshwari Mahavidyalaya, Ambajogai - 431 517.

Studies on food and feeding habits of an organism are one of the foremost aspects in biology (Qasim, 1972), and the analysis of stomach content has become a standard practice providing important insight into fish feeding pattern and quantitative assessment of food habits is part of fisheries management. Accurate description of diets and feeding habits also provide the basis for understanding trophic interactions in aquatic food webs. Diets of an organism represent an integration of many important ecological components that include: behaviour, condition, habitat use, energy intake and inter/intra specific interactions.

The food requirements at various stages of life history of fishes differ in time and space beyond doubt as several studies on the food and feeding habits of fishes from various habitats reflect. Research on the diet helps in understanding suitably the production, habits, intensity of feeding and the ecological role of fish population, which are helpful in defining the trophic status and the pattern of growth rate of fish (Mohanraj, 2000).

The diet of fishes changes with a number of factors which are extrinsic or intrinsic and thus information on diet of fishes is important to understand the basic functioning of fish assemblages which are important for developing ecosystem based fisheries management models (Hanson and Chouinard 2002; Kulbicki *et al.* 2005).

A better understanding of the relationship between the fish species and its food item is essential for forecasting the abundance and exploitation of the stock. Information on the principal prey organism and the preference or dietary overlap between years, classes or different species dwelling in the same or comparable habitats can be gained through food and feeding studies (Legand and Rivaton, 1969; Clarke, 1980). The quantity and quality of food consumed help to determine the fecundity of the year classes as well as the growth rate and the time of sexual maturity, survival of larval stages and ultimately the lifespan of fish (Nikolskii, 1969).

Some fishes feed on plants (herbivorous), others feed on animals (carnivorous), while a large number of fishes derive their requirements from animals as well as plants (omnivorous). A few fishes depend for their nutrition entirely on zooplankton and phytoplankton. These fishes are known as plankton feeders. The plant material consumed by fishes included unicellular algae, filamentous algae, and portions of higher aquatic plants. The animals consumed by fishes are the mussels, insects, larvae, smaller fishes, worms, crustaceans, frogs and tadpoles. This article has been prepared with a view to sum up all those previously documented information on food and feeding habits of marine fishes.

1. *Harpodon nehereus:* Prawns and shrimps formed the most predominant food of the fish. 60.3 per cent of the bulk of its food consisted of this item. The young ones formed 17.5 per cent of the total gut contents which shows the marked cannibalistic habits of the fish. 19.6 per cent of the guts had this item. Other fishes (*Coilia dussumieri, Coilia ramcartii, Anchoviella tri, Anchoviella sp, Mugil parsia, Mugil tade, Mugil speigleri, Trichiurus haumela, Gadusia chapra, Pama pama, Bregmacerus macclellandi, Pseudapocryptes lanceolatus*) together forms the next item of importance as an article of diet and constituted 10.9 per cent of the total gut contents. Megalopa larvae formed 7.1 per cent of the bulk of the gut contents and occurred in 10.3 per cent of the guts examined. Other items that were consumed by the fish were plant matter and detritus (Pillay, 1953).

Vinaya Kumar *et al.* (2012) analysed diet composition, feeding dynamics and proximate composition of *H.nehereus* along Sunderban area of West Bengal. They observed prawns, small Bombay duck fish, small pelagic fishes, plant matter, zooplankton, crustacean larvae, sand, mud and miscellaneous items in the gut of *H.nehereus*.

2. *Rastrelliger kanagurta:* Studies on food and feeding of mackerel indicated a planktonic diet with dominance of copepods and presence of diatoms, dinophysids, crustaceans, molluscan larvae, algae, amphipods and miscellaneous items (Bimachar and George 1952; Pradhan 1956; Rao and Rao 1957; Noble 1962; Venkataraman and Mukundan 1970; Sivadas and Bhaskaran, 2009).

It feeds on pelagic crustaceans including copepods, fishes, sand and scales (Nath *et al.* 2015). The presence of sand grains and fish scales in mackerel stomach has been reported by Devanesan and Chidambaram (1953) and Kutty (1965).

According to Devanesan and Chindambaram (1953), mackerel supplements its diet of planktonic organisms by feeding occasionally on dead and decaying fishes at the bottom and at times, fish scales and sand grains.

Noble (1962) studied the food and feeding habits of the *Rastrelliger kanagurta* at Karwar and reported plankton as the exclusive diet of mackerel. The main food components recorded in the gut were diatoms, algae, dinoflagellates, tintinnids, *Noctiluca miliaris*, polychaete larvae, molluscan larvae, eggs and larvae of decapods crustacean, eggs and nauplii of copepods, cirripede nauplii and cypris larvae, cladocerans, copepods, chaetognathus, appendiacularians, other zooplankton elements, fish eggs and larvae, fish scales and sand.

Ganga (2010) observed highest active feeding during monsoon. Among maturity stages, feeding activity was high even in ripe and spent stages. The feeding intensity declined in the largest size groups (>231 mm) during the monsoon and post monsoon seasons but in the pre-monsoon season even large size groups were found to be actively feeding.

3. *Sardinella longiceps:* It is pre-dominantly a phytoplankton feeder which is indicated by the presence by extremely fine straining mechanism provided by the well developed gill rakers (Kagwade, 1964).

It mainly feeds on diatoms (*Coscinodiscus* spp., *Fragilria oceanica*, *Biddulphia* spp., *Pleurosigma* spp., *Nitzschia* spp and *Rhizosolenia* spp., *Asterlonella japonica*, *Bacteriastrum hylum*, *Dithylum* sp., *Hemidiscus* sp, *Planktonella* sp., *Thalassiothrix* sp and *Triceratium* sp), Dinophyceae (*Dinophysis caudate*, *Prorocentrum micans*, *Ceratium fusus*, *Ceratium furca*, *Ceratium massiliense*, *Caratium tripos*, *Peridinium*, *Pyrophacus*, and *Ornithocercus*) and tintinnids (Dulkhed, 1962). Zooplankters usually occurred only in a very small numbers and among them copepods are important (Dulkhed 1962; Kagwade 1964).

The abundance of diatom *Fragilaria oceanica* is said to indicate abundance of oil sardine in coastal waters (Jayaprakash, 2004). The food of adults of Madras coast consist of small sized crustaceans like: copepods, ostracods, lucifer and larval prawns; larval bivalves, polychaete larvae, sorgestids and a few diatoms and algae. Food of post larvae of oil sardine consist of diatoms and algae (Jayapraksh, 2004).

4. *Terapon jarbua:* Manoharan *et al.* (2012) studied stomach content analysis of this species from Parangipettai coast and classified the species as euryphagus carnivorous. It feeds on polychaetes, fish, crustaceans, phytoplankton, bivalves, gastropods, zooplankton, sand grains and miscellaneous items like: algal filaments and other plant and animal materials.

5. *Cynoglossus macrostomus:* The food and feeding habits of Malabar sole *Cynoglossus macrostomus* occurring along the coastal seas off Kerala was

documented by Jayaprakash (2000). The fish is mainly adapted to a bottom habitat feeds on polychaetes and detritus, amphipods, copepods, small molluscs and foraminifera. The occurrence of these items indicated that the fish is a carnivorous detritus feeder (Jayaprakash, 2000). Active feeding was found immediately after spawning during October-November and February-March. Since the detritus is an important food component followed by other macrobenthos the fish can safely be placed between trophic level I and II (Jayaprakash, 2000).

In malabar sole the visual factor is not involved when feeding detritus, but this is an important factor while feeding on polychaetes, copepods and amphipods (Jayaprakash, 2000).

The diet of this species primarily consists of detritus, fishes, crustaceans, molluscs, foraminiferans, worms, diatoms and sand. Detritus was the most important item of gut (Abdu Rhiman, 2006). Fishes with poor feeding condition dominated in all the seasons. During the pre-monsoon and monsoon seasons, fishes with poor feeding condition were more compared to the post-monsoon. Generally, actively feeding fishes were very rare in all seasons (Abdu Rahiman, 2006).

6. *Cynoglossus arel:* Khalil and Ibrahim (2016) studied the pattern of food and feeding habits of *Cynoglossus arel* from Karachi coast of Pakistan. *C. arel* is a carnivorous in nature, which mainly feed upon crustaceans, molluscs, polychaetes, and fishes. Crustaceans and molluscs are the most favored diet of *C. arel*. Analysis of stomach contents showed the occurrence (in percentage) of polychaetes (8.12%), crustaceans (17.56%), molluscs (9.31%), fish (0.84%), sand-mud (10.39%) and miscellaneous items (53.76%).
7. *Sillago sihama:* Taghavi *et al.* (2012) reported from Northern Persian Gulf that *S. sihama* is planktivorous and feeding on a wide range of food of planktonic and benthic organisms. Diatoms, blue-green algae, and dinoflagellates constituted main food of plant origin. Diatoms were found to be the most preferable food of plant origin where it occurred in more than 60.8 per cent of food item by number and 59.5 per cent by occurrence. Crustacean including crabs and their larvae, shrimps, copepods, eggs and larval forms comprised the maximum part of the food of animal origin.

This species is carnivorous (Khan *et al.* 2014) which feeds on crustaceans, teleosts, molluscs, echinoderms and polychaetes. Fish changes its food habit with the change in season. Juveniles of *Sillago sihama* feed mainly on crustaceans like prawns and crabs and polychaetes and occasionally on echinoderms and molluscs. The adults mainly feed on crustaceans, molluscs, polychaetes, echinoderms and teleosts and occasionally on poriferans, oligochaetes and other minor phyla (Khan *et al.* 2014).

According to Yeragi and Yeragi (2015) diatoms act as the most preferable food of plant origin in both the life stages like juvenile and adult in all the season, Diatoms, blue-green algae and dinoflagellates constituted main food of plant origin. Diatoms were found to be the most preferable food during starvation period of monsoon due to unexpected water currents. During monsoon, the habit of food and feeding was disturbed for short time. The feeding intensity of juvenile was notice that on increasing along with increase in size group. Crustacean including shrimps, crabs, their larvae, copepods eggs, and larval forms comprised the maximum part of the food of animal origin. It was concluded that *Sillago sihama* in the coastal waters of Mithbav is planktonivorous and feeding on a wide range of food of planktonic and benthic organisms (Yeragi and Yergai, 2015).

8. *Scomberomorus guttatus:* Devaraj (1998) carried out systematic investigation on the food and feeding habits of the spotted seer *S. guttatus* from the Northern Gulf of Mannar and Palk Bay along the southeast coast of India. The spotted seer is essentially a surface feeder. It feeds on a limited number of species, of which the sardines are the most important and the whitebaits the next. The shift from whitebaits which constitute the exclusive diet of the young, to sardines which form the major food of the adult.
9. *Euthynnus affinis*: It is a coastal tuna, occurring in waters of 0 to 200 meters depth range in the pelagic realm. Diet of *E. affinis* predominately consisted of three groups *i.e.*, fish, crustacean larvae and molluscs. Crustacean larvae dominated the prey list both by number and occurrence. The crustacean larvae included brachyuran megalopa larvae and crablets (45%), stomatopod alima larvae (21%), shrimp larvae (13%) and phyllosoma larvae of scyllarid lobsters (0.1%). Fishes and molluscs contributed only about 4 per cent and 2 per cent respectively in total diet. Crustacean larvae predominately occurred in the guts across all the size group samples (Gupta *et al*. 2014). Earlier reports on *E. affinis* from the south-west coast indicate lesser quantity of crustacean larvae (Kumaran, 1964).
10. *Lepturacanthus savala*: Pakhmode and Mohite (2014) studied the feeding biology of *L. savala* off Ratnagiri coast, Maharashtra and reported this species as carnivorous. It feeds on fish, crustaceans, cephalopods etc. Fishes were observed to form important food item and were mainly recorded in *L.savala* of the size group 30-40 cm to 60-70 cm. Cannibalism has also been recorded by the presence of juvenile ribbonfishes in the gut of bigger *L. savala*. Index of fullness showed a peak in September but it was low during April and November suggesting probable cessation of feeding during spawning season. The period of low digested matter empty guts coincided with the two spawning peaks, suggesting that the fish preferred not feed during the spawning months (Pakhmode and Mohite, 2014).

The food of this species is mainly constituted by prawns (*Parapeneeopsis sculptllis*) and fishes (*Harpondon nehereus, Setipinna* sp; *Anchoviella* sp; *Trichiurus* sp, *L. savala*). Cannibalism was also noticed (CMFRI, 1986).

The food and feeding habits of this species from the Palk Bay and Gulf of Mannar were studied by James (1967). The results indicated that fishes form its major diet, followed by: Acetes, and prawn. Squilla, Lucifer, Octopus, Sepia and zoea larvae were preyed upon whenever available.

11. *Trichiurus lepturus*: Pillai (1974) studied food and feeding habit of *T. lepturus* from the Trawler catches off Tuticorin (Gulf of Mannar) and reported intensive feeding of this species during the months of October and November. In August and December the feeding is observed moderate. During the remaining period feeding appears to be poor.

Food and feeding of the ribbonfish *T. lepturus* off Karnataka, south-west coast was studied by Rohit *et al.* (2015). *Acetes* sp., *Stolephorous devisi, Loligo* sp., *Saurida tumbil, Sardinella longiceps* and *Decapterus russelli* were the major food items. Juveniles of *T. lepturus* and unidentified fish as well as shrimp remains were found occasionally in the gut indicating cannibalistic behaviour. Higher feeding intensity in terms of stomach fullness index was observed during April, June and October and lower values during November and December.

Venkataraman (1944) and Prabhau (1955) observed prawns as one of the main food elements of *T.lepturus*.

Vijaraghavan (1951) from Madras listed teleostean, acetes, lucifer, mysids, amphipods, copepods, ostracods, aergestids, zoea of brachyera, megalops of crabs, polychaetes, Leptocephalus along with algae, green matter, prawns, cumacea, hermit crabs, Squilla, copepod nauplii, Sepia, larval gastropods and bivalve larvae.

12. *Thunnus albacares:* The food of yellowfin tuna, *Thunnus albacores* caught by longlines off the east coast of India was studied by Rohit *et al.* (2010). *T.albacares* caught by the longline were found to be non-selective feeders, foraging on micronektonic, pelagic or benthic organisms available in the epipelagic waters. Teleosts, crabs, squids and shrimps were the major component of food items. *Priacanthus harmrur* was the most preyed upon fish, followed by the swimming crab *Charybdis smithii*, the squid *Sthenoteuthis ovalaniensis* and prawn *Solenocera hextii*. Being a large pelagic predator, it formed an important link in the food chain of the ocean system and also formed a good collector of the less exploited micronekton organisms of the deep scattering layer (Rohit *et al.* 2010).

Rohit and Rammohan (2009) studied fishery and biology of this species along Andhra coast and reported crustaceans (42.5%), fishes (34.7%), and cephalopods (15.5%) as the main food components of this fish.

13. *Thunnus obescus:* Fishes, cephalopods and crustaceans formed the major food items. This species feed all the time where during the day they swim more in deeper waters and at night they swim at the surface. The tuna swims or moves vertically through the water to catch their prey. This strategy allows them to swim further into the water to catch their prey. They feed mostly in the deeper waters during the day and feed more to the surface of the water at night.
14. *Epinephelus diacanthus:* Crustaceans and fish formed the major prey category. Molluscs and detritus were the least preferred diet component. Gravimetric analysis of stomach contents revealed that 30.2 per cent of the diet consist of benthic crabs. Thus the most important crustacean component was benthic crabs, followed by: *A.indicus* and *Oratosquilla nepa*. Unidentified fishes formed the major teleost component. Teleosts appeared in minor quantities were *Trichiurus lepturus, Nemipterus japonicus, Stolephorus* spp and soles.

    Active feeding was noticed in the pre-monsoon season when a relative decrease in empty stomach was observed. Fishes in poorly fed condition were relatively higher throughout the season. There was no significant variation in the feeding intensities among seasons (Abdu Rahiman, 2006).
15. *Pseudosciaena diacanthus:* Prawns appear to be the most favourtie food item of the juvenils, the common species met with being *Parapenaeopsis stylifera, P. sculptilis, Penaeus* sp., and *Palaemon* sp., followed by teleosts *Otolithus ruber, Johnius dussumieri, J.carutta* and *Opisthopterus tardoore*, crabs and stomatopods. *Acetes indicus* and some molluscs formed a small portion in the diet. Feeding intensity was slightly higher during the period of September to November (Suseelan and Nair, 1969). Rao (1963) observed a period of high feeding intensity during September-December.

    The adult fish is piscivorous, teleosts constituting more than 63 per cent in the total food. The common species were *Ilisha filigera, Thrissocles sp., Opisthopterus tardoore, Otolithus ruber, Johnius dussumieri, Nemipterus japonicus, Lactarius lactarius, Caranx* sp., and *Leiognathus* sp. Prawns (*Metapenaeus affinis* and *Palaemon tenuipes*) were next in importance and other organisms recorded were stomatopods, crabs, bivalves, gastropods and cephalopods (Suseelan and Nair, 1969).
16. *Otolithoides brunneus:* It is carnivorous, feeding mainly on prawns, *Acetes* and teleosts, with small quantities of cephalopods and other crustaceans. The prawns were found to consist mostly of *Parapenaeopsis stylifera* and *Solenocera* sp. The feeding intensity of the juveniles was poor during October to February. Stomach content analysis of a few adults indicated a diet consisting mainly of teleosts and a fair amount of prawns along with some cephalopods. The fishes met with were *Coilia dussumieri, Trichiurus* sp., and *Harpodon nehereus*. The prawn species recorded were *Metapenaeus* sp and *Palaemon tenuipes* (Suseelan and Nair, 1969).

17. *Otolithes ruber:* Pillai (1983) studied biometry, food and feeding and spawning habits of this species along the Porto Novo coast and reported this species as highly carnivorous and selective feeder. Food intake was intense in lower size groups. The larger size groups of fishes exhibited more or less moderate feeding, where as the intermediate size groups were in poor feeding condition.

The main food components observed by Pillai (1983) were prawn remains, mysids, Acetes, Squilla, apogonid fishes and juveniles of sciaenids. The unidentifiable food items were categorised as semi-digested matter due to their extreme degree of digestion.

Nair (1979) also studied food and feeding habit of *O.ruber* from Calicut and observed irregular periodicity in feeding. According to him the young ones feed mainly at the surface on *Acetes* and mysiids, while the adult fish feeds at the bottom chiefly on prawns and teleosts.

18. *Otolithus argenteus:* According to Bapat and Bal (1952) prawns from the main diet of *O.argenteus*. It appears to be a surface plankton feeder. In the more advanced forms it appears that the fish food is taken in increasing percentages until finally it forms the major item of the food of the adult. The fish food mainly consisted of *Bregmaceros macclellandi* and *Pellona* sp.

19. *Johnius dussumieri:* This is a carnivorous fish, preferring a benthic habitat, as evidenced by the presence of polychaetes, gastropod shells, sand grains and mud in the stomach. Prawns, *Metapenaeus* spp and teleosts, *Bregmaceros mcclellandi* and *Leiognathus* sp formed an important component of the diet with fairly high percentage of stomatopods. The other organisms that formed part of its diet were Acetes, crabs, amphipods, copepods, gastropods, cephalopods and nereid polychaetes. The feeding intensity was low except during post spawning periods, September to October and March to May (Suseelan and Nair, 1969).

20. *Johnius carutta:* It is carnivorous, feeding mainly on free living crustaceans at the bottom like: penaeid prawns, *Acetes indicus*, portunid crabs and amphipods, fishes and molluscs like: pteropods and gastropods (Suseelan and Nair,1969).

Swamy Kumar *et al.* (2015) categorised this species as euryphagic. Free living crustaceans formed the major food in which squilla, shrimps, Acetes spp and small crabs dominated. Other crustacean identified were *Parapenaeopsis* sp, *Metapenaeus monoceros, Penaeus monodon, Aristeus* spp., *Solenocera* sp., *Argulus* sp., *Albunea symnista*, hermit crab, megalopa (crab larvae), shrimp post-larvae, amphipods, isopods and copepods. The other food items identified were teleost fish, polychaetes, molluscs, brachiopods and miscellaneous items (Swamy Kumar *et al.* 2015).

21. *Johnius axillaris:* According to Suseelan and Nair (1969), this species is carnivorous feeding mainly on fishes and invertebrates living at bottom. The diet of *J.axillaris* seems primarily based on teleosts and prawns supplemented by a wide variety of other organisms like: Acetes, stomaopods, amphipods, isopods, copepods, polychaetes, cephalopods and salps (Suseelan and Nair, 1969).

The feeding intensity was found to be slightly higher in the months of May and December although gorged stomachs were observed occasionally in other months also (Suseelan and Nair, 1969).

22. *Johnius glaucus:* The proportion of fishes with active and moderate feeding reduced with increasing length. There was a gradual decrease in the occurrence of crustacean in the diet of various size groups. The percentage composition ranged from 53.4 per cent in the size group 200-209 mm TL to 42 per cent in the size group 240-249 mm TL. The percentage occurrence of fishes was 51 per cent in the size group 220-229 mm TL. The fish is a carnivore preferring a benthic habitat. The food of *J.glaucus* is mainly composed of fishes and crustaceans.

Acetes spp., prawns, *Metapenaeus* spp., and *Squilla* were representatives of the crustacean group. Fishes comprised *Bregmaceras* sp, *Coilia* sp., *Cynoglossus* sp., and ribbon fish. The other organisms that formed part of the diet were crabs, copepods, *Sepia* sp., *Loligo* sp., and *Squilla*. The feeding intensity was low except during the post-spawning periods (September to October and March to May) (Thangavelu *et al.* 2012).

Raje (2000) studied the gut content of *J.glaucus* and reported crustaceans and fishes in the diet of this species. According to him, *Acetes* spp., *Solenocera* spp., and other penaeid prawns constituted the crustacean duet, while *Coilia dussumieri* and fish larvae formed the fish component.

23. *Grammoplites suppositus*: In this species crustaceans and fishes are the important food items. Molluscs, sea urchins and detritus were insignificant in the diet. When considering the frequency of occurrence, penaeid prawns (28.3%), followed by benthic crabs (26.4%) and unidentified fishes (16%) were dominant. The most abundant prey by number was benthic crabs (27.9%), followed by: *Acetes indicus* (23.2%) and *S.choprai* (16.2/5).

The highest percentage of empty stomach was observed during the pre-monsoon. The diet of *G.suppositus* of 141-165mm length group comprised largely of unidentified fishes and *C.macrostomus*. Fishes larger than 165 mm showed higher percentage of crustae and initially for *O.nepa* (166-190 mm) and later for *S. choprai* and benthic crabs. Cannibalism was found in 141-155 mm and 216-240 mm length groups. The preferred diets of fish of 216-240 mm were benthic crabs, followed by *S. choprai* and penaeid prawns.

Consumption of benthic crabs and *S.choprai* increased above 166 mm length. In the length group 241-265 mm *S.choprai* and benthic crabs were dominant and fish groups were considerably reduced (Abdu Rahiman, 2006).

24. *Priacanthus hamrur*: The gut content analyses indicated a highly carnivorous nature of this fish (Thangavelu, *et al.* 2012). It feeds on crustaceans, cephalopods and polychaetes. *Acetes indicus* was the most important crustacean. Other crustaceans occurred in minor quantities were *Solenocera choprai*, penaeid prawns, benthic crabs, copepods, amphipods and crustacean larvae. Cephalopods represented by *Loligo duvauceli* and polychaetes occurred rarely. Most of the young ones of *P.harmrur* fed on small sized *A.indicus* (Abdu Rahiman, 2006).

During pre-monsoon and post-monsoon seasons, *P.hamrur* is monophagous to *A.indicus*, whereas, in the monsoon, detritus followed by amphipods were largely consumed. Unidentified fishes and *L.duvauceli* respectively constituted the second rank in the post-monsoon and pre-monsoon seasons (Abdu Rahiman, 2006).

25. *Johnieops sina:* Fishes, molluscs, crustaceans, foraminiferans, diatoms and detritus formed the diet of *J.sina.* Crustaceans were the most important and highly preferred food followed by: fishes. Polychaetes, foraminiferans and diatoms were the least ranked food items. *Acetes indicus*, *Oratosquilla nepa* and unidentified fishes were the highly preferred prey component in the diet of *J.sina* (Abdu Rahiman, 2006).

The diet of *J.sina* during the pre-monsoon season was characterised by the large proportion of crustacean (especially crustacean appendages and *Acetes indicus*). Similarly, largest proportion of detritus was observed in the pre-monsoon season. During the monsoon season largest proportion of fishes with the dominance of unidentified fishes and cycloid scales. Copepods and detritus also formed significant proportion in the monsoon season (Abdu Rahiman, 2006).

Large sized crustaceans were dominant in larger fishes and small sized crustaceans were observed in smaller fishes (Abdu Rahiman, 2006).

J. sina mainly feed on crustaceans followed by teleosts fishes and the juveniles mainly feed on Acetes. Highest percentage of penaeid prawns and fishes was observed in 190-199 mm and 160-169 mm length groups, respectively. Intense feeding in male fishes was observed during April, September, October and November, whereas the females fed intensively during December and January (Venugopal *et al.* 2014).

26. *Otolithes cuvieri:* It is a carnivore feeding on a mixed diet consisting of teleosts fishes and crustaceans (Thangavelu *et al.* 2012).

According to Manojkumar (2003) *O.cuvieri* is carnivorous, mainly feeding on *Acetes* spp., penaeid prawns, deep sea prawns, fishes, stomatopods, molluscs, isopods, copepods and fish larvae. The fishes showed preference for teleost fishes as they grew. The intensity of feeding was higher during the pre-monsoon and post-monsoon months. It was poor in juveniles and mature fishes.

According to Telvekar *et al.* (2006) this species is carnivorous and it feeds mainly on fishes and crustaceans. The identifiable food items constituted fishes like: *Harpodon nehereus, Cynoglossus arel* and *Coilia dussumieri*. Higher feeding intensity coincided with the advancement of the reproductive process and poor feeding with commencement of the spawning activity.

Gut content of this species comprised mainly fishes, crustaceans, cephalopods and detritus. *Acetes indicus* was the most important prey of *O.cuvieri*. Among the fishes, *N. mesoprion* and *Stolephorus* spp., were the most important prey. Diet during the pre-monsoon season was mainly constituted by *A.indicus* and penaeid prawns and among teleosts, other teleosts and *Bregmaceros* spp., were significant. In addition to *A.indicus,* which formed bulk of the diet in the post-monsoon, proportion of teleosts such as: *N.mesoprion* and *Stolephorus* sp., was also significant to *O.cuvieri* (Abdu Rahiman, 2006).

27. *Nemipterus japonicus:* According to Suresh Kumar and Mohite (2013) this species is a predaceous bottom feeder carnivore and feeds mainly on crustaceans and fishes. Molluscs, polychaetes, unidentified matter and semi-digested matter were the other minor food items. In size groups 40-60mm, 60-80 mm, 100-120 mm to 160-180 mm size group, crustaceans dominated over the other items of food. Increase in the feeding intensity was observed during February-March and August. This can be associated with the higher requirement of energy for the development of gonads and the spawning.

Food of *N.japonicus* consists of fishes, crustaceans and molluscs (Abdu Rahiman, 2006). Crustaceans were the most important prey category, *Solenocera choprai, Acetes indicus* and benthic crabs being the most important of gut contents. Teleosts were second in rank, *Stolephorus* spp., and unidentified fishes being the most important. Among molluscs, *Loligo duvauceli* was significant in the diet. The diet composition of *N.japonicus* varied season wise. In the pre-monsoon season *A.indicus* and *S.choprai* were almost equally ranked first followed by: *L.duvauceli* and benthic crabs. Juveniles of large predators such as: *S.tumbil, S.undosquamis, N.mesoprion* and *Pseudorhombus spp.,* appeared only in monsoon. In the post-monsoon season, *Stolephorus* spp., were highly preferred, but was only next to *S.choprai* and benthic crabs. Proportion of *A.indicus* considerably reduced in the post-monsoon season due to thr increasing consumption of benthic crabs and fish groups (Abdu Rahiman, 2006).

Thangavelu *et al.* (2012) observed crustaceans (Acetes spp., penaeid prawns, crabs, squilla), juvenile of fishes (flatheads, lizard fishes and fish larvae) in the stomach contents of *N.japonicus*. The study revealed that *N.japonicus* is a carnivore.

28. *Nemipterus mesoprion: Acetes* spp formed the most dominant food item followed by: penaeid prawns, other crustaceans, fishes and molluscs (Thangavelu *et al*. 2012). Authors revealed that *N.mesoprion* is a demersal carniovore, whose diet is mainly composed of crustaceans, fishes and molluscs.

Joshi (2005) reported that *N.mesoprion* off Cochin were mainly feeding on fishes (*Stolephorus* spp., and *Leiognathus* spp.,) and crustaceans such as: prawns, mysids, crabs, squilla, *Acetes* spp., and deep sea prawns.

According to Raje (1996) *N.mesoprion* off Veraval is a carnivore and the diet composed of crustaceans, fishes, molluscs and annelids.

Rao (1989) also reported that *N.mesoprion* off Visakhapatnam is carnivorous, feeding on crustaceans and teleosts.

It mainly feeds on fishes, crustaceans and molluscs (Abdu Rahiman, 2006). Crustaceans formed the most important prey group, followed by teleosts fishes and molluscs. Of the crustaceans, *Acetes indicus* and *Solenocera choprai* were most important. Fish with active feeding was observed to be higher in the monsoon and post-monsoon seasons and, fishes with poor feeding were higher in the monsoon. The diet of *N. mesoprion* was uniform throughout the year. *A.indicus* and *S.choprai* were highly important to the fish. In the pre-monsoon season, *A.indicus* followed by *S.choprai* and *Bregmaceros* spp formed the major diet. Low level of cannibalism was observed in the pre-monsoon when it fed on the juveniles of the same species. During the monsoon, both *A.indicus* and *S.choprai* formed the main component of diet. In the post-monsoon, *A.indicus* was highly preferred followed by *S.choprai* and unidentified fishes. Importance of *L.duvauceli* and unidentified fishes gradually increased from the pre-monsoon to post-monsoon season (Abdu Rahiman, 2006).

29. *Pampus argenteus:* Diet of this fish consists of crustaceans, fishes, diatoms, worms and detritus. *P.argenteus* fed most often on crustaceans and copepods. Among fish items, cycloid scales and in diatoms, *Nitzschia* spp were important. The most frequently occurred prey item was detritus, followed by: copepods and cycloid scales.

The proportion of fishes with poor feeding condition was high throughout the season. Their proportion was highest in the pre-monsoon followed by the monsoon season. Percentage of empty stomachs was higher in large fishes of length group 271-300 mm. Fishes with active feeding was observe to be highest in 241-270 mm. Fishes with moderately fed stomachs were highest in younger fishes. Percentage of poorly fed fishes was higher in all length groups.

The small sized fishes (<120 mm) ate mainly detritus and copepods; mysids and *Nitzschia* spp., were also important for this group and cycloid scales ranked 3rd and 4th important prey respectively in 121-150 mm size groups. Fishes of the size group 151-180 mm exclusively fed on detritus. In sizes >150 mm copepods formed an important item in the diet and simultaneously a relatively decrease in proportion of detritus was observed. Detritus and copepods dominated the diet of fishes between 181-210 mm and 211-240 mm. Among the diatoms, *Conscinodiscus* sp formed 3rd ranked prey item in 241-270 mm size group. However, in fish >270 mm, fish remains and amphipods contributed to 3rd and 4th ranked item after copepods and detritus (Abdu Rahiman, 2006).

A Systematic investigation on the food and feeding habits of *Pampus argenteus* was undertaken by Pati (1980) from Bay of Bengal along the Orissa coast. Copepod formed the main food item followed by smaller jelly fishes and phytoplankters. A variety smaller crustacean, polychaetes, fish eggs and fish larvae occurred in minor quantities. The post larvae feed on phytoplankton and a variety of zooplanktonic organisms are added to the diet during subsequent growth.

30. *Parastromateus niger:* Sivaprakasam (1967) studied the food and feeding habits of *P.niger* from Saurashtra coast and observed highly macreted food which was in advanced stage of digestion. Because of this, the specific identification of the food items was difficult and there was also a high proportion of pulpy semi-digested matter (Sivaprakasam, 1967). The study revealed that *P.niger* is carnivorous. It feeds mostly on zooplankton.

The diet of *P.niger* consisted of Thaliceans (42.8%), prawns (14.8%), fish scales (6.7%), crustacean larvae (4.0%), amphipods (3.7%), other crustaceans (1.1%), cuttle fish remains (0.7%), polychaetes (0.4%), medusa (0.2%), semi-digested matter (25.6%).

The smaller fish preferred prawns and stomatopod larvae while the larger fish preferred thaliaceans, amphipods and other crustaceans.

Feeding intensity in general was low. The incidence of empty stomachs was low during October to December and high in the other months (Sivaprakasam, 1967).

31. *Rhyncobatus djiddensis:* This species exhibited monophagy to the extent that crustaceans were the main food of *R.djiddensis*. *A.indicus* was primarily eaten by *R.djiddensis* and formed the most important food item. The second most important component was *Solenocera choprai*. Stomatopods represented by *Oratosquilla nepa* constituted the third most important prey of stomachs. Penaeid prawns and crabs were also observed in stomachs. Feeding was generally higher in smaller length group. Proportion of poorly fed fishes was generally higher in smaller length groups.

During the pre-monsoons and post monsoon seasons, feeding was monophagous to the most important prey, *A.indicus*. Prey items like: crab, unidentified fishes and *C.macrostomus* recorded their highest proportion in pre-monsoon. During the monsoon season, *O.nepa* followed by *S.choprai* and unidentified prawns were highly preferred. Consumption of *L.duvauceli* as well as *Stolephorus* spp., was higher in the monsoon season.

A.indicus formed the most important prey till 601-675 mm length group. For the smaller length group (<300 mm), *O.nepa* was the second most important prey. *S.choprai* consistently made-up the second most important prey from 301-375 mm to 526 to 600 mm length groups. Individuals of 601-675 mm length group preferred *A.indicus* in addition to large proportion of *L.duvauceli* as well as crabs and unidentified fishes. Fishes of the largest length group (>675 mm) were typically piscivorous that fish groups mainly represented by *C.macroctomus* and unidentified fishes were largely consumed to the diet, in addition to the substantial proportion of *A.indicus* (Abdu Rhiman, 2006).

32. *Dascyllus trimaculatus:* It is carnivorous, feeding mainly on crustaceans, amphipods, isopods, polychaetes, nematodes, mollusca, detritus, mud and miscellaneous items (Priyadharsini *et al.* 2012).

Crustaceans formed the major food item of *D.trimaculatus*, followed by polychaetes. Crustaceans exhibited highest percentage during March and food consumption was also highest in March (Al-Zibdah *et al.* 2009).

33. *Stolephorus commersonii:* Arun Kumar *et al.* (2015) have reported the feeding dynamics of this species along the coastal waters of south Andaman and confirmed this species as planktivorous carnivore. It mainly feeds in the pelagic realm on planktonic crustaceans, bivalves, gastropods, and miscellaneous food items. The copepods formed the main prey item. No significant seasonal variation in feeding preference was observed. Lower length classes exclusively fed on planktonic copepods and amphipods whereas the higher length classes fed mainly on postlarval shrimps and planktonic crustaceans. Active feeding was observed during monsoon season.

34. *Arius thalassinus:* It is carnivorous, chiefly feeds on organisms of the benthic epifauna and infauna along with fishes. The diet of this species is mainly opportunistic and carnivorous such as: crustaceans, squids, fishes, detritus, echinoderms, amphipods, sand and mud. The stomach content included a higher percentage of crabs, prawns, polychaetes, bivalves, gastropods and cephalopods (Mohanraj and Prabhu, 2012).

According to Thangavelu *et al.* (2012) this species is carnivorous and food comprises higher percentage of detritus and mostly organisms of the benthic epifauna along with fishes.

Chacko (1949) described this species as omnivorous, feeding at the surface and also browsing at the bottom.

35. *Arius maculates:* It is euryphagus carnivorous fish, mainly feeding on a broad range of planktonic and benthic marine organisms. Manikandarajan *et al.* (2014) reported stomach content analysis of this fish from Parangipettai coast of Tamil Nadu. In the gut portion various food items like: crustaceans, fish and polychaetes, phytoplankton, zooplankton, sand grains, digested matter and miscellaneous were recorded. The feed compositions were in the following order: miscellaneous<crustaceans<fish< polychaetes <sand grains< digested matter <zooplankton <phytoplankton.

According to Mazlan *et al.* (2008) *A.maculatus* is an excellent benthic feeder in muddy water environment. They classified food items in three major categories *i.e.*, macro-zoobenthos, benthic crustacean and mixture of wide spectrum of macro/micro benthic faunas. The presence of maxillary barbells served as an important sensory organ in search for embedded prey in the muddy sediment of the mangrove forest.

36. *Arius jella:* According to Rao (1964) it is omnivorous and voracious feeder. He recorded from its stomach benthic forms like: anemones, polychaetes, crabs, amphipods, anomurans, stomatopods, bivalves and gastropods and indicated the bottom feeding nature.
37. *Arius dussumieri:* It is carnivorous and bottom feeder. Crustaceans and small sized fishes formed the major food item of this fish. Molluscs, polychaetes, sea stars, brittle stars, amphipods, ostracods etc., formed a minor component of the diet of *A.dussumieri* (Deo *et al.* 2010). Devanesan and Chidambaram (1953) mentioned this species as carnivorous benthic feeder, mainly feeding on crustaceans (crabs and prawns). Maximum feeding intensity was observed during post-breeding period (Deo *et al.* 2010).
38. *Lethrinus miniatus:* It is carnivorous. It feeds mainly on crustaceans, echinoderms, molluscs, fishes, crabs and sea urchins. The gut content of this species showed a high percentage of echinoderms and crabs along with shrimp, bivalves, gastropods and fishes (Mohanraj and Prabhu, 2012).
39. *Leiognathus brevirostris:* The main food component was plankton constituted by copepods *Calanus sp.,* and *Eucalanus sp*; amphipods *Melita sp., Eriopsia sp., Podoceru sp.,* diatom *Conscinodiscus sp.,* and *Squilla sp.,* which formed 59.75 per cent of the diet whereas the benthos (nematodes, polychetes, *Nereis sp.,* and Eunice sp., and foraminiferans) and others (shell pisces, sand,mud, fish scales) formed 22.05 per cent and 18.19 per cent respectively (Sebastian *et al.* 2011).

40. *Leiognathus berbis:* Food and feeding habit of *Leiognathus berbis* collected from trawl catches at Toothukudi fishing harbor was studied by Nagarajan (2014). Phytoplanktons, zooplanktons and microinvertebrates constituted the major food of the fish and females were found to be more active feeder than males. Active feeding in males were observed in February and that for females in November. Active feeding was observed in size groups from 81-90 to 111-120 mm in males and 81-90 to 131-140 mm in females. The maturing and matured females fed more actively than the immature and gravid females. Copepods constituted the major food items and were observed in all the months. No remarkable variation in size related selection of food items was observed. The other minor constituents of the diet were foraminiferans, diatom, nematodes, polychaetes, coelenterates, amphipods, Lucifer, fish scales, zoea, mysis and dinoflagellates (Nagarajan, 2014).

41. *Gazza minuta:* The diet of *G.minuta* consists of fish (*Stolephorus devisi, Pseudorhombus sp., Cynoglossus sp., Apogon sp., and Thryssa sp.,*) and small quantity of cuttle fish (*Sepia sp.,*) which together constitute 48.04 per cent while the benthos (*Neris sp., Eunice sp.,* nematodes, *Peneus indicus, Penaeus monodon* and *Parapenaeopsis stylifera*) and plankton (*Calanus sp., Acartia, Conscinodiscus sp., and Asterionella sp., Squilla sp.,* algae) constitute 27.80 per cent and 24.16 per cent respectively (Sebastian *et al.* 2011).

42. *Saurida tumbil:* They are mainly piscivorous, squids and prawns coming next in importance. Among the fish items *Leiognathus sp., Stolephorus spp., Trichiurus spp., Rastrelliger kanagurta, Johnius spp., squrida spp.,* were important (Rao, 1981).

The food of the size group <16 cm consisted of small fishes especially, *Stolephorus spp., Leiognathus spp., Sardinella spp.,* while that of 16-30 and 31-45 cm size groups consisted more of large fishes, comprising mainly *Trichiurus* spp., *Leiognathus* spp., *Upeneus spp., Rastrelliger kanagurta* and carangids.

Cannibalism was observed in all the size groups but it was more pronounced in the size group 31-45 cm. It feed on organisms found on or near the bottom. The feeding intensity increased with the size of the fish (Rao, 1981) The feeding intensity of *S.tumbil* has been found to be low during the spawning period *i.e.,* October-November. Tiews *et al.* (1972) did not observed any seasonal variation in the diet or feeding frequency of *S.tumbil* from Philippine waters. Rao (1981) found that the intensity of feeding in *S.tumbil* was highest in the morning and thereafter gradually declined in the evening followed by a slight rise in the night.

43. *Saurida undosquamis:* Fishes (52.3%) formed the primary food item of *S. undosquamis* mainly comprised of *Decapterus* spp. (23.8%), *Nemipterus* spp. (4.8%) and *Saurida* spp. (2.7%) followed by molluscs (46.8% dominated by *Loligo* spp.) and crustaceans (0.6%) represented by

Solenocera spp., *Parapenaeopsis scuptilis* and *Metapenaeopsis stridulans*. Fishes, molluscs and crustaceans formed the regular food in almost all the months. Fish were the dominant food items during February-May, July-October and December; molluscs in January, June and November; and crustaceans in July (Raje *et al*. 2012).

Teleosts were the dominant food items in the stomach of all the size groups. The presence of bottom dwelling fishes (*Nemipterus* spp., *Saurida* spp., *Apogon* spp., sciaenids, soles, prawns, crabs etc)., and pelagic fishes (*Decapterus* spp., *Stolephorus* spp., *Trichiurus* spp., carangids etc.,) in the gut indicates that *S.undosquamis* feed at the subsurface as well as bottom (Raje *et al*. 2012).

Kadharsha *et al*. (2013) studied feeding and reproductive biology of *Saurida undosquamis* from Parangipettai coast of southeast coast of India. According to them fish is a main food item of this species. The gastrosomatic index was found maximum during post monsoon and minimum during the monsoon season.

44. *Pseudapocryptes elongatus:* The important food substances of this species were found to be benthic diatoms, followed by: blue green algae, detritus, miscellaneous items, plant materials and fish eggs (Mahadevan, 2015).

Among the diatoms the genus *Navicula, Pleurosigma, Gyrosigma, Nitzschia* and *Pinnularia* contributed significantly. The blue green algae consumed are *Anabina sp., Trichodesmium sp., Oscillatoria sp., Lyngba sp.,* and *Chroococcus sp.* The plant materials (root and leaves) of mangrove, salt marsh and seaweeds were also recorded in the gut of *P.elongatus*. *P.elongatus* also feed on juvenile shrimps in aquarium for months.

45. *Bolephthalmus boddarti:* According to Ravi (2013) diatoms formed the major food item in the gut of *B. boddarti* and found around 55 per cent of its diet. Nematodes, polychaetes, algae and fish eggs also found constituting lower percentage. Detritus and mud/sand particles were present in moderate percentages. Active feeding was noticed during January (post monsoon to May (summer) but it was below 50 per cent during June (summer) to September (pre monsoon), whereas during October and monsoon the feeding intensities were found very low. The poor feeding may be due to flood in the mudflats during monsoon season.

46. *Upeneus tragula:* The presence of a pair of barbells just below the symphysis of the lower jaw attached to the tip of the ceratohyal suggests the bottom feeding habits of this species. It feeds on prawns (*Penaeus indicus, P.monodon, Metapenaeus monoceros*), crabs (*Thalamita* sp., *Portunus* sp., *Charybdis* sp., *Porcellana* sp.), Fishes (*Therapon* sp; *Leiognathus* sp., *Anchoviclla* sp.), Isopods (*Sphaeromatriste, S. lerebrans*), copepods (*Acartia* sp., *Calanopia* sp.), bivalves (*Nuculana* sp., *Lithodomus* sp.), decapods larvae (zoea and megalopa stages).

The feeding intensity in case of mature fish was found to be very poor during the months of July to September in first year and June to September in the second year with the exception of August. This low feeding activity in case of mature fish may not be due to the shortage of food items available as the immature fish were found to feed actively during these months on those food items also which occur in case of mature fish coincides with the peak spawning season of the species and suggest a slackening in feeding during spawning seasons (Thomas, 1969).

47. *Upeneus vittatus:* Rabindra Nath (1966) stated that *U.vittatus* feeds voraciously on crustaceans, teleosts, molluscs and polychaetes. The crustacean items were mainly *Acetes erythraeus*, prawns, mysids, lucifers and copepods. He also observed that during the season of zooplankton abundance the fish feed largely on crustaceans while during the period of phytoplankton abundance, it depends almost entirely on teleosts and polychaetes.

Thomas (1969) observed crustaceans as the major food of *U. vittaus*. Among crustaceans prawns, crabs and isopods dominated the stomach contents. The two species of prawns frequently met with were *Penaeus indicus* and *Metapenaeus monoceros*. The common crabs in the food items were *Portunus* sp., and *Thalamita* sp. Isopods were mainly represented by *Sphaeroma* sp., (Thomas, 1969).

The percentage occurrences of bivalves and fishes were comparatively higher in stomach contents of *U. vittaus* than in *U. tragula*. About 19.17 per cent had bivalves and 15.78 per cent had fishes as the major items of food. The fishes recorded in the stomach contents were *Leiognathus* sp., and *Anchoviella* sp., Majority of the bivalves were *Nuculana* sp and *Modiolus* sp. Other molluscs found in a few stomachs were *Cerathium* sp., *Epitomium* sp and *Dentalium* sp. Amphipods, mysids, polychaetes and stomatopods also were found in small quantities. Echinoderms were represented by *Amphipholis squamata* and *Ophiactis* sp., and they were accidental inclusions (Thomas, 1969).

48. *Upeneus luzonius*: Bivalves were found to be the dominant food item (Thomas, 1969). The stomach contents were exclusively bivalves, mostly *Nuculana* sp and *Modiolus* sp. Prawns and crabs were found only in 9.09 per cent and 5.45 per cent of fishes. Isopods, copepods, amphipods, decapod larvae and polychaetes were also found in a few specimens. Fishes were totally absent in the stomach contents (Thomas, 1969).

49. *Upeneus sulphureus*: A detailed investigation on the food spectrum and feeding habit of *Upeneus sulphureus* from coast of Nizampatnam of Andhra Pradesh revealed that this fish is pre-dominantly omnivorous nature, and abundant and important food fish in this area (Krishna *et al.* 2015). The stable food item for this fish was crustaceans and their

larvae, small fishes, polychaetes worms, miscellaneous matter and digested food. The monthly Gastro somatic index ranged from 3 to 12 and the higher values were recorded in the months of June and July months (Krishna *et al.* 2015).

50. *Pteoris volitans:* Priyadharsini *et al.* (2013) stated that *P. volitans* mainly consume crustaceans, fish, polychaetes, nematodes, zooplankton, phytoplankton, bivalves, gastropods, sand, digested matter and miscellaneous items. They also observed a slight difference in feed composition in the males and females. In male *P. volitans* stomach contents as identified feed composition were in the following order *viz;* crustaceans (22.71)>fish (21.11)>zooplankton (17.88)>phytoplankton (13.70)>miscellaneous (13.42)>bivalves (10.98)>polychaetes (10.54)> gastropods (8.55)>sand (8.18)>nematodes (7.93)>digested matter (4.52) and the female fish of *P. volitans* stomach contents as identified feed compositions in the following order *viz;* crustaceans (45.43)>fish (42.22)>zooplankton (35.77)>phytoplankton (27.41)>miscellaneous (26.84)>bivalves (21.97)> sand (16.36)>nematodes (15.85)>digested matter (9.05) respectively.

51. *Pterois russelli:* Priyadharsini *et al.* (2014) studied the food and feeding habits of *Pterois russelli* from South East coast of India and reported fish, crustacean, zooplankton, phytoplankton, polychaetes, nematodes, gastropods, bivalves, sand, digested matter and miscellaneous as the main food items in both the sexes.

In male fish stomach contents were identified in the following order *viz;* fish (25.20%)>crustacean (13.70%)> miscellaneous (13.4%)>zooplankton (9.91%)> phytoplankton (8.32%)>polychaetes (6.60%)> nematodes (6.23%)> gastropods (5.90%)>bivalves (5.88%)>sand (5.67%)>digested matter (3.48%) and the stomach of female fish contents was identified in the following order *viz;* fish (26.50%)>crustacean (11%)>miscellaneous (9.39%)> phytoplankton (8.76%)>zooplankton (8.50%)> polychaetes (7.44%)>nematodes (6.91%)> gastropods (6%)> bivalves (5.91%)>sand (5.79%)>digested matter (3.68%) respectively.

52. *Megalaspis cordyla*: It is carnivorous. Jaiswar and George (1991) described *Acetes indicus* and small sized fishes such as: *Stolephorus* species as primary food items of this fish. In addition it also feeds on juveniles of *Trichiurus, Apogon, Coilia, Sardinella, Nemipterus, Thryssa* and *Sciaenids.* The food of *M. cordyla* also comprises the youngones of molluscs, especially Loligo and Sepia, and occasionally ostrcods. The choice of food is *Acetes indicus.* Food of adults of both the sexes of *M. cordyla* was composed of *A. indicus,* juveniles of fishes, cephalopods, prawn larvae and ostracods. The juveniles and maturing fishes of *M. cordyla* were found to feed primarily on small crustaceans like: Acetes and prawn larvae. Fully ripe

fishes were not feeding. Some spent fishes and adults were feeding on *Acetes indicus* and juveniles of fishes.

Feeding intensity was highest in young fishes, moderate in maturing and mature fishes. Ripe fishes were found with empty stomachs; spent fishes had high feeding intensity but some of the spent fishes were found with empty stomachs. There was no difference in the intensity of feeding between two sexes.

Srinivasan (1978) reported from Vizhingam bay that this fish is carnivorous feeding mainly on fishes. Chacko and Mathew (1955) from Malabar reported this fish to feed mainly on *Anchoviella, Sardinella fimbriata, Metapenaeus dobsoni.*

53. *Polynemus heptadactylus:* Food and feeding habits of *P.heptadactylus* from fish landing stations of Bombay was reported by Kagwade (1972). *P.heptadactylus* is carnivorous and its food composition varied widely crustaceans raking first, followed by: fishes, polychaetes, molluscs and echinoderms. The planktonic forms, dominted by copepods, were observed in the food of juveniles alone. Crabs, molluscs and echinoderms were absent in the food of juveniles but present in that of adults. Among the crustaceans, *Acetes indicus* and *Squilla* spp., dominated in juveniles and penaeid and carid prawns followed by *Squilla* spp in adults. Amongst the fish food, *B. macclellandi* ranked high in both the juveniles and adults. *Acetes indicus* and *Acetes* sp formed the major item of *Polynemus heptadactylus* (Bapat and Bal,1952).

54. *Polynemus tetradactylus:* Prawn larvae and copepods constitute the main food of the young forms. More advanced forms take to polychaetes and squilla larvae. This has to be substantiated with more material. The polychaetes were mostly taken during the rainy season (Bapat and Bal, 1952).

55. *Serranus diacanthus:* The young forms of this fish during the first and second stages appear to feed mainly on copepods, prawns and amphipods. It is of interest that the percentages of copepods and prawns decrease and those of amphipods increase during the second stage. Prawn larvae and copepods were consumed more during the rainy season (Bapat and Bal, 1952).

56. *Scatophagus argus:* The main food of the smaller specimens (<70 mm) consisted of different species of unicellular algae and detritus. The components of detritus were mud, sand, minute broken shells of molluscs and other inorganic matter. Fish scales, diatoms, copepods and fish eggs were also found. The percentage occurrence of algae (58.2-88.1%) and detritus (12.3-32.4%) were higher than diatoms (7.2-19.3%), copepods (0.8-28.3%) fish scales (1.2-9.1%) and fish eggs (0.7-5.3%) were also observed (Sivan and Radhakrishnan, 2011).

Larger sized specimens (>70mm) have the most diversified food items in their diet. Multicelluar algae were the predominant food of the adult fish throughout the period of observation. Algae (48.4%-86.3%), detritus (12.4-46.9%), diatoms (8.9-28.3%), fish scales (2.8-15.9%), crustaceans (1.2-13.6%), fish eggs (0.2-11.3%), bivalves (1.1-8.2%), copepods (0.7-16.3%), rotifers (0.4-5.2%), sea anemones (0.2-4.9%), sponges (0.4-3.1) and polychaetes (0.2-2.9%) were observed in the gut contents (Sivan and Radhakrishnan, 2011).

The feeding intensity of *S. argus* did not follow regular pattern. During the months of January-April majority of the fishes had actively fed. May showed decreased feeding. In July-August active feeding was observed, followed by decrease in feeding during September. October-December again the number of actively fed was more (Sivan and Radhakrishnan, 2011).

Gandhi (2002) studied the food and feeding of *S. argus* from the marine environment in and around Mandapam and reported that in addition to unicellular algae, higher plants, protozoa, sponges, crustaceans, fish scales, sand and mud, the other food items such as: coral polyps, bivalves, Lepas, prawns, sea anemones and alphaeids were also present in the gut.

57. *Tachysurus tenuispinis:* Raje (2003) studied some biological aspects of this species from Veraval and reported this fish as carnivorous bottom feeder. It mainly feeds on crustaceans, polychaetes, molluscs, fishes and echinoderms. The crustaceans were represented by *Acetes* spp; *Squilla* spp; prawns and crabs. Polychaetes were dominated by *Neries* spp. Molluscs were represented by *Loligo* spp and bivalves and fishes diet comprised sciaenids, *Nemipterus* spp., *Leiognathus* spp., and catfish eggs. The echinoderm noticed in the gut was a single brittle star.
58. *Liza melinoptera:* Quantitative and qualitative analysis of the gut contents of *Liza melinoptera* revealed that this species feed mainly on decayed organic matter, diatoms, algae and sand grains indicating a bottom feeding habit. Intensive feeding was observed during October-February and poor feeding activity during pre-monsoon months of March to June. Sand particles and decayed organic matter showed more or less an increasing trend with the increasing fish size. But this was not seen in the case of diatoms, algae, semi-digested matter and miscellaneous matter. These results suggest that the fish is a bottom feeder and more or less depends upon detritus and decayed organic matter for feeding (Somashekara *et al.* 2012).
59. *Pennahia macrophthalmus:* Food and feeding habits of *P.macrophthalmus* occurring in the trawl catches of Visakhapatnam was studied by Rao (1980). According to him this species is a macrophagous carnivore feeding on teleosts and prawns. Among the teleosts, *Bregmaceros macclellandi* and *Anchoviella* sp are predominant. Prawns (*Penaeus* sp.,

Metapenaeus sp., *Acetes* sp.,) are found to be the major components among the crustaceans. *P. macrophthalmus* become more ichthyphagous with age .Low feeding between February-April, moderate feeding between May-July and high feeding during the rest of the months seemed to prevail (Rao, 1980).

60. *Cheimerius nufar:* Al-marzouqi (2012) studied the food and feeding habits of this species from the Arabian Sea coast of Oman. The common food items found in the gut of *C. nufar* largely belonged to fishes, crustaceans, cephalopods and polychaetes. About 41.21 per cent of food items were found to be semidigested whereas sardine, crustaceans, cephalopods, polychaetes and other fish represent 37.66 per cent, 1.88 per cent, 2.09 per cent, 1.05 per cent and 16.11 per cent of food items respectively (Al-Marzouqi, 2012).

The semi-digested matter was the dominant item in the gut of fish during most of the months and the percentage contribution ranged between 89 per cent (January) and 37.8 per cent (December). While the contribution of sardine varied from 30 per cent (March) to 89 per cent (December), 'other fish' varied from nil (January) to 36 per cent (December). The other food items such as: crustaceans (0% -11.1%) and cephalopods (0% -14%) occurred for few months. A total of 847 fish with empty stomachs were recorded (Al-Marzouqi, 2012).

Feeding intensity in relation to different sizes of *C. nufar* showed inconsistency of feeding among fish. The percentage of empty stomachs ranged from 55.6 per cent (51-55 mm size group) to 75 per cent (41-45 mm size group). Active feeding was observed in fish of sizes 61-65 mm (66.7%) and 71-75 mm (100%) (Al-Marzouqi, 2012).

61. *Gerres filamentosus:* It is an omnivorous, showing more preference towards animal materials as food. Presence of sand and mud in the gut content indicates the bottom feeding habit of the species subsisting mainly on crustaceans, tunicates, polychaetes, filamentous algae, diatoms, molluscan shell, fish scales and miscellaneous items (Aziz *et al.* 2012). Crustaceans were the dominant items that contributed 27 per cent of the total gut content. There was no appreciable difference in the intensity of feeding between males and females. Feeding index in relation to maturity stages depicted that in the third stage, the fishes showed more feeding intensity (Aziz *et al.* 2012).

62. *Decapterus russelli:* According to Poojary *et al.* (2010), the main diet of *Decapterus russelli* comprises crustaceans and fishes with *Acetes indicus* being the most dominant food item. The second most dominant food item was fishes which comprised of *Lactarius lactarius*, silverbellies, myctophids, *Nemipterus* spp., *Saurida tumbil*, *Boleophthalamus* sp.,

Polynemus indicus, Bregmaceros mcclellandi, Polynemus heptadactylus, Cynoglossus spp., *Trichiurus lepturus, Stolephorus* spp., and eels. Penaeid prawns, cephalopods, crabs and plankton were encountered rarely. The juveniles feed on *A. indicus* and sometimes on plankton, whereas the adult feeds on large quantities of *A. indicus* and teleosts. Fish component entered the diet when the species was 100-109 mm in size. The fish component was found to increase with the increase in size of fish, with *A. indicus* still being the preferred food item as it was found in large quantities even in the higher length groups. The percentage of males and females showing low feeding intensity was higher during all the months except in January for females. It was seen that feeding intensity gradually increases as the fish increases in size indicating that as the fish continues to grow it eventually becomes a more active predator. No seasonal variation was observed in feeding intensity of *D. russelli* (Poojary *et al.* 2010).

Decapterus russelli is a carnivore, subsisting mainly on crustaceans, fishes, polychaetes, salps, molluscs and miscellaneous items. Crustaceans were the most dominant item in different size groups. The fish showed preference to other food fishes as they grew. The intensity of feeding was high during most of the months. Feeding intensity was high in juveniles followed by immature, maturing and spent fishes (Manojkumar, 2007).

63. *Psettodes erumei:* Fishes constituted the main food item. Among the fishes, *Apogon* sp., Sciaenids and *Leiognathus* sp., were commonly observed. *P. erumei* generally swallows the prey entirely. In some cases, the length of the prey was equal or longer than the fish itself. Molluscs formed the second major food. *Loligo* sp only has been observed to constitute this food item. Prawns and crabs constituted the arthropod diet and formed the third major food item. Echinoderms formed a minor component of the diet. No clear change in the feeding habit with the increase of body length has been noticed. Of course, in the fish of smaller size, *i.e.*, 71-140 mm, fish and molluscs formed the major food items, whereas, in the fish beyond this size, certain amount of arthropods and echinoderms are also added to their diet. No clear seasonal change in the feeding habit was seen. Higher rate of feeding was observed during January to April in comparison to rest of the months of the year (Das and Mishra, 1990).

Monthly variation of gastrosomatic index indicated high values during January to April. So far as the body length was concerned, the gastrosomatic index was highest in the body length group 71-140 mm and reduced gradually with the increase of body length (Das and Mishra, 1990).

64. *Atropus atropos:* Fishery and biology of *Atropus atropos* from Veraval was studied by Raje (1994).This fish is pelagic carnivore. *Acetes* spp., formed most important food item followed by: cephalopods, teleosts, *Squilla* spp and copepods. *Acetes* spp formed 46.25 per cent of the diet and only small sized *Acetes* spp were observed in the diet. Among the cephalopods, *Loligo* spp and *Sepia* spp., formed 17.08 per cent. The teleost food items comprised 16.11 per cent in the diet of *A. atropos* were juveniles of ribbon fish, *Myctophids* spp and other fish larvae. *Squilla* spp was represented by Alima larvae of *Squilla* spp and formed only 9.50 per cent of diet. Copepods formed only 3.22 per cent which were obtained either in whole form or in the form of reddish pulp (Raje, 1994).
65. *Alepes djedaba:* Raje (1993) observed *Acetes* spp as the dominant food item followed by: copepods, fish *Myctophum* spp., and *Squilla* spp. The contribution of *Acetes* sp., was more than 50 per cent in all the months, whereas fish, copepods, *Myctophum* spp., and *Squilla* spp., formed significant part of the diet during May, January, February and November respectively.
66. *Halaelvrus hispidus:* According to Nair and Appukuttan (1973) it is carnivorous, feeding mostly on fishes, squids and crustaceans. Food was found in a highly macerated condition and most of the components were in advanced stages of digestion rendering the specific identification of the different items difficult.

Fish constituted the major food item and formed 60.5 per cent of the total volume of stomach contents. The common fishes observed were *Myctaphum* sp; *Gonostoma* sp., flat fishes and Eels. Generally small sized fishes dominated in the diet.

Squids ranked second in importance. They were also found to be in advanced stage of digestion. Their percentage by volume was 16.9 per cent.

The next important item of food was the crustaceans including the deep sea prawn *Solenocera hextil*, alima larvae of stomatopods, zoea larvae and other unidentified and digested crustaceans. They formed as much as 16.17 per cent of the total volume of food.

Among the miscellaneous items of food, gastropods formed 0.2 per cent and sea grass 0.1 per cent of the total volume.

67. *Eridacnis radcliffei:* Nair and Appukuttan (1973) studied the food and feeding habits of this fish. Fish ranked first in abundance constituting 55.4 per cent of the total volume. The common fishes observed were *Myctophum* sp., *Gonostoma* sp., and Eels. Crustaceans formed the next important food item forming 28.3 per cent of the total volume of stomach contents. Crustaceans were mainly represented by deeps sea prawn *Solenocera hextii* and alima of stomatopod and zoea larvae in lesser magnitude.

Squids were the next important food of this shark. Squids formed 13.7 per cent of the total volume of stomach examined. Other food items recorded were bivalves and mud.

68. *Iago omanensis:* Nair and Appukuttan (1973) observed fish as the major food item. *Myctophus* sp., was the only fish which could be identified. Digested fish, which could not be identified. Digested fish, which could not be identified due to the advanced stage of digestion. This also included fish bones, scales and eye lenses.

The next important food of *I. omanesis* were squids, which formed 31.5 per cent by volume of total food. The deep sea squids were the main component. Crustaceans ranked third in abundance and the most important crustacean was *Solenocera hextii*. Other miscellaneous items of food were bivalves, gastropods and pieces of sea grass (Nair and Appukuttan, 1970).

69. *Scoliodon laticaudus:* Devadoss (1989) studied the food and feeding habits of this shark. The young sharks preferred prawn diet rather than fish and moulluscs. As they grow up, the feeding preference is gradually shifted to fishes and fast moving molluscs like squids and cuttle fishes.

Adolescent sharks (250-300 mm) had 28.6 per cent of the stomachs empty and as they grow to maturity size the percentage of empty stomachs were limited to below 40 per cent.Once they reached maturity size at 350 mm in total length and started carrying the developing embryos in their uteri, the percentage of starvation was more pronounced.

Crustaceans were dominant in the diet throughout the year except January to March. There was a slight decline of this group in the diet during September to November. Prawns (*Penaeus indicus, Metapenaeus dobsoni* and *Parapenaeopsis stylifera*) were found pre-dominantly more. In addition to prawns, other crustaceans recorded were small crabs, *Squilla* spp., and young *Thenus* sp. They were well represented in the diet in all the months.

Molluscs represented by squids and cuttle fishes were fairly taken during January and September.

Fish diet taken in were mackerel, oil sardine, silverbellies, anchovies, soles, sciaenids and small ribbon fishes. Young ones of soles, silverbellies and anchovies were eaten by young sharks, while oil sardine, mackerel, ribbon fish and sciaenids were taken in by fairly larger sharks of above 400 mm during the months of September to February when these fishes were available abundantly (Devadoss, 1989).

70. *Mugil cephalus:* Rao and Babu (2013) studied the food and feeding habits of *Mugil cephalus* at east coast of Andhra Pradesh. In adult fish the analysis of the gut revealed that the chlorophyceae, myxophyceae, bacillariophyceae, dino-flagellates, copepods and polycheatae worms along with sand and mud were the main component of diet. Where as

in juveniles the volume of the gut varied according to season. The bacillariophyceae (diatoms) and micro algae, *cladophora* (green algae) and myxophyceae were prominent. The volume of the gut in Juveniles maximum in the months of October and September, low in the month of April was observed.

71. *Plotus canius:* Brachyuran carbs of the families sesarmidae, and other brachyurans (Ocypodidae and Porcellanidae) were the most frequently occurring and important food items consumed by this fish (Leh *et al.* 2012). Among the sesarmids *Perisesarma eumolpe* de Man, *Perisesarma onychophorum* de Man, *Episesarma versicolour* Tweedie and Cleistocoeloma merguiensis de Man were the dominant food items while *Typhlocarcinus* sp., was of equal importance. Prawns of the genera Penaeus, Metapenaeus and Sergestid Acetes were also consumed. Other food items consumed in lesser amounts were hyperiid amphipods, copepods, isopod sphaeroma, gastropods Littoraria, Nerita, Syncera, bivalve Gelonia, bottom living *Glossogobius* sp., nekton fish Thryssa and mangrove detritus. Miscellaneous food items found were shell fragments of barnacles and oyster, eggs of horse shoe crab, animal tissues, and small amounts of sand particles (Leh *et al.* 2012).

72. *Hyporhamphus xanthopteurs:* Algal filaments and other vegetable matter formed the major portion of the food of juveniles. They include *Spirogyra* sp., and *Ulothrix* sp., of chlorophyceae, *Oscillatoria* sp., *Lyngbia* sp and *Nostoc* sp of cyanophyceae, *Skeletonema* sp., *Coscinodiscus* sp., *Nitzschia* sp., *Biddulphia* sp., *Thalassiosira* sp and *Pleurosigma* sp., of bacillariophyceae (Varghese, 2005).

Adults consume algae like: *Spirogyra* sp., *Ulothrix* sp., *Oedogonium* sp., *Oscillatoria* sp., *Lyngbia* sp., *Spirulina* sp., *Nostoc* sp., *Coscinodiscus* sp., *Fragillaria* sp., *Pleurosigma* sp., *Navicula* sp., *Skeletonema* sp., *Nitzschia* sp., *Melosira* sp., *Campylodiscus* sp., *Biddulphia* sp., Leptocylindrus sp., *Thalassiosira* sp., *Gyrosigma* sp., *Guinardia* sp and *Pinnularia* sp. The prawns include *Parapenaeopsis stylifera, Metapenaeus dobsoni* etc. Other crustaceans such as: copepods and mysids were also present in lesser quantities. However, nematode worms were encountered occasionally. Insect parts, prawn larvae and other crustacean larvae also formed minor fractions of the diet. Digested matter comprising animal and vegetable matter formed another major group whereas mud and sand formed a small category. This shows that *H. xanthopterus* is omnivorous (Varghese, 2005).

The Gastro-somatic Index of *H. xanthopterus* showed variations during different months of the year. During the June to August the GSI values were low coinciding with the decrease in feeding intensity of the fishes. In all other months the GSI values were high which may be due to the active feeding. The decrease in feeding intensity coincided with the spawning season of the fish (Varghese, 2005).

73. *Hyporhampus limbatus*: Juveniles feed on smaller food items. In early stages they consume algae. Prawns (mainly *Penaeus* sp.,) constituted the most abundant food item of adult, followed by: algae, other crustacean parts, polychaete worms, nematode parts, digested animal and vegetable matter and mud particles (Varghese, 2005).

Gastro-Somatic Index varied from month to month. A sharp fall in the GSI value was seen in March and April, followed by an increase in May to October. Succeeding this peak, a general decrease in the value was noted in November and December. The rise and falls in the GSI value coincide with the spawning season of the fish (Varghese, 2005).

74. *Chlorophthalmus agassizi:* According to Hashim (2012) fishes constitute major component (78%) of food, followed by myctophid (9.4%), squid (8.3%), elver (3.3%), leptocephalus (0.5%) and flat fishes (0.5%).
75. *Neoepinnula orientalis:* Fish ranked first in abundance constituting 80.7 per cent. Squid formed next important food item (7.1%), followed by cubiceps (5.4%), myctophid (4.8%) and octopus (2%) (Hashim, 2012).
76. *Bembrops caudimacula:* Crustaceans formed 45.3 per cent of the total gut contents. Squid and shrimp contributed 36.9 per cent and 17.7 per cent of the total gut contents respectively (Hashim. 2012).

REFERENCES

Abdu Rahiman, K.P. (2006). Studies on Food and Feeding of Marine Demersal Finfishes with Special Reference to Trophic Interactions, Ph.D. thesis, Faculty of Marine Sciences, Cochin University of Science and Technology.

Al-Marzouqi, A. (2012). Food and Feeding Habits of Santer seabream *Cheimerius nufar* (Val., 1830) from the Arabian Sea coast of Oman. *J. Mar. Biol. Ass. India*, 54 (1), 108 - 112, Available online at: www.mbai.org.in doi: 10.6024/jmbai.2012.54.1.01702-14.

Al-Zibdah, M. and Nemeh Kan'an. (2009). Aspects of Growth, Reproduction, and Feeding Habit of Three Pomacentrid Fish from Gulf of Aqaba, Jordan. *Jordan Journal of Biological Sciences*, 2(3):119-128.

Arun Kumar, M., Padmavati, G. and Venu, S. (2015). Food and Feeding Dynamics of *Stolephorus commersonnii* (Lacepede, 1803) (Family: Engraulidae) from South Andaman. *Journal of Marine Biology*, Volume 2015, Article ID: 870919,8 pages.

Aziz, Megha., Ambily, V. and Bijoy Nandan, S. (2012). Food and Feeding Habits of *Gerres filamentosus* (Cuvier, 1829) from Kodungallur - Azhikode Estuary, Kerala, India. *Fishery Technology* 49 (2012): 10-13.

Bapat, S.V. and Bal, D.V. (1952). The Food of Some Young Fishes from Bombay. Proceedings of the Indian Academy of Sciences, Section B, 35:78-92.

Bhimachar, S. and P.C. George. (1952). Observations on the Food and Feeding of Indian Mackerel *Rastrelliger kanagurta* (Cuvier). *Proc. Indian Acad. Sci.*, 36B (3): 105-117.

Chacko, P.I. (1949.) Food and Feeding Habits of the Fishes of the Gulf of Mannar. *Proc. Indian Acad. Sci.*, 29:83-97.

Chacko, P.I. and Mathew, M.J. (1955). Biology and Fisheries of the Horse Mackerel of the West Coast of Madras State. Cent. Mar. Biol. Stn. West Hill, Malabar Coast No.2 :1-22 Government Press, Madras.

Clarke, T.A. (1980). Diets of Fourteen Species of Vertically Migrating mesopelagic Fishes in Hawaiian Waters. *Fish. Bull., U.S.* 78(3):619-640.

CMFRI. (1986). The Present Status of Ribbonfish Fishery in India, CMFRI Special Publication No. 24, Central Marine Fisheries Research Institute, Cochin, India.

Das, M. and Mishra, B. (1990). On the Biology of *Psettodes erumei* (Bloch and Schn.), an Indian Halibut. *Indian J. Fish*; 37(2):79-92.

Deo, A.D., Venkateshvaran, K. and Devaraj, M. (2010). Relative Condition Factor and Food and Feeding Habits of Two Arid Catfishes from Mumbai Waters. *J. Indian Fish. Associ.*, 37:57-64.

Devadoss, P. (1989). Observations on the Length-Weight Relationship and Food and Feeding Habits of Spade Nose Shark, *Scoliodon laticaudus* Muller and Hence. *Indian J. Fish.*, 36(2):169-174.

Devanesan, D.W. and Chidambaram, K. (1953). The Common Food Fishes of Madras Presidency. Madras Government Publication, 207 p.

Devaraj, M. (1998). Food and Feeding Habits of the Spotted Seer, *Scomberomorus guttatus* (Bloch and Schnedier) in the Gulf of Mannar and Palk Bay. *J. Mar. Biol. Ass. India*, 40 (1&2):105-124.

Dulkhed, M.H. (1962). Observations on the Food and Feeding Habits of the Indian Oil Sardine, *Sardinella longiceps* Val. *Indian J. Fish.*, 2(1):A:34-47.

Gandhi, V. (2002). Studies on the Food and Feeding of the Cultivable Butter Fish, *Scatophagus argus* (Cuv. and Val.). *J. Mar. Biol. Ass. India*; 44(1-2):115-121.

Ganga, U. (2010). Investigations on the Biology of Indian Mackerel *Rastrelliger kanagurta* (Cuvier) along the Central Kerala coast with Special Reference to Maturation, Feeding and lipid Dynamics. Ph.D. thesis, Cochin University of Science and Technology, Kochi - 682016.

Gupta, K.S., Shoba Joe Kizhakudan, Joe K. Kizhakudan, K.S.S.M. Yousuf and S. Raja. (2014). Preliminary Observation on Dominance of Crustacean Larvae in the diet of Little Tunny *Euthynnus affinis* (Cantor, 1849) Caught off Chennai and Cuddalore Coasts. *Indian J. Fish*; 61(2):40-44.

Hanson, J.M. and G.A. Chouinard. (2002). Diet of Atlantic Cod in the Southern Gulf of St. Lawrence as an Index of Ecosystem Change, 1959–2000. *J. Fish Biol.*, 60: 902–922.

Hashim, M. (2012). Distribution, Diversity and Biology of Deep sea Fishes in the Indian EEZ. Ph.D. thesis, Faculty of Marine Sciences, Cochin University of Science and Technology, Cochin.

Jaiswar, A.K. and George, J.P. (1991). Food and Feeding Habits of *Megalaspis cordyla* (Linnaeus, 1758) along the Northwest coast of India. *Journal of the Indian Fisheries Association*, 21:5-10.

James, P.S.B.R. (1967). The Ribbon Fishes of the Family Trichiuridae of India. Memoir 1. Marine Biological Association of India: 226 pp.

Jayaprakash, A.A. (2000). Food and Feeding Habits of Malabar sole *Cynoglossus macrstomus* Norman. *J. Mar. Biol. Ass. India*, 42(1&2):124-134.

Jayaprakash, A.A. (2004). Trends in World Sardine Fisheries and India's Status, Ocean Life, Food and Medicine, Expo 2004, Central Marine Fisheries Research Institute, Kochi, Kerala.

Joshi, K.K. (2005). Biology and Population Dynamics of *Nemipterus mesoprion* (Bleeker) off Cochin. *Indian J. Fish.*, 52 (3): 315-322.

Kadharsha, K., Mohanchander, P., Lyla, P.S. and Khan, S.A. (2013). Feeding and Reproductive Biology of *Saurida undosquamis* (Richardson, 1848) from Parangipettai coast, Southeast Coast of India. *Pak. J. Biol. Sci.*, 16(22):1479-1487.

Kagwade, P.V. (1964). The Food and Feeding Habits of the Indian Oil Sardine *Sardinella longiceps* Valenciennes. *Indian J. Fish.*, 11: 345-370.

Kagwade, P.V. (1972). Food and Feeding Habits of *Polynemus heptadactylus* Cuv. and Val. *Indian J.Fish.*, 16(1&2):188-197.

Khalil, Bushra and Farzana Ibrahim. (2016). Food and Feeding Habits of *Cynoglossus arel* (Family: Cynoglossidae) from Karachi Coast, Pakistan. *International Journal of Fauna and Biological Studies*. 3(1): 91-96.

Khan, M.A., Kiran Yousuf and Shagufta Riaz. (2014). Food and Feeding Habits of *Sillago sihama* (Forsskal, 1775) (Family: Sillaginidae) from Karachi coast. *International Journal of Fauna and Biological Studies*, 1(3):27-31.

Krishna P.V; Panchakshari. V., and K . Prabhavathi. (2015). Food and Feeding Habits of Goat Fish *Upeneus sulphureus* from Nizampatnam Coast, Andhra Pradesh, India. *International Journal of Advanced Research*, 3: (11): 1066-1070.

Kulbicki, M., Y-M. Bozec, P. Labrosse, Y. Letourneur, G. Mou-Tham and L. Wantiez. (2005). Diet Composition of Carnivorous Fishes from Coral Reef lagoons of New Caledonia. *Aquat. Living Resour.*, 18: 231-250.

Kumaran, M. (1964). Studies on the Food and Feeding of *Euthynnus affinis* (Cantor), *Auxius thazard* (Lacepede) *Auxis thynnoides* Bleeker and *Sarda orientalis* (Temminck and Schlegel), Proceedings of the Symposium on Scombroid Fishes, Part II, Marine Biology Association of India, 12-15 January 1962, Mandapam.

Kutty, M.N. (1965). Obervations on the Indian Mackerel *Rastrelliger kanagurta* (Cuvier) from the trawl Catch along the Bombay coast. *Indian J. Fish*; 9(2)A: 590-603.

Legand, M. and Rivaton, J. (1969). Cycles Biologiques des Poissons mesopelogiques dans l'Est de l'Ocean Indien. Troisieme Note: Action predatrice des Poissons microtechniques. *Cah. ORSTOM, Ser. Oceanogr*; 7(3):29-45.

Leh, M.U.C., Sasekumar, A. and Chew, L.L. (2012). Feeding Biology of eel catfish *Plotosus canius* Hamilton in a Malaysian mangrove estuary and mudflat. *The Raffles Bulletin of Zoology*, 60(2):551-557.

Mahadevan, G. (2015). Studies on Biodiversity of Mudskippers (Gobiidae: Oxudercinae) and Biology of the *Pseudpocryptes elongatus* (Cuvier, 1816) from the Mudflats of Sunderban, India. Ph.D. thesis, CAS in Marine Biology, Annamalai University, Parangipettai, pp. 258.

Manikandarajan, T., Ramamoorthy, K., Srilatha, G., Sankar, G. and Kathirvel, K. (2014). Stomach Content Analysis of Catfish-Arius Maculates (Thunberg, 1972) from Parangipettai Coast, South East Coast of India. *Asian Journal of Biomedical and Pharmaceutical Sciences*; 4(38):50-56.

Manoharan, J., Gopalakrishnan, A., Varadharajan, D., Thilagavathi, B. and Priyadarsini, S. (2012). Stomach Content Analysis of *Terapon jarbua* (Forsskal) from Parangipettai coast, South East Coast of India. *Advances in Applied Science Research*, 3(5):2605-2621.

Manojkumar, P.P. (2003). Obersvations on the Food and Feeding Habits of *Otolithes cuvieri* (Trewaves) off Veraval. *Indian J. Fish*; 50(3):379-385.

Manojkumar, P.P. (2007). Food and Feeding Habits of *Decapterus russelli* (Ruppell, 1830) along the Malabar coast. *Indian J. Fish.*, 54(4): 427-431, 2007.

Mazlan, A.G., Abdullah, S., Shariman, M.G. and Arshad, A. (2008). On the Biology and bioacoustic Characteristic of Spotted Catfish Arius maculates (Thunberg 1792) from the Malaysian estuary. *Research Journal of Fisheries and Hydrobiology*, 3(2):63-70.

Mohanraj, G. (2000). Studies on the Biology and Population Dynamics of the Goatfishes (Pisces: Mullidae), *Upeneus bensasi* and *Upeneus moluccensis* of Madras coast, Ph.D. thesis, University of Madras, India.

Mohanraj, T. and Prabhu, K. (2012). Food Habits and Diet Composition of Demersal Marine Fishes from Gulf of Mannar, Southeast Coast of India. *Advances in Biological Research*, 6(4):159-164.

Nagarajan, D. (2014). Food and Feeding Habits in *Leiognathus berbis* (Valenciennes) from Tuticorin Southeast coast of India. *International Journal of Research in Fisheries and Aquaculure*, 4(3):126-133.

Nair, R.V. and Appukuttan, K.K. (1973). Observation on the Food of deep sea sharks *Halaelurus hispidus* (Alcock), *Eridacnis radcliffei* smith and *Iago omanensis* Compagno and Springer. *Indian J. of Fisheries*, 20(2):575-583.

Nair, Somasekharan, K.V. (1979). Food and Feeding Habits of *Otolithes ruber* (Schneider) at Calicut. *Indian J. Fish.* 26 (1&2): 133-139.

Nath, S.R., Beraki, T., Abrahman, K. and Berhane, Y. (2015). Gut Content Analysis of Indian Mackerel (*Rastrelliger kanagurta*). *J. Aquac. Mar. Biol.* 3 (10): 00052. DOI: 10. 15406/ jamb.2015.03.00052.

Nikolskii, G.V. (1969). Theory of Fish Population Dynamics as the Biological Background for Rational Exploitation and Management of Fishery Resources. R. Jones (Ed.), Oliver and Boyd, Edinburgh, p. 323.

Noble, A. (1962). The Food and Feeding Habits of the Indian Mackerel *Rastrelliger kanagurta* (Cuvier) at Karwar. *Ind. J. Fish.*, 9A (2): 701-713.

Pakhmode, P.K. and Mohite, S.A. (2014). Feeding Biology of Ribbonfish, *Lepturacanthus savala* (Cuvier, 1929) off Ratnagiri coast, Maharashtra. *International Journal of Fisheries and Aquatic Studies*, 1(3):123-129.

Pati, S. (1980). Food and Feeding Habits of Silver Pomfret *Pampus argenteus* (Euphrasen) from Bay of Bengal with a Note on its Significance in Fishery. *Indian J. Fish*; 27 (1&2):244-256.

Pillai, P.K.M. (1974). A Note on the Food and Feeding Habit of the Ribbon Fish, *Trichiurus Leptuturs*. *Indian Jr. of Fisheries*. 21(2): 597-600.

Pillai, P.K.M. (1983). On the Biometry, Food and Feeding and Spawning Habits of *Otolithes ruber* (Schneider) from Porto Novo. *Indian J. Fish.*, 30(1):69-73.

Pillay, T.V.R. (1953). The Food and Feeding Habits of the Bombay duck, *Harpodon nehereus* (Ham.) in the river Matlah (Bengal). *Proceedings of the National Institute of Sciences of India*. 19:427-435.

Poojary, Nalini, Tiwari, L.R. and Jaiswar, A.K. (2010). Food and Feeding Habits of the Indian scad, *Decapterus russelli* (Ruppell, 1830) from Mumbai waters, north-west coast of India. *Indian J. Fish.*, 57(4): 93-99.

Prabhu, M.S. (1955). Some Aspects of the Biology of the Ribbon Fish *Trichiurus haumela* (Forskal). *Indian J. Fish.*, 2:132-163.

Pradhan, L.B and V.C. Palekar. (1956). Key to the Stages of Sexual Maturity of *Rastrelliger kanagurta* (Cuvier). *Indian J. Fish.*, 3(1): 183-185.

Priyadharsini, S., Manoharan, J., Varadharajan, D. and Kumaraguru Vasagam, K.P. (2014). Food and Feeding Habits of *Pterois russelli* from Cuddalore South East Coast of India. *J. Earth Sci.Clim. Change*, 5:191.doi:10.4172/2157-7617.1000191.

Priyadharsini, S., Manoharan, J., Varadharajan, D. and Subramaniyan, A. (2012). Interpretation on the Food and Feeding Habits of *Dascyllus trimaculatus* (Rupell, 1829) from Gulf of Mannar, South East Coast of India, *Archives of Applied Science Research*, 4(4):1758-1762.

Priyadharsini, S., Subramaniyan, A., Manoharan, J. and Varadharajan, D. (2013). Food and Feeding Habits of Red Lionfish *Pterois volitans* from Cuddalore Coast, South East Coast of India. *J. Aquac. Res. Development*. 4:184.doi:10.4172/2155-9546.1000184.

Qasim, S.Z. (1972). The Dynamics of Food and Feeding Habits of some Marine Fishes. *Indian J. Fish.*, 19:11-28.

Rabindra Nath, P. (1966). Biology and Seasonal Distribution of the Pelagic Food Fishes of Travancore Coast. Kerala University Publication, 140 pp.

Raje, S.G. (1993). Some Aspects of Biology of *Alepes djeda* (Forsskal) from Veraval, Gujarat. *Indian Journal of Fisheries*, 40(3):189-192.

Raje, S.G. (1994). Fishery and Biology of *Atropus atropos* (Bloch and Schneider) from Veraval. *J. Mar. Biol. Ass. India*. 36 (1&2):181-187.

Raje, S.G. (1996). Some Observations on the Biology of *Nemipterus mesoprion* (Bleeker) from Veraval (Gujarat). *Indian J. Fish.*, 43 (2): 163-170.

Raje, S.G. (2000). Some Aspects of the Biology of *Otolithes cuvieri* (Trewavas) and *Johnius glaucus* (Day) from Veraval.*J. Indian Fish. Ass.*, 27: 1-6.

Raje, S.G. (2003). Some Aspects of the Biology of *Tachysurus tenuispinis* day from Veraval. *Journal of the Indian Fisheries Assocation*. 30:97-103.

Raje, S.G., Dineshbabu, A.P., Thakur Das, Sujit Sundaram and Chavan, B.B. (2012). Biology and Population Dynamics of *Saurida undosquamis* (Richardson) from Mumbai Waters, Northwest Coast of India. *J. Indian Fish. Assoc.*, 39: 1-13.

Rao. K. Srinivasa. (1964). Food and Feeding Habits of Fishes of Trawl Catches in the Bay of Bengal with Observations on the Diurnal Variation in the Nature of the Feed. *Indian J. Fish*; 11(1):277-314.

Rao, K.V. Narayana and K.P. Rao. (1957). Differences in the Food of the Young and the Adult Indian Mackerel, *Rastrelliger kanagurta* (Cuv.). *Nature*, 180: 711-712.

Rao, K. Venkatasubba. (1963). Some Aspects of the Biology of 'Ghol' *Pseudosciena diacanthus* (Lacepede). *Indian J. Fish.*, 10A(2): 413-459.

Rao, K.V.S. (1981). Food and Feeding of Lizard Fishes (*Saurida* spp.) from North Western Part of Bay of Bengal. *Indian J. Fish.*, 28(1&2):47-64.

Rao, R.K. and Babu, K.R. (2013). Studies on food and feeding habits of *Mugil cephalus* (Linnaeus, 1758) East Coast off Andhra Pradesh, India. *Canadian Journal of Pure and Applied Sciences*, 7(3): 2499-2504.

Rao, T.A. (1980). Food and Feeding Habits of *Pennahia macrophthalmus* Bleeker at Visakhapatnam. *Indian Jr. of Fisheries*, 27(1&2):61-65.

Rao, T.A. (1989). Fishery of Threadfin breams at Waltair with Notes on some Aspects of Biology of *Nemipterus mesoprion* (Bleeker). *J. Mar. Biol. Ass. India*, 31 (1&2): 103-109.

Ravi, V., (2013). Food and Feeding Habits of the Mudskipper, *Boleophthalmus boddarti* (Pallas, 1770) from Pichavaram Mangroves, Southeast Coast of India, *International Journal of Marine Science*, 3(12): 98-104 (doi: 10.5376/ijms.2013.03.0012).

Rohit, Prathibha and K. Rammohan, K. (2009). Fishery and Biological Aspects of Yellowfin Tuna *Thunnus albacares* along Andhra Coast, India. *Asian Fisheries Science* 22 (2009): 235-244, Asian Fisheries Society, Manila, Philippines, Available online at www.asianfisheriessociety.org

Rohit, Prathibha, G. Syda Rao and K. Rammohan. (2010). Feeding Strategies and Diet Composition of Yellow fin tuna *Thunnus albacores* (Bonnaterre,1788) caught along Andhra Pradesh, East coast of India. *Indian J. Fish*; 57(4):13-19.

Rohit, Prathibha, RAJESH, K.M., Sampathkumar, G. and Karamathulla, Sahib, P. (2015). Food and Feeding of the ribbonfish *Trichiurus lepturus* Linnaeus off Karnataka, South-west Coast of India. *Indian J. Fish.*, 62 (1): 58-63, 2015.

Sebastian, Honey, Inasu, N.D. and Tharakan, Jeeja. (2011). Comparative Study on the Mouth Morphology and diet of three co-occurring Species of Silver bellies along the Kerala Coast, *J. Mar. Biol. Ass. India.*, 53(2):196-201.

Sivadas, M. and M.M. Bhaskaran. (2009). Stomach Content Analysis of the Indian Mackerel *Rastrelliger kanagurta* (Cuvier) from Calicut, Kerala. *Indian J. Fish.*, 56(2) 143-146.

Sivan, Gisha and Radhakrishnan, C.K. (2011). Food Feeding Habits and Biochemical Composition of *Scatophagus argus*. *Turkish Journal of Fisheries and Aquatic Sciences*, 11:603-608.

Sivaprakasam, T.E. (1967). Observations on the Food and Feeding Habits of *Parastromateus niger* (Bloch) of the Saurashtra coast. *Indian J.Fish*. 10:140-147.

Somashekara, S.R., Shivaprakash, S.M., Benakappa, S., Anjaneyappa, H.N., Shrinivas H. Hulkoti and Kamlesh Panda. (2012). Food and Feeding Habit of the grey mullet, *Liza melinoptera* (Velanciennes) from Mangalore waters. In: Perspectives in Ecology (Eds.V.B. Sakhare and J.S. Mohite), pp. 1-8, Oxford Book Company, Jaipur, India.

Sreenivasan, P.V. (1978). Observations on the Fishery and Biology of *Megalaspis cordyla* at Vizhingam. *Indian J. Fish*.25 (1&2):122-140.

Suresh Kumar, P.S. and Mohite, S.A. (2013). Study of Food and Feeding Habit in *Nemipterus japonicus* along the Ratnagiri coast of Maharashtra. In: Advances in Aquatic Ecology (Volume 7), Edited by Vishwas B. Sakhare and B. Vasanthkumar, pp. 89-96. Astral International (P.) Ltd., New Delhi.

Suseelan, C. and Somashekaran, Nair, K.V. (1969). Food and Feeding Habits of Demersal Fishes off Bombay. *Indian J. Fish;* 16(1&2): 56-74.

Swamy, Kumar M., G. Rajeswari and B. Kishore. (2015). Food and Feeding Habits of *Johnius carutta* (Bloch, 1793) off Visakhapatnam, East Coast of India. *Fishery Technology*. 52:88-94.

Taghavi Motlagh, A., Hakimelahi, M., Ghodrati Shojaei, M. Vahabnezhad, A. and Taheri Mirghaed, A. (2012). Feeding Habits and Stomach Contents of Silver Sillago, *Sillago sihama*, in the Northern Persian Gulf. *Iranian Jr. of Fisheries Sciences*, 11(4):892-901.

Telvekar, Prashant, A., Chakraborty, S.K. and Jaiswar, A.K. (2006). Length-weight Relationship and Food and Feeding Habits of *Otolithes cuvieri* (Trewavas, 1974) from Mumbai. *Indian J. Fish.*, 53(4): 131-134.

Thangavelu, R., Anbarasu, M., Zala M.S., Mohamed Koya, K., Sreenath, K.R., Suresh Kumar Mojjada and Shiju, P. (2012). Food and Feeding Habits of Commercially Important Demersal Finfishes off Veraval coast. *Indian J. Fish.*, 59(4):77-87, 2012.

Thomas, P.A. (1969). Goat Fishes (Family: Mullidae) of the Indian seas, Memoir III, Marine Biological Association of India, pp. 174+Plates I to VIII.

Tiews, K., A. Mines and I.A. Ronquilo. (1972). On the Biology of *Saurida tumbil* (Bloch, 1801), Family: Synodontidae in Philippine waters. *Proc. Indo-Pacific Fish. Court*; 13(11):100-120.

Varghese, A.S. (2005). Sytematics and Biology of Fishes of the Family Hemiramphidae of Cochin coast, Ph.D. thesis, The Cochin University of Science and Technology, Cochin - 682016.

Venkataraman, G. and C. Mukundan. (1970). A Note on the Food of Young Mackerel. *J. Mar. Biol. Ass. India.*, 12(1&2): 230-232.

Venkataraman, R.S. (1944). The Food of Ribbon Fishes *Trichiurus* spp. *Curr.Sci.*, 13(9): 239.

Venugopal, N., N.G.K. Pillai and D. Prakasan. (2014). Food and Feeding Habits of *Johnieops sina* (Cuvier, 1830) along Cochin Coast of India, *Indian J. Fish.*, 6(1):103-107.

Vijayaraghavan, P. (1951). Food of the Ribbon Fishes of Madras. *J. Madras Univ.*, 21:81-85.

Vinaya Kumar, V., Devivaraprajad Reddy, A., Ch. Balakrishna, Satyanarayana, Y. and Sudhir Kumar Das. (2012). Analaysis of Diet Composition, Feeding Dynamics and Proximate Composition of Bombay Duck, *Harpodon nehereus* along Sunderban area of West Bengal, India. *Arch. Appl. Sci. Res.*, 4(2): 1175-1182.

Yeragi, S.S. and Yeragi, S.G. (2015). Food and Feeding of an Economically Important Estuarine Fish, *Sillago sihama* (Forsskal). *Int. J. of Life Sciences*, 3(2): 147-151.

Page 34-55

PLANKTON AND FISHERIES
Edited by : **V.B. Sakhare; H.K. Jadhav** and **S.S. Jadhav**
Edition : **2017**
ISBN : 978-93-5056-811-8
Published by : **Discovery Publishing House Pvt. Ltd., New Delhi (India)**

2 Inland Fisheries of India

Vishwas Balasaheb Sakhare
Post Graduate Department of Zoology
Yogeshwari Mahavidyalaya, Ambajogai - 431 517.

India is the third largest fish producer in the world contributing to 6.3 per cent of global fish production. Indian aquaculture also ranks second in the world after China. Indian fisheries and aquaculture sector play an important role in the socio-economic upliftment of fishermen community. This sector contributes to 1.1 per cent of the GDP and 5.15 per cent of the agricultural GDP. More than 65 per cent of the fish production comes from inland sector. The volume of fish and fish products have presently emerged as the largest group in agricultural exports of India, with 10.51 Lakh tonnes in terms of quantity and Rs. 33422 crores in value. This accounts for around 10 per cent of the exports of the country and nearly 20 per cent of the agricultural exports. It is estimated that more than 50 different types of fish and shell fish products are exported to 75 countries around the world.

According to the National Sample Survey (NSS), the annual per capita fish consumption was 2.45 kg., in 1983; it increased to 3.45 kg., in 1999-2000. Only 35 per cent population in India was estimated to be fish eater and their annual per capita fish consumption was 9.8 kg., in 1999-2000. However, wide regional variations do exist in fish consumption across regions, states and income classes.

The country has 429 Fish Farmers Development Agencies (FFDAs) and 39 Brackish water Fish Farmers Development Agencies (BFDAs) for promoting freshwater and coastal aquaculture. Training is mainly dealt with by these agencies. They also provide package of assistance for popularizing aquaculture technologies. With more than 2.4 Lakh fishing crafts operating in the coast, six major fishing harbours, 62 minor fishing harbours and 1511 landing centers are functioning to cater the needs of over 3.9 million fisherfolk.

Fishery Resource

The country has a long coast line of 8129 kms., and large areas under estuaries, backwaters, lagoons etc. With the declaration of the Exclusive Economic Zone (EEZ) in 1977, an area of 2.02 million sq.km., (comprising of .086 million sq.km., on the west coast, 0.56 million sq.km., on the east coast and 0.60 sq.km., around the Andaman and Nicobar Island) has come under our jurisdiction with right of exploring, exploiting and natural utilization of living resources falling within it.

The inland fishery resources include 1,91,024 km., stretch of rivers and canals, 3.15 million ha of reservoirs, 2.35 million hectare of ponds and tanks, 1.3 million ha of oxbow lakes and derelict water bodies and 1.24 million ha of brackish water areas (Table 2.1).

Table 2.1: Fishery Resources of India

1	Coastal line (kms.)	8129
2	Exclusive Economic Zone (million sq.km.)	2.02
3	Continental shelf (million sq.km.)	0.506
4	Rivers and canals (kms.)	1,19,024
5	Reservoirs (million ha)	3.15
6	Ponds and tanks (million ha)	2.32
7	Oxbow lakes and derelict waters (million ha)	1.3
8	Brackish waters (million ha)	1.24
9	Estuaries (million ha)	0.29

Inland Fisheries of India

Fish production of water bodies depends on the basic productivity of the ecosystems, the efficiency of energy flow at different trophic levels and the degree of human intervention in monitoring the biotic communities. Capture fisheries refer to the pen water systems where the options for changing the habitat variables and biotic communities are limited (Jhingran, 1990), while aquaculture is practiced in captive ecosystems allowing sufficient scope for human interventions in the biological production processes. Presently, the annual fish production in India is estimated at 7.6 million t, of which nearly 4.6 million t (60.56%) comes from inland sector. The significant growth in inland fish production highlighted its role in fisheries sector of our country. The contribution of inland fisheries towards upliftment of socio-economic status of fisher community is also vital, considering the number of fishers engaged in this enterprise. The main inland fisheries resources of

India comprise *(i)* Capture fisheries of rivers, lakes and estuaries, *(ii)* Culture fisheries of ponds and tanks and *(iii)* Capture-cum-culture based fisheries of reservoirs and oxbow lakes, where the management norms of both capture and culture fisheries grade into each other.

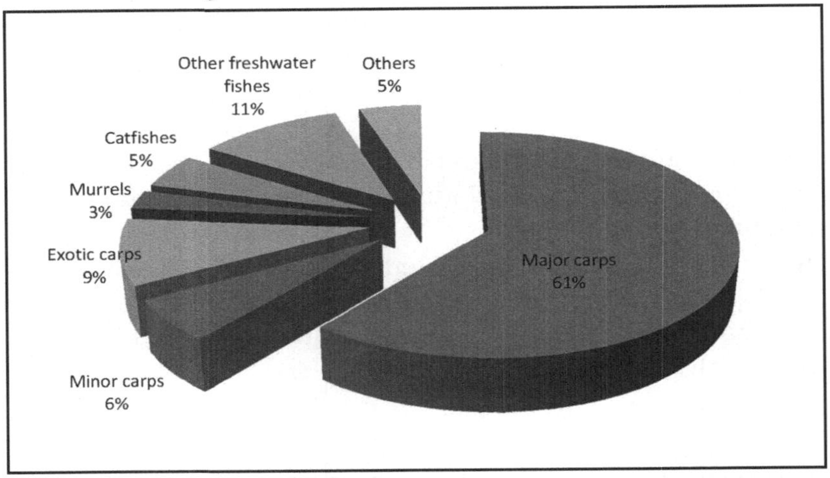

Fig. 2.1: **Percentage contribution of Inland fish landings in India (Year 2012)**

Table 2.2: Inland Fish Landings (by States/Union Territories) for Year 2012

Sr. No.	State/Union Territories	Landings in Tonnes
1	2	3
1.	Andhra Pradesh	1396148
2.	Arunachal Pradesh	3475
3.	Assam	250200
4.	Bihar	344470
5.	Chattisgarh	250482
6.	Goa	4087
7.	Gujarat	94708
8.	Haryana	111480
9.	Himachal Pradesh	8561
10.	Jammu and Kasmir	19700
11.	Jharkhand	107920
12.	Karnataka	168241
13.	Kerala	135936
14.	Madhya Pradesh	84855
15.	Maharashtra	137461

Contd...

1	2	3
16.	Manipur	24992
17.	Meghalaya	5389
18.	Mizoram	5450
19.	Nagaland	6840
20.	Orissa	286615
21.	Punjab	99131
22.	Rajasthan	32760
23.	Sikkim	500
24.	Tamil Nadu	189117
25.	Tripura	57460
26.	Uttarakhand	3847
27.	Uttar Pradesh	449750
28.	West Bengal	1323276
29.	Andaman and Nicobar Islands	193
30.	Chandigarh	46
31.	Dadra and Nagar Haveli	108
32.	Daman and Diu	133
33.	Delhi	690
34.	Lakshadweep	00
35.	Puducherry	5673
	Total	5609694

Table 2.3: Species-wise Inland Fish Landings in India (Year 2012)

Sr. No.	Category	Landings in Tonnes
1.	Major carps	3418794
2.	Minor carps	338252
3.	Exotic carps	535844
4.	Murrels	150081
5.	Catfishes	279684
6.	Other freshwater fishes	622722
7.	Others	264317
	Total	5609694

Major carps: Catla, Rohu, Mrigal, Calbasu.
Exotic carps: Common carp, Silver carp, Grass carp.
Murrels: Ophicephalus spp.
Catfishes: Wallago attu, Pangasius, Bagarius.

Capture Fisheries

Rivers: The different river systems in the country provide a traditional source of livelihood to thousands of fishermen and the riverine fish contribute significantly to the country's total inland fish production.

1. *Ganga river system*: Out of 14 large rivers, the Ganga river system is the largest river system of India with a combined length of about 12500 kms., draining near about one million sq.km., area. It flows through the states of Hariyana, Uttar Pradesh, Bihar, West Bengal, Madhya Pradesh, and Rajasthan. The different tributaries of Ganga are Gomti, Ghagra, Gandak, Kosi, Yamuna (Jamuna), Son, Punpun and Damodar. The river Yamuna is the largest tributary of the river Ganga. It covers 42.5 per cent of the total Ganga basin area.

Ganga river system accounts for 29 per cent of river length in the country. Ganga supports a wealth of fish fauna both in terms of variety and richness. The river is home for more than 140 fish species, of which many are commercially important. It is the original habitat of Indian major carps and several economically important catfishes. Ganga is also a major source of the riverine spawn, which meets the carp seed requirements of the culture sector to the tune of 30 per cent.

The commercially important fishes are: *Catla catla, Labeo rohita, Labeo calbasu, Cirrhinus mrigala, Cirrhinus reba, Labeo bata, Labeo dero, Mystus aor, Mystus seenghala, Silonia silondia, Wallago attu, Pangasius pangasius, Rita rita Clupisoma ganua Eutropiichthys vacha, Ailia coila, Amblypharyngodon mola, Plotosus canius, Polydactylus indicus, Hilsa ilisha, Ompak bimaculatus, Ompak pabda, Setipinna phasa, Setipinna brevifilis, Gadusia chapra, Notopterus chitala, Notopterus notopterus, Channa marulius, Channa striatus, Mastacemeblus armatus, Mastacembelus panchalus, Macrognathus aral, Terapon jarbua, Tor tor, Tor mosal, Tor putitora, Xenentodon cancila* and *Rhinomugil corsula.* Exotic fish species like: *Oreochromis mossambicus, Oreochromis niloticus, Cyprinus carpio, Hypophthalmichtys moiltirx, Aristichthys nobilis* and *Clarias gariepinus are also found in different tributaries of the river.* Along with the above mentioned fish species, the different prawn species recorded in the Ganga river are: *Macrobrachium rosenbergii, M.biramanicum chopral, M. lamarrei, M. malcomsonii, Metapenaeus brevicornis, M.monoceros, Penaeus monodon, P. indicus and P. semisulcatus.*

Different types of fishing gears and crafts are used in Ganga water. The important gears used in Ganga water are drag net (with or without pocket), gill net, purse net, hook and line, cast net, scoop net and trap. The crafts used for fishing are mostly indigenous, non-mechanized and locally built, except for mechanized boat in few stretches. The simplest and most primitive types of boat used for fishing in the river are the rafts and dongas, which are operated in calm waters. In the larger rivers subject to strong current and tidal movements, sturdier plank built boats are used. The boats operated in river Ganga are generally made of wood or tin (CIFRI, 2006).

The catch from the river is declining day-by-day. The average catch per km., of stretch worked out from the data collected at Allahabad centre depict that in 1950's the catch was as high as 1344 kg., whereas the catch declined to 362 kg., during 2000s. The production potential of Ganga, in its lower reaches, is estimated at 198.3 kg/ha/yr, whereas the actual fish yield is 30 kg/ha/yr. Thus, only 15.2 per cent of the potential is harvested (Sinha, 1999).

2. *Brahmaputra river*: The Brahmaputra river system with a combined total length of 4023 km., has a catchment area of 51 million hectare, an average and annual runoff of 38 million hectare meter and an average annual rainfall of 122 cm. The river is known as 'tsangpo' in the upper reaches, originates in Kubiangiri, east of the Mansarover lake in Tibet. It flows eastward at an elevation of 3600m MSL through southern Tibet for a distance of 1600 km., parallel to Himalayas. The river than turns abruptly south in a sharp – bend, at an elevation of 2830 m, and flowing in Arunachal Pradesh for a distance of 180 km., enters the valley of Assam at Pasighat, at an elevation of 150 m. In the plains it is joined by two other Himalayan rivers, Dibang and Luhit. Flowing further westward through Bangladesh for its last 480 km., joining the Ganga at Gualando. The Brahmaputra on its way to Bangladesh is joined by a large number of tributaries, both from the north as well as south. Characteristically the northern tributaries are large with steep shallow braided channels carrying high silt discharge, whereas, those on the southern bank are deeper with meandering channels, low gradient and lesser silt load.

Fishery of Brahmaputra is supported by: *Labeo rohita, Catla catla, Cirrhinus mrigala, Labeo calbasu, Labeo gonius, Labeo bata, Cirrhinus reba, Wallago attu, Channa gachua, Silonia silondia, Pangasius pangasius, Mystus cavasius, Mystus seenghala, Mystus aor, Mystus menoda, Mystus tengra, Mystus vittatus, Rita rita, Clarias batrachus, Heteropnestues fossilis, Bagarius bagarius, Ompak pabda, Ompak bimaculatus, Settipinna phasa, Gudusia chapra, Notopterus notopterus, Notopterus chitala, Mastacembelus armatus, Mastacembelus aculeatus, Xenentedon cancila, Glossogobius giuris, Amblypharyngodon mola, Nemacheilus* spp., *Ambassis* spp.

Biologically and economically important species have started showing a declining trend. The average fish production in Brahmaputra also declined from 196.93 kg/day in 1973-79 to 137.4 kg/day in 1996-98 (Sinha, 2000).

3. *Godavari river*: River Godavari is the largest of the peninsular rivers. It starts from Trambekeshwar and towns like: Nashik, Kopargaon, Gangakhed, Paithan, and Nanded are situated on the banks of this rivers. After flowing a distance of 1,465 km., it joins the Bay of Bengal in Andhra Pradesh. The main tributaries of the river are: Warna, Pravara, Sindhphana, Manjra, Pranhita, Dudhna and Dakshinpurna. Fish species such as: *Catla catla, Cirrhina mrigala, Labeo rohita, Labeo calbasu, P. sarana, Wallago attu, Channa* spp., are common in Godvari. The fish like: *Mystus*

spp., forms the food for poor people. Some fishes like: *Chanda nama, Chanda ranga, Glossogobius* etc., comparatively of small size, are useful in public health as larvicidal fishes. The crafts used in the Godavari are of primitive type, and no modern craft has been introduced for fishing. The gears most commonly used are the gill-nets, cast-nets and hook and lines.

4. *Indus river system*: It comprises the main river Indus and its major tributaries like: Kabul, Swat, Kurrum, Jhelum, Chenab, Ravi, Beas and Satlaj. River Indus is the main river of this system with a total length of 2,880 km. It originates in Tibet near the Mansarovar lake at an elevation of 5,180 m and passes through inaccessible mountain ranges in Northern Kashmir and emerges out of the hills near Attock (Pakistan). From Attock to its mouth in the Arabian sea, south of Karachi, the Indus transverses the plains of Pakistan for a length of about 1,610 km. The fish fauna of the upper reaches of Indus river has not been fully explored because of its inaccessibility. The main fish species present in the river are: *Labeo gonius, Rita buchanani, Exostoma stolicizkae, Trichogaster* sp., *Nemacheilus* spp., and *Schizopygopsis stoliczkee.*
5. *Krishna river*: This river starts from Mahabaleshwar in Maharashtra and after flowing for a distance of 1,400 km., from its origin; it joins the Bay of Bengal. It flows through the states of Maharashtra, Karnataka, and Andhra Pradesh. Its length in Maharashtra is 282 kms. Tributaries of river Krishna are the Koina, Warna and the Panchgganga. The fishery is mainly supported by: *Labeo rohita, Cirrhina cirrhosa, Thynnichthys* sp., *Aspidoparia* spp., and *Mystus seenghala.*
6. *Cauvery river*: It originates from Brahmagiri hills on the western ghats at an elevation of 340 m. After flowing 800 kms., it joins the Bay of Bengal in Tamil Nadu. It has the total catchment area of 87900 sq.km. It flows through the states of Kerala, Karnataka and Tamil Nadu. It is known to devout Hindus as 'Daksina Ganga (Ganges of the South)' and its entire course is considered holy ground. It is celebrated for its scenery and sanctity in Tamil literature. The Cauvery basin is with many tributaries including the Shimsha, the Hemavati, the Arkavati, Honnuhole, Lakshmana Tirtha, Kabini, Bhavani River, the Lokapavani, the Noyyal and the Amaravati River.

The major fishes present in the river are: *Catla catla, Cyprinus carpio, Labeo kontius, L. rohita, L. ariza, Cirrhina cirrhosa, C. mrigala, Mystus aor, M. seenghala, Wallago attu, Silonia silondia, Channa marulius, Notopterus Notopterus, Pangasius pangasius* and *Tor mussullah, Tor putitora.* The Mettur dam across the river Cauvery marked the end of the wild run of the anadromous Cauvery hilsa. Today, the hilsa has disappeared from the Cauvery region (Rama, 2014). The coracle is the most common craft and cast nets and drag nets are commonly used gear used for fishing.

7. *Narmada river*: It is one of the important rivers peninsular India. It originates in the Amarkantak hills at an elevation of 1.057 m in Bilaspur district of Madhya Pradesh. It has a length of 1,312 kms., and total catchment area of 98,7963 sq.km. It is mainly fed by seasonal rains. It flows through the states of Madhya Pradesh, Maharashtra and Gujarat. In its last 160 km., course, it flows through the plains and fall into the Gulf of Cambay (Arabian sea). The main fisheries of river is supported by *Labeo rohita, L. calbasu, L. fimbratus, L. bata, Tor tor, Cirrhina mrigala, C. reba, Puntius sarana, Mystus seenghala, M. cavasius, Clupisoma garua, Ompak bimaculatus* and *Wallago attu*. Other miscellaneous fishes are *Channa* spp., *Mastacembelus* spp., and *Notopterus notopterus.*
8. *Mahanadi river*: It originates from Sihawa hills to the extreme south-west of Raipur district of Madhya Pradesh and flows through Orissa, Bihar and Maharashtra. The total length of the river is 857 km. The fishery of river comprise the carps, catfishes, live fishes, featherbacks, prawns and miscellaneous species. A list of common fishes of river Mahanadi is depicted in Table 2.4.

Table 2.4: Fish Fauna of River Mahanadi

Catla catla, Cirrhinus mrigala, Cirrhinus reba, Labeo calbasu, Labeo boggut, Labeo bata, Labeo gonius, Labeo rohita, Ctenopharyngodon idella, Cyprinus carpio, Hypophthalmichthys molitrix, Osetobrama cotio, Danio rerio, Esomus danricus, Garra gotyla gotyla, Garra mullya, Puntius sarana, Puntius chola, Puntius ticto, Salmostoma bacaila, Salmostoma phulo, Noemacheilus botia, Mystus aor, Mystus seenghala, Mystus bleekeri, Mystus cavassius, Mystus tengra, Mystus vittatus, Rita rita, Bagarius bagarius, Pangasius pangasius, Clarias batrachus, Clarias gariepinus, Xenentodon cancila, Rhinomugil corsula, Channa gachua, Channa marulius, Channa orientalis, Channa striatus, Channa punctatus, Badis badis, Anabus testudineus, Colisa fasciatus, Glossogobius giuris, Tetradon cutcutia.

9. *Medium and minor rivers of India*: India is having 44 medium rivers with a total drainage area of 0.24 million sq.km. Nine of these rivers flows through more than one state and are considered as interstate rivers. Seventeen medium rivers flow towards west into the Arabian sea, and twenty-three towards the Bay of Bengal while four rivers in Mizoram and Manipur flow into Bangladesh and Burma.

Reservoirs: Indian reservoirs have a total area of 3.15 million ha, out of which small reservoirs occupy 1.49 million ha followed by large (1.14 million ha) and medium (0.52 million ha) ones. Among variously sized reservoirs, maximum annual production is reported from small reservoirs (50 kg/ha/yr) followed by medium (12.5 kg/ha/yr) and large (11.4 kg/ha/yr) with an average of 20.13 kg/ha/yr, although potential exists for manifold increase as demonstrated in some small, medium and large reservoirs in the country. Poor appreciation of the biological and limnological functions governing the production regimes of reservoirs and lack of stocking programmes have rendered below-optimal utilization of the fisheries potential of the reservoirs. It is expected that through sustained supplementary stocking of quality fingerlings, augmenting the fish stocks through auto stocking, adoption of appropriate mesh sizes, optimum fishing effort and enforcement of closed areas and closed seasons the average productivity could be increased to a level of 500 kg/ha/yr from small reservoirs; 200 kg/ha/yr from medium reservoirs; and 100-150 kg/ha/yr from the large reservoirs.

The total water spread area of Indian reservoir is about 3 million hectares, which forms about 50 per cent of the total reservoir area in South East Asia. Indian Institute of Management, Ahemadabad listed 975 reservoirs in India, in size range of 1000 ha to 10,000 ha covering an area of 1.7 million hectares. According to Sugunan (1995), the present total area under the reservoirs in India is 3.1 million hectares (Table 2.5).

Table 2.5: Distribution of Small, Medium and Large Reservoirs in India

Type	Small Reservoir	Medium Reservoir	Large Reservoir	Total
Number	19134	180	56	19370
Area (ha)	1485557	527541	1140268	3153366

Data pulled from Sugunan (1995): FAO Report.

Table 2.6: A State-wise Number of Reservoirs in India

States	Small Reservoirs		Irrigation Tanks		Medium Reservoirs		Large Reservoirs	
	Number	Area (Ha)	Number	Area (Ha)	Number	Area (Ha)	Number	Area (Ha)
Tamil Nadu	58	15,663	8837	300278	9	19,577	2	23,222
Karnataka	46	15,253	4605	213404	16	29,078	12	1,79,556
Andhra Pradesh	98	24,178	2800	177749	32	66,429	7	1,90,151
Gujarat	115	40,099	561	44025	28	57,748	7	1,44,358
Uttar Pradesh	40	20,845		1,97,806	22	44,993	4	71,196
Madhya Pradesh	6	1,72,575			21	1,69,502	5	1,18,307
Maharashtra	NA	1,19,515			NA	39,181	NA	1,15,054
Bihar	112	12,461			5	12,523	8	71,711
Orissa	1433	66,047			6	12,748	3	1,19,403
Kerala	21	7,957			8	15,500	1	6,160
Rajasthan	389	54,231			30	49,827	4	49,386
Himachal Pradesh	1	200			NA	NA	2	41,364
West Bengal	4	732			1	4,600	1	10,400
Haryana	4	282			NA	NA	NA	NA
NE States	4	1,639		600	2	5,835	NA	NA
Total	2331	5,51,677	16,803	9,33,862	180	5,27,541	56	11,40,268

Unfortunately, majority of reservoirs are not being scientifically managed for fisheries. Only a handful of than have so far has been harassed along scientific lines, while the others are either half-heartedly managed or not managed at all. As compared to several developed countries, the per hector fish production in Indian reservoirs is very poor, being only about 20 kg/yr as against 88 kg/yr in the USSR, 100 kg/yr in Sri Lanka and 64.5 kg/yr in large reservoirs of Thailand. Lot of progress has been made in several developed countries in deep water fishing in reservoirs and management of their fisheries.

Fig. 2.2: **Fishing raft used in reservoir**

Since the reservoirs are constructed primarily for hydel and irrigation purposes, the fish production from them is treated as of bye-product importance. This relegation is one of the reasons of poor fish yield from reservoirs. So much so, the reservoir fish industry could not make any remarkable progress as yet. Because of the country's growing demand for irrigation and power, new reservoirs have been coming up and thus this potential is expected to grow further giving ample opportunities of culture based capture fishing practices, provided these water bodies are managed scientifically for development of fisheries at an optimally sustainable level.

Reservoirs are generally classified as small (<1000 ha), medium (1000-5000 ha) and large (>5000 ha), especially in the records of the Government of India.

Fig. 2.3: **Tilapias dominating in Indian Reservoirs**

The exotic fishes like: *Cyprinus carpio, Ctenopharyngodon idella, Hypophthalmichthys molitrix, Oreochromis mossambicus, Oreochromis niloticus, Salmo trutta fario, Salmo salar, Onchorynchus nerka, Onchorhynchus mykiss, Aristichthys nobilis, Clarias gariepinus* etc., were import and introduced in Indian reservoirs. The transplantation of these fishes into Indian reservoirs has not been a very good experience.

It is observed that introductions of tilapia and common carp has oblitered *Puntius spp.,* in Krishnarajasagar reservoir of Karnataka (Ramkrishna, 2008). Tilapias has entered the reservoirs of all the river systems of Karnataka state and affected the faunal composition of indigenous fishes in the reservoirs, posing a great challenge for its effective control and management.

In North Indian reservoirs establishment of silver carp has already affected the performance of catla and rohu because of overlapping in feeding niches (Devaraj *et al.* 2008).

According to Karamchandani and Mishra (1980) silver carp and catla share a common niche and compete with each other for food in a reservoir ecosystem. Percentage composition of phytoplankton in the guts of both the fishes caught during the same time from Kulgarhi reservoir was more or less the same. Zooplankton, the favourite menu of catla, formed 21 per cent of the gut contents of silver carp. The authors concluded that silver carp hampered the growth of catla in the reservoir and advocated caution before its stocking in Indian reservoirs.

Common carp is not suitable for stocking in Indian reservoirs, especially the larger ones, for diverse reasons. Being a sluggish fish, its chances of survival in a predator-dominated reservoir are very poor. Due to its slow movement and bottom dwelling habit, they are not frequently caught in a passive fishing gear like gill net. It is no wonder, despite a regular stocking for 13 years, not a single common carp was ever caught from Nagarjunasagar reservoir of Andhra Pradesh. The stocked fishes failed to survive among the predators. A more important disqualification is its propensities to compete with some economically important indigenous carps like: *Cirrhinus mrigala, Cirrhinus cirrhosa* and *Cirrhinus reba* with which common carp shares food niche. The presence of common carp has resulted in the decline of Cirrhinus species in Girna reservoir (Maharashtra) and Krishnarajsagar reservoir (Karnataka).

Estuaries: An estuary may be defined as a region where river water mixes with seawater and considerably dilutes it. It is the most variable and dynamic aquatic ecosystem, which is influenced by factors like: water movements, tides, mixing of sea and river water, salt load and salinity regime. India has an estimated estuarine waters spread area of 0.29 million hectare. The estuarine fisheries are above subsistence level and contribute significantly to the production. The average fish yield varies from 45 to 75 kg/ha. The major estuarine systems in India are the Hooghly Matlah estuarine system in west Bengal; the Rushikulya estuary in Orissa; the Godavari and Krishna in Andhra Pradesh; the Adyar, the Cauvery; velar and Vaigai estuaries in Tamil Nadu, the Narmada and the Tapti in Gujarat, Asthamudi in Kerala, Kalinadi in Karnataka and Mandovi-zuari system of Goa.

1. *Hooghly – Matlah estuarine system*: The Hooghly-Matlah estuarine system located in west Bengal between latitude 21°-23°N and longitude 88°-90°E. The Hooghly-Matlah estuarine complex has the largest deltaic region in the world. The total approximate area of this estuarine system with its innumerable tributaries and network of creeks is 2340 sq. km. The mangrove vegetation grown in the deltaic region harbours a potential grazing ground for the estuarine fishes and prawn species. The estuarine sources are highly productive. About 50,000 tonnes of fish are landed annually, 70 per cent being from high salinity zone. Maximum sustainable yield has been estimated to be 3, 56,741 t that is about 200 kg less than what was landed in 1996-97.

The important fish species in bag net catches during winter migratory fishing are: *Harpodon nehereus, Settipinna* spp., *Trichiurs* spp., *Hilsa ilisha, Lates calcarifer,* and prawns mainly *Parapenaeopsis* spp.

2. *Mahanadi estuarine system*: The Mahanadi estuary lies in Cuttack and Puri districts of Orissa and drains into the Bay of Bengal. The tidal influence extends up to about 42 km., from the mouth of the river. As an estuarine

complex including the brackishwater lagoons of about 12000 ha, Mahanadi estuarine system covers about 30,000 ha area with an estimated annual production of about 550 tonnes/year. The fishery of this estuary includes clupeoids, mullets, and prawns. The important fishes present are: *Hilsa ilisha, Nematolosa nasus, Sardinella* spp., *Mugil cephalus, M.cunnesius, M.parsia, Lates calcarifer, Sillago* spp., *Epinephelus spp, Malabaricus* spp., *Ambassis* spp., *Leiognathus* spp., *Lutianus johnii, Datnoides quadrifasciatus* and *Sparus berda*.

3. *Godavari estuarine system*: It is the major estuary in peninsular India. It has an area of about 18000 hectares. Goutami is the main source of the estuarine complex in which tidal influence extends only up to 40-50 km., upstream from the mouth region. Formation of sand bars in the estuarine mouth restricts the entrance of tidal waters.

About 200 species of fishes have been recorded from the estuary, of which 72-80 per cent are nearly euryhaline, 12-20 per cent almost marine and 15 per cent freshwater in origin. Mullets form nearly 2/3rd of the total fish landing and are represented by: *M. cephalus, M. speigleri, M. dussumieri, L. troschelii, L. oligolepis*, and *L. seheli*. The other fishes of commercial importance are: *Pristiopama hasta, Leiognatus* sp., *Gerres filamentous, Caranx sp., Sillago sihama, Lates calcarifer* etc. Mullets and prawns form the major catch of the system. *M. monoceros, M. dobsoni, M. affinis, M. brevicornis, P. monodon*, and *P. indicus* are the important prawn species available in lower reaches of the estuary.

4. *Other estuarine systems*: Other than Godavari estuarine system there are eight small estuaries in peninsular India namely: Vasishtha, Vainatheyam, Adyar, Karuveli, Ponniyar, Godilam, Paravan, Vellar, Killai and Coferoom.

The 40 km., long the Adyar river meets the Bay of Bengal at Adyar within the southern limits if Madras city. The tidal influence is felt in the river up to a distance of 6.4 km., from its mouth. The estuary is connected to the sea only during monsoon and post monsoon months. When freshwater discharge reduces by the end of January, sand bar is formed at the river mouth and the estuary gets totally cut off from the sea. Among important fishes the estuary is having mullets, *Sillago sihama, Tilapia mossambica*, catfishes and prawns.

The Vellar river drains into the Bay of Bengal at Port Novo. The total length of the river is 480 km. The Vellar estuary is located in between latitude 11°-29'N and longitude 79°-46'E. The estuary covers an area of 262 ha. The important fishes of the estuary are *Mugil* spp., *Leiognathus* spp., *Sardinella gibbosa, Johnius spp., Polynemus tetradactylus, Engraulis malabaricus*, catfishes and prawns and shrimps.

5. *Narmada estuarine system*: River Narmada is having an estuarine stretch of about 120 km., which ends in Gulf of Cambey. Gradual decline in tidal ingress is being observed due to development of sand bars at the mouth region of the estuary. However, from ten years records during 1973-82 the average annual production of the estuarine system has been estimated to be about 4000 tonnes in which as a group hilsa contributed (40-45% average 1662.4 tonnes) followed by mullets (15-20% average 686.95 tonnes) and prawns (5-8% average; 286.55 tonnes). Miscellaneous species contributed 30-38 per cent (average 1520 tonnes) of the total landings. The fishing potential estimated in a survey during 1986-87 indicated that 2884 fishermen are actively engaged in fishing activities in the system with 103 boats (non-mechanised) and about 28000 nets. Gill nets are in maximum use (26414 nos.) in the lower zone of the estuary. Hilsa forms the major catch of these gill nets (80-85%). Cast nets are mainly used for prawn fishing. Besides these, the seedling of freshwater giant prawn (*M. rosenbergii*) form an important fishery resource in mixoligohaline and limnetic zones of the system.

On account of a cascade of dams under construction on the Narmada river system with the world Bank aid the entire ecosystem and its productivity are bound to be greatly affected. Pre-impoundment surveys have been initiated by the Central Inland Fisheries Research Institute (CIFRI), Barrackpore (West Bengal) in 150 km., stretch of the river Narmada in the state of Gujarat.

Lakes

- *Pulicat lake*: Pulicat lake is second largest lagoon on east coast spreading in the Nellore district of Andhra Pradesh and the Chingleput district of Tamil Nadu where it is connected with Bay of Bengal by narrow mouth near the Pulicat village. In length it is 60 km., and the width varies from 1-18 km., with total area of 77700 ha but with water spread area of 36900 ha rest being dry and becoming marshy during monsoon. Geographically, the lake lies between the latitudes 13°26′ to 13°43′N, and longitudes 80°03° to 80°18′E. Topographically, the lake has been steadily shrinking both in its water spread area as well as in its depth, due to monsoon siltation and summer evaporation.

Anthropogenic developmental activities like the several industries, around Ennore in the south (North Chennai), add chemical, oil and thermal pollution, along with fly-ashy slurry from the two thermal power plants, and the dredged out silt from the Ennore megaport, all observed to be the most major threats for the survival of fisheries and water birds in the southern region of the lake, in recent times. It is connected to sea by a narrow mouth, whose position, depth and width vary with season. Two seasonal rivulets-Rayala vagu and Kalangi river drain into the lake. In the lake, there are several islands the important being pernadu, venadu and Irakkam. The average amplitude of the tide at lake mouth is only 25 cm and its influence is felt up to 6 to 10 km., from the mouth. The average depth is 1.5 m. During the period 1970-77 total catch varied from 759.6 t (1975) to 1371.4 t (1972) yield ranging from 20.6 to 37.2 kg/ha; of the water spread area.

The lake is surrounded by nearly 66 fishing villages, 52 of which are on the lake-side, 22 in Andhra Pradesh and 30 in Tamil Nadu. The rest of the villages are on the sea-side in Tamil Nadu. Prior to the tsunami-2004, there were a total of 43,022 fisherfolk of whom 10730 were active fishermen.

There is no organized data collection of the capture fisheries on the Pulicat lake. During 1970 prawns accounted for 566.5 t of which the main contributors were *Penaeus indicus* (335.9 t), *M . monoceros* (76.1t) and *M. dobsoni* (54.4t). Mullets accounted for 214.6t the main species being *M. cephalus* (136.2t). Perches amounted to 87.4t. Clupeids accounted for 125.6t, the main species being *Nematolosa nasus* (70.2t), crabs were represented by 4 *Neptonus pelagicus* (70.2t) and *Scylla serrata* (48.8t).

Mullets and prawns are the major fisheries of the lake. Fishes like: *Mugil cephalus, M. macrolepis, Sillago sihama, Gerres oyena, Nematalosa nasus* and *Chanos chanos*; prawns like: *Penaeus semisulcatus, P. monodon, P. indicus, Metapenaeus monoceros* and *M. dobsoni*; crabs like: *Scylla serrata* and *Portunus pelagicus* and oyster like: C*rassostrea madrasensis* are also found in the lake.

- *Chilka lake*: The Chilka lake located along the east coast of India between the latitudes 19028'-19024'N and longitudes 85067' and 85035' E is a pear shaped brackish water lagoon in between the district of Puri, Kaurda and Ganjam has an average water spread area of 1050 sq.kms. It covers an area of 1165 sq.kms., in monsoons and 906 sq.kms., in summer. This lake is designated as an important Ramsar site (No. 229) of India.

The lake is fed with main two tributaries of river Mahanadi called river Daya and river Bhargavi at the northern side and connects with the Bay of Bengal near Arakhakuda village through a zig zag long outer channel of 35 kms., long. Similarly the lake has connected with the Bay of Bengal at the southern end near Purunabandha village through 16 kms., long canal called as 'palur canal'. As a result of this, the entire lake becomes a freshwater during monsoons. This peculiar phenomenon change provides a congenial features for survival of freshwater flora and fauna up to December and afterwards the salinity gradually increases touching maximum in July.

The lake is divided in to four ecological sectors namely: the southern sector, the central sector, the northern sector and the outer channel sector. The northern sector is freshwater dominated zone, central sector is a brackish water zone and southern sector is a higher saline area. The outer channel sector is marine in nature with saline water but during monsoon, the water becomes fresh due to discharge of flood water to the sea (Parida *et al.* 2013).

Table 2.7: Fish Species in Chilka lake

Ailia coila, Ambassis commerconii, Aplocheilus panchax, Bagarius bagarius, Caranx sexfasciatus, Caranx ignobilis, Caranx melampygus, Catla catla, Chanda nama, Channa punctata, Channa striata, Chanos chanos, Chela labuca, Clarias batrachus, Crossocheilus latius, Cynoglossus lingua, Echeneis naucrates, Elops machnata, Esomus danricus, Etroplus suratensis, Gazza minuta, Gerres filamentosus, Gerres setifer, Gerres limbatus, Gerres phaiya, Glossogobius giuris, Gudusia chapra, Heterompeustes fossilis, Hilsa kelee, Labeo ariza, Labeo calbasu, Labeo rohita, Lates calcarifer, Liza macolepis, Liza parsia, Liza tade, Macrognathus aral, Mastacembelus armatus, Megalops cyprinoides, Mugil cephalus, Mystus cavasius, Mystus gulio, Mytus vittatus, Nematalosa nasus, Notopeturs notopterus, Ompak bimaculatus, Ompmak pabda, Pangasius pangasius, Plotosus canius, Plotosus lineatus, Pristis pectinata, Pteoris radiate, Puntius sophore, Puntius ticto, Puntius vittatus, Rasbora daniconius, Rasbora rasbora, Rhinomugil corsula, Salmostoma bacaila, Sardinella melannura, Scoliodon laticaudus, Silonia silondia, Sphyraena putnamae, Tenualosa ilisha, Tenualosa toil, Hilsa kelee, Terapon jarbua, Tetradon cutcutia, Wallago attu, Xenentodon cancila, Anguilla bengalensis, Anguilla bicolor bicolor, Danio rerio, Hippocampus fuscus, Otolithes ruber, Oreochromis mossambicus, Butis butis etc.

Chilka lake has more than 132 fishing villages with a total population of more than 0.15 million. About 30 per cent of the fishing village population are active fishermen. Khorda net, gill net, drag net, sieve net, scoop net and cast net are the main gears used in Chilka lake. Gill net fishing and Khonda fishing together registered to about 80 per cent of the total fishing in the lake (Pardia *et al*. 2013).

- *Kolleru lake*: Kolleru lake is the second largest freshwater ecosystem in peninsular India. It is located between 16°32′ latitudes of 16°47′N and longitudes of 81°2′ and 81°4′E in the state of Andhra Pradesh. The lake was formed as a natural depression between river Godavari on the north and river Krishna on the south near their tail-end region, before they open into Bay of Bengal. Several irrigation canals originating from the dams on river Godavari at Dhowlaiswaram and river Krishna also open into the lake. Lake also receives water through a number of large and medium sized, seasonal rivulets and streams that drain the surrounding upland areas. The lake is connected to Bay of Bengal through a narrow natural channel Upputeru, about 62 km long. The water spread area of 901.3 sq.km., at maximum and 135 sq.km., at 1m (M.S.L.). The total catchment area of the lake was estimated to be about 4700 sq.km. Depending upon the seasonal inflow the depth of lake varies between 1m to 4m. During summer the marginal shallow areas of the lake become completely dry. The lake area receives annual average rainfall of 99.95 cm. The relative humidity varies between 64 per cent in June and 83 per cent in February. The lake experiences brackishwater conditions in the months when the inflow of freshwater into the lake is low. The saline water reaches up to the middle regions of the lake, while in the northern parts freshwater conditions exist. On the onset of southwest monsoon in the mid seasonal drains and streams.

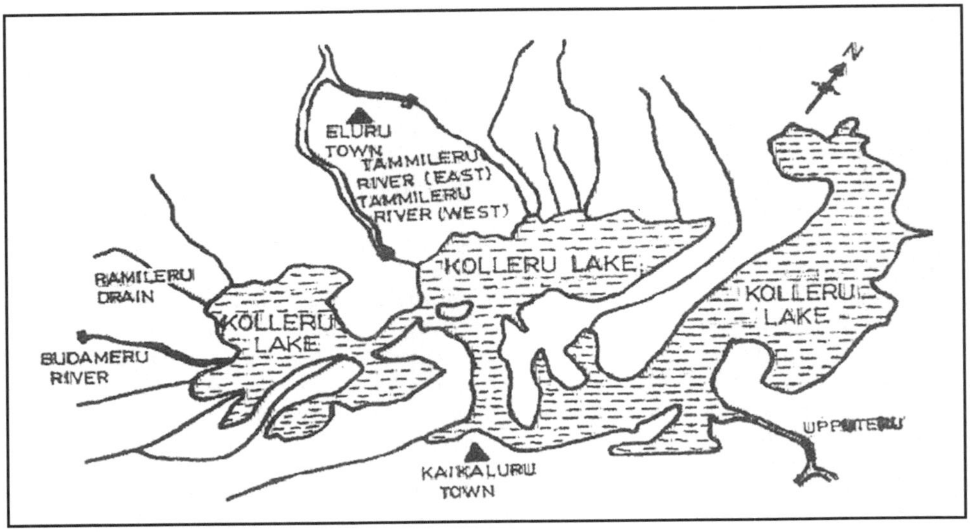

Fig. 2.4: **Map of Kolleru Lake, Andhra Pradesh**

Near about 105 species of fish and 7 species of commercially important prawns were recorded so far from the lake, out of which 19 species of fish were encountered in brackish waters in the tidal zone. The lake supports a rich fishery of air breathing fishes. Traditionally live fish captured in the lake area exported to markets in the north-eastern India. The Indian climbing perch (*Anabus sp.*) dominate the catch. The commercially important catfish include: *Clarias batrachus, Heteropnesutes fossilis* and *Wallago attu*. The murrels such as: *Channa striatus* and *Channa punctatus* supports a good fishery. Carp landings are represented by: *Catla catla, Labeo rohita, Cirrhinus mrigala* and *Puntius sarana sarana*. Other important fish species are: *Mugil cephalus, Etroplus suratensis, Etroplus maculates, Mastacembelus armatus armatus, M. pancalus, Macrognathus aculeatus* and *Anguilla bengalensis*. The commercially important prawns are: *Penaeus monodon, Penaeus indicus, Metapenaeus monoceros, M. dobsonii, Macrobrachium rosenbergii, M. rude,* and *M .macolmsoni.*

The marginal areas of the lake have been converted into fishponds. World Banks extended financial assistance to farmers for the construction and management of fishponds. In the last decade nearly 24000 hectares area have been converted into the fishponds. This has resulted in the degradation of natural habitat in the lake proper over the years affecting the fishery. The area of the lake has diminished and the breeding areas of the many species are affected.

Dutt and Murthy (1976) studied the fisheries of Kolleru lake for 1970-72, when the ponds were not constructed. During this period the total fish landings were estimated to be around 720 tonnes. Of these fish *Anaus oligolepis* and *A. testudineus* dominated the landings forming nearly 28 per cent. Carps contributed to 18 per cent and murrels to about 16 per cent. Rao *et al.* (19991) based on a study of the landings to be around 1800 to 2800 tonnes. The total landings during the period between 1976 and 1987 increased three fold. It is mainly due to an increase in the fishing activity in the lake.

A comparative study of the major fish groups on the fisheries of Kolleru lake between the periods before and after the changes in ecology suggests perceptible changes in the fisheries of Kolleru lake. Catfish landings when compared to earlier period also increased. The landings of the climbing perches and murrels remained stable, while that of carps declined remarkably. This could be attributable to the decrease in the lake area, where the juveniles are distributed and also the increased capture of juveniles of carps for stocking in the nearby fish ponds. Normally the juveniles got recruited from the streams and irrigational channels opening into the lake. Increaseed exploitation of juveniles could be one of the reasons for the decline in fishery.

- *Dal lake*: The Kashmir valley has a number of freshwater lakes notably Dal lake, Wular Lake, Haigam Rakh, Mirgund and Hokarsar. These lakes are unique in their flora and fauna, their beauty and their biological production. The Dal lake is situated within the Srinagar city lying with a latitude of 34.7°N and longitude of 74.52°E. It is a Himalayan urban lake which is mainly used for tourism. Fishery is of secondary importance. The lake is one of the most beautiful lakes of India. The maximum depth of the Dal lake is around 1.37 meter. Thirty seven species of fish have been recorded and important species inhabiting the Dal lake are: *Schizothorax esocinus, Schizothorax niger, Schizothorax curuifrons, Labeo dero, Crossocheilus sp., Botia birdi, Nemacheilus kashmirensis, Gambussia afffinis, Glyptothorax, Glyptosternum* etc.

Besides the above mentioned fishes, the exotic fishes like: scale carp (*Cyprinus carpio communis*) and mirror carp (*Cyprinus carpio specularis*) constitute the major catch of commercial fishery of Dal lake. Common carp introduced in the year 1957, constitutes about 70 per cent of the total catches where as *Schizothorax* contributes for about 10 per cent and other fishes including catfishes form 20 per cent of total landings.

- *Loktak lake*: Loktak lake is the largest freshwater wetland in North-Eastern India. It is also known as the only floating lake in the world due to the floating phumdis on it. Loktak is a shallow and somewhat acidic freshwater lake. It is the largest wetland in the North-Eastern region of India and has been referred as the lifeline of the people of Manipur due to its importance in the socioeconomic and cultural life. The lake is situated 38 kms., south of Imphal city of Manipur state. It covers an area of about 286 sq.kms., at the elevation of 768.5 m located between longitudes 93° 46′ and 93° 55′ E and latitudes 24° 25′ and 24°

42′ N. The depth of water during dry season ranges between 0.5 m to 1.5 m. The total water spread area of about 490 sq.kms., was recorded in 1966. Loktak lake plays an important role in the ecological and economic security of the region. The Lake has been the source of water for generation of hydroelectric power, irrigation and water supply. A large population living around the lake depends upon the lake resources for their sustenance. The lake is included on Montreux record in 1993 as a result of ecological problems such as: deforestation in the catchment area, infestation of water hyacinth, and pollution.

The fish fauna of lake comprises 64 species. Loktak lake serves as the breeding ground for several species of migratory fishes such as: *Labeo dero, L. angra, L. bata, Cirrhinus reba* and *Osteobrama belangeri*. These riverine species migrate from the Chindwin Irrwaddy river system in Burma to the upstream areas of Manipur river and breed in various shallow lakes in the valley. These fishes disappeared from the lake since the construction of Ithai barrage which has blocked their migratory route. The fisheries of lake is also supported by: *Hypopthalmichthys molitrix, Ctenopharyngodon idella, Cyprinus carpio, Cirrhinus mrigala, Labeo rohita, L.calbasu, L.gonius, Catla catla, Puntius spp., Esomus danricus, Heteropnestes fossilis, Ambassis* sp., *Osteobrama cotio, Channa* spp., *Glossogobius* spp., *Notopterus* spp., *Amblypharyngodon mola, Anabus testudineus, Lepidocephalus* spp., *Clarias batrachus* and *Tilapia sp.*

Loktak lake serves as the breeding ground for several species of migratory fishes such as: *Labeo dero, Labeo angra, Labeo bata, Cirrhinus reba* and *Osteobrama belangiri* (Singh *et al.* 2011).

- *Sasthamcotta lake*: It is the largest freshwater lake in Kerala state, extending to about 3.42 sq.km. The lake is situated at 09° 02′N and 76° 37′. The ancient Sastha temple of the lake is an important pilgrimage center. It is spring fed lake and is the source of drinking water for half a million people in the Kollam district of Kerala. The lake is a designated wetland of international importance under the Ramsar Convention since November 2002. More than 27 fish species and two genera of prawns are reported from the lake. The fisheries of lake is supported by: *Puntius ticto, Puntius amphibious, Puntius filamentosus, Mystus oculatus, Parambassis dayi, Xenentodon cancila* and the lake is famous for catches of fishes like: *Etroplus suratensis, Etroplus maculates, Ambassis dayi* and *Horabagarus brachysoma*. Gill nets, cast nets and encircling nets are operated for fishing. Despite its large area, Sasthamcotta lake supports a negligible fishery, which is mainly artisanal. Drastic reduction of large sized species from the lake is reported by Girijakumari (2007). Large sized species like: *Horabagrus brachysoma, Wallago attu, Channa marulius* and *Channa micropeltus* etc., which were once present in large quantities were reduced considerably or even absent (Girijakumari, 2007).

Culture Fisheries

- *Freshwater Aquaculture:* Ponds scattered in different parts of the country can produce a higher production level ranging from 3-10 t/ha, but the average yield is too much low *i.e.* 50-500 kg/ha. Problems like: non-availability of quality seed, feed, chemicals and fertilizers often retard then pond productivity. The composite fish culture of Indian major carps (Catla, Rohu and Mrigal) with three exotic carps (common carp, silver carp and grass carp) is one of the best known examples of fin fish polyculture. The polyculture technology proved to be the turning point in the history of carp culture in India which played an important role in augmenting aquaculture production beyond 10 t/ha/yr. Fin fish culture in earthen ponds in the inland areas has shown tremendous progress. It can be further improved by providing quality inputs such as: seed, feed and by providing better infrastructure support for water management, aeration and feeding. There is a wide scope for improvement in the average production to 3-4 t/ha/yr, from the present level of less than 2 t/ha/yr. In Andhra Pradesh and Punjab fish farmers have demonstrated that production of fin fish from ponds could be enhanced to about 15 t/ha/yr, by resorting to proper management techniques (Thampy, 2002).
- *Brackish water fish farming:* Very limited area of brackish water resources is used for aquaculture, mainly in West Bengal, Orissa, Kerala and Andhra Pradesh. The important commercial species of brackish water fishes are: *Chanos chanos, Liza tade, Liza parsia, Lates calcarifer* and *Mugil cephalus.* The ancient practice of trapping prawn seed from the tidal belt into the adjoining paddy fields is in vogue in West Bengal, Kerala and Karnataka (Jhingran, 1990).

1. *Oxbow lakes*: India has extensive riverine wetlands in the form of oxbow lakes, variously named as beel, jheel, mauns, chaurs etc. These lakes in the states of West Bengal, Assam and Bihar constitute an important resource for fishery exploitation. By adopting scientific management yield about 1.2 million t of fishes can be achieved. But, flood control measures, water abstraction, siltation, habitat destruction and heavy weed infestation have restricted the yield to about 120-200 kg/ha/yr (Jhingran, 1990). These lakes are also suitable for pen and cage culture. The oxbow lakes are facing major problems like excessive enrichment of nutrients from external sources and locking of nutrients in hydrophytic chains as well as in the bottom biota dominated by molluscs.

REFERENCES

Central Inland Fisheries Research Institute (CIFRI), Barrackpore. 2006. Report of ICAR A.P. Cess Fund Scheme "Techno-socio-economic Status of Fishers of River Ganga" 80p.

Devaraj, K.V., Basavaraju, Y. and Seenappa, D., (2008). Introduced Food Fishes of Karnataka: An Overview, pp. 235-241, In: Fish Introductions in India: Status, Potential and Challenges (Eds. W.S. Lakra, A.K. Singh and S. Ayyapan), Narendra Publishing House, Delhi.

Dutt, S. and V.S.R. Murthy. (1976). On the Fish and Fisheries of the Lake Kolleru, Andhra Pradesh. *Mem. Soc. Zool.*, Guntur 1:17-21.

Girijakumari, S. (2007). Resource Potential of Sasthamkotta Lake with Special Reference to Fish Fauna and their Sustainability, Ph.D. thesis, Mahatma Gandhi University, Kerala.

Jhingran, A.G. (1990). Recent Advances in Inland Fisheries Development in India, In: Technologies for Inland Fisheries Development (Eds. V.V. Sugunan and Utpal Bhaumik), pp. 1-13, Central Inland Capture Research Institute, Barrackpore, West Bengal.

Karamchandani, S.J. and Mishra, D.N., (1980). Preliminary Observations on the Status of Silver Carp in Relation to Catla in the Culture Fishery of Kulgarhi Reservoir. *J. Bombay Nat. Hist. Soc*; 77:261-269.

Parida, S., Karna, S.K., Bhatta, K.S. and Guru, B.C. (2013). Distribution of Fishing Gears in India's Largest Brackish Water Lagoon, India. *Bull. Env. Pharmacol. Life Sci.*, 2(7):62-67. Paper available on http:/www.bepls.com.

Rama Swayamprakash. (2014). Fishing the Cauvery River: How Mettur Changed it all. South Asia Network on Dams, Rivers and People, 1-14.

Ramakrishna, N.R. (2008). Exotic Fishes in Karnataka: Their History, Status and Prospects. In: Fish Introductions in India: Status, Potential and Challenges (Eds. W.S. Lakra, A.K. Singh and S. Ayyapan), 249-254, Narendra Publishing House, Delhi.

Rao, K.V., R.S. Panwar, M.Rama Krishnaiah, J.B. Rao, T.S. Rama Raju, K.S. Rao and G. Ch. Rao. (1991). Studies on Ecology and Fisheries of Kolleru lake Ecosystem and Development of Suitable Management Measures for Obtaining Sustained Fish Production. Annual Report, Central Inland Fisheries Research Institute, Barrackpore: 26-30.

Singh, A.A., Debtanu Barman, Asem Sanjit Singh and S.C. Mandal. (2011). Loktak Lake: A Dying Wetland of Manipur in N.E. India: Development Measure for its restoration). *Fishing Chimes*, 31(1):88-90.

Sinha, M. (1999). Vision of Inland Fisheries of India of Twenty First Century. In: S.H. Abidi, N.K. Thakur, R.S. Biradar and L. Shenoy (eds.), Vision on Indian Fisheries of 21st Century, Central Institute of Fisheries Education, Mumbai, pp. 154-168.

Sinha, M. (2000). In: Proc. Seminar on Fishery Technologies and their Commerclization, p. 35-43, CIFE, Mumbai.

Sinha, M. (2000). In: Environmental Impact Assessment of Inland Waters for Sustainable Fisheries Management and Conservation of Biodiversity, (Sinha, M., Jha, B.C. and Khan, M.A. Eds.), p. 1-9, Bulletin Number 101, Central Inland Fisheries Research Institute, Barrackpore, West Bengal.

Sugunan, V.V. (1995). Reservoir Fisheries of India, FAO Report Number 345, Daya Publishing House, Delhi.

Thampy, D.M. (2002). Role of Professionals in the Development of Inland Fisheries in India. In: Riverine and Reservoir fisheries of India (Boopendranath, M.R., Meenakumari, B., Joseph, J., Sankar, T.V., Pravin, P. and Edwin, L., Eds.), p. 351-358, Scoiety of Fisheries Technologists (India), Cochin.

Page 56-62

PLANKTON AND FISHERIES
Edited by : V.B. Sakhare; H.K. Jadhav and S.S. Jadhav
Edition : 2017
ISBN : 978-93-5056-811-8
Published by : Discovery Publishing House Pvt. Ltd., New Delhi (India)

3 Disco Fish Trawl (46 m) of Ratnagiri, Maharashtra

N.N. Sawant & **A.S. Mohite**
Department of Fisheries Engineering, College of Fisheries,
(Dr. B.S. Konkan Krishi Vidyapeeth, Dapoli), Ratnagiri - 415 629.

ABSTRACT

Trawling is one of the popular fishing methods along the west coast of India. However, there are regional variations in trawl net design, construction and operation. The present study deals with the general characteristics and specifications of fish trawl (46 m) operated along the Ratnagiri coast of Maharashtra. The material used for the fish trawl is HDPE (High Density Polyethylene) and the knot type used for construction is a single trawl knot. Blue colour netting twine material is normally used having twine diameter of 1.50 mm for construction of netting of wing and belly; while 1.0 mm twine is used for cod end. The mesh size of the cod end section was 18 mm while the upper and lower edge of cod end had 100 meshes in width and 150 meshes in depth.

Keywords: Trawling, Fish trawl, Disco Dol.

INTRODUCTION

Trawling, though an efficient method of fishing is known to be one of the most non-selective methods of fish capture. Trawl is an important marine fishing gear; nearly 20 per cent of marine fish landed in the world is caught by this gear (Sreekrishna and Shenoy, 2001). The major factors influencing on the fish catch is the vertical opening of the net (Takayama and Koyam, 1959 and Parrish 1959). In a known fishing ground the quantity of fish caught by trawl gear has direct bearing on the volume of water filtered during a certain period of operation and depends on both the horizontal and vertical opening of the net while in operation (Deshpande, 1960).

The trawl nets are operated from Ratnagiri as per the prevailing local practices largely based on the individual fishing experience (Mohite, 1999). The nets are fabricated as per the requirement of individual fisherman and local tradition. Thus variations in design pattern and rigging practices of trawl nets are observed. Therefore, the present study is an attempt to document the observation with respect to net specifications, material used, mesh size, mode of operation, etc., of the fish trawl (46 m) operated along the Ratnagiri coast of Maharashtra.

Materials and Methods

The detailed information regarding the specifications and construction of fish trawl (46 m) operated along the Ratnagiri coast of Maharashtra was collected by physically sampling the units in operation. The data were recorded according to Sreekrishna and Shenoy (2001) and Akerman (1986).

Results and Discussion

The fish trawl (46 m) operated along the Ratnagiri coast of Maharashtra is commonly known as *Disco Dol* (20 *Angli*). The number of *Angli* locally refers to the width of the mesh size equivalent of that many numbers of fingers. Different sections are fabricated separately and then assembled as per the specifications. *Disco Dol* (20 *Angli*) was a two seam high opening bottom trawl net operated along the coast of Ratnagiri specifically to catch Ribbonfish, Squid, Croaker, Pomfret etc. It was mainly made up of two panels *i.e.*, upper and lower panel, side panel was absent in this type of trawl net. The average total length of the 20 *Angli Disco Dol* was found to be 46 m. Specification of the 20 *Angli Disco Dol* net are presented in the Table 3.1.

There were two wings present in the *Disco Dol* comprising of upper panel and lower panel on each wing. Each wing was divided in three sections *viz;* A, A_1 and A_2, The dimensions for the each section was recorded separately. The material used for wing was Blue coloured HDPE twine. The knot type used for the construction of wing section was single trawl knot. The diameter of twine used for construction of netting was 1.00 mm. The mesh size of wing section in 20 *Angli Disco Dol* was 400 mm. The number of meshes observed in A and A_1 sections of wing for upper and lower panel were same; *i.e.* 1 and 50 numbers respectively. Depth meshes for this section was also found same; *i.e.* 25. While the baiting rate observed in A and A_1 was same; *i.e.* 1:1. The hanging coefficient for A and A_1 observed was 0.63 and 0.66, respectively. The mesh size of wing section in 20 *Angli Disco Dol* was 400 mm. The number of meshes observed in wing section for upper and lower panel was same; *i.e.* 50 numbers. Depth meshes were 25 and 31 in upper and lower wing respectively. The hanging coefficient observed in upper wing and lower wing was 0.63 and 0.66, respectively. The wing length observed of upper and lower panel was 40.23 and 38.40 m, respectively.

Table 3.1: Specifications for fish trawl 46 m (*Disco Dol*, 20 *Angli*)

Name of the gear: Disco Dol	**Main species caught:** Ribbonfish, Squid, Croaker, Pomfret etc.	**Operation:** Day	**Trawling speed:** 10- 12 RPM
Locality: Ratnagiri, Maharashtra India.		**Trawling period:** 4 Hrs	**Water depth to warp ratio:** 1: 25
Vessel: OAL: 40 -50	**H.P:** 90-100		

PARTICULARS OF WEBBING

Webbing	A	A_1	A_2	B	B_1	B_2	C	D	E	F	G	H	I	J	K	L	M	N
Sections/ Local name	Wing/*paay*						Square/*pat*	Belly/*Ghanpat*										Codend/ *Khola*
Material/ preservation	High Density Polyethylene (HDPE)/ Nil																	
Knot type/ colour	Single Trawl Knot/ Blue/ Green																	
Twine Ø mm	1																	
Mesh size, mm	400	400	400	400	400	400	400	320	240	200	160	120	80	60	40	30	25	18
Upper edge	1	1	50	1	1	50	180	180	180	180	180	180	180	250	200	100	100	100
Lower edge	50	50	50	50	50	50	180	180	180	180	180	180	180	200	100	100	100	100
Depth, meshes	25	25	25/31	25	25	25/31	12/6	8	12	12	25	25	50	50	100	150	150	150
Baiting /creasing rate	1:1	1:1		1:1	1:1	-								2:1	2:1	-		
Hanging coefficient	0.63	0.66	0.63/0.66	0.66	0.63	0.63/0.66	0.63/0.66	-										

PARTICULARS OF LINES AND ROPES

	Top wing section		Bottom wing section		Wing end section	Lateral sides
	Bolsh rope	**Head rope**	**Bolsh rope**	**Foot rope**	**Wing line**	**Side rope**
Material	NA	HDPE	NA	HDPE	HDPE	HDPE
Number		1		1	2, One on either end	2, One on either side
Diameter, mm		10		10	5	4
Length, m		46		52	18	52 x 2

PARTICULARS OF OTHER GEAR ACCESSORIES

	Floats	**Sinkers**	**Otter boards**
Diameter, mm	152, 203,254,305	6-8	
Number/quantity	5-7	500-600	2
Material	PVC	Iron	Wooden planks fitted with iron plates and iron shoe
Shape	Round	Ellipse ring	Flat Rectangular
Indicator float	-	-	-
Style of attachment/ Dimension, mm	2+1+2 3+1+3	Each loop consists of 17 ellipse rings. Each loop is attached with a gap of 4-5 feet interval	1372 x 838 x 32 at top & 64 at bottom (Length x Breadth x width)
Weight in air, kg	0.250, 0.500, 1.5,2	30-35	70-75

The square section of *Disco Dol* was made up of 1.50 mm blue coloured HDPE twine, with single trawl knot. The mesh size of square section in 20 *Angli Disco Dol* was 400 mm. The observed numbers of meshes in upper and lower edge were same; *i.e.* 180 mesh. Depth meshes were 6 in number. The hanging coefficient observed in square section was 0.63.

The Belly portion comprised of 11 different sections starting from lower edge of the square portion up to the upper edge of codend portion. The belly of *Disco Dol* was made up of 1.00 mm blue coloured HDPE twine with single trawl knot. Different mesh size was observed ranging from 400 to 25 mm mesh size. The second to eleventh sections the mesh size observed was 400, 320, 240, 200, 160, 120, 80, 60, 40, 30 and 25 mm. The observed numbers of meshes in upper and lower edge of first to seventh section were same; *i.e.* 180 mesh. Eight and Ninth section comprised 250 meshes in upper edge and 200 meshes in lower edge. The tenth section was observed with 200 meshes in upper edge while 100 mesh in lower edge in both the panels. Last two sections had same number of meshes in upper edge and lower edge; *i.e.* 100 mesh. Depth meshes in first sections was 6 in number. Second section comprised of 8 numbers of meshes. Third and Fourth section comprised of 12 meshes each. While fifth and sixth sections had 25 meshes each. Seventh and Eighth sections were found with 50 depth meshes each. Ninth section had 100 mesh depths while 150 depth meshes were found in tenth and eleventh sections each. The baiting rate observed in eight and ninth section of the belly was 2:1 each.

Codend of 20 *Angli Disco Dol* was also made up of 1.00 mm blue coloured HDPE twine with single trawl knot. The mesh size in this section of net observed was 18 mm. The observed numbers of meshes in upper and lower edge were same; *i.e.* 100 mesh. Depth meshes found in codend section were 150 in number.

In the *Disco Dol*, head rope (46 m) and foot rope (52 m) of 10 mm diameter made up of HDPE was used. Hollow spherical shaped HDPE floats were used along the headline to maintain vertical opening and fishing height in the water column. *Disco Dol* was rigged with 5-7 numbers of float having 152 mm, 203 mm, and 254 mm or 305 mm diameter. Weight of floats ranged between 0.250-2.0 kg. Chain was used as sinking material which was in tandem with the floats to maintain vertical opening and to increases the sinking speed. Total weight of the chain used for the fish trawl net was observed to be 30-35 kg.

Locally fabricated flat rectangular wooden otter boards with iron fittings, heavy metal shoe, two triangular collapsible brackets (the front one being shorter than the back one) and two aft ward back strop rings fitted to outer surface of boards are commonly used. The dimension of the otter board comprised of length, breadth and width of the otter board were observed to range between 1372-1524, 838-1067, and 32 at top and 63.5-64 mm at bottom respectively. The boards, which usually weigh 70-75 kg., the weight of the boards was adjusted by varying the quantity of metal fittings.

The *Disco Dol* is operated on the trawlers having overall length (OAL) from 12.19 to 15.24 m., breadth from 4.5 to 5.4 m and depth from 1.9 to 2.4m, with their tonnage varying from 5 to 50 tonnes. Generally, their wheel house is situated at amidships and masts with their boom and derrick arrangement at aft. They are fitted with 6 cylinder water cooled diesel engines of 90-165 BHP (Brake Horse Power), a pair of stern gallows provided with towing blocks, a horizontal stowing bar for arranging the net behind the cabin and a four drum power take off winch. Commercial and Palghar type winches which are perpendicular type of winches, are fitted on front side of cabin having two net drums and warping heads are used.

The crew members in each fishing vessel for trawling operation ranges from 5 to 8. Trip duration ranges from single day operations to multiday; with actual trawling operation carried out for 12-18 hrs per day. The stern based trawling is generally of 3-4 hours per haul with the trawler speed being maintained at 4-6 knots.

On the comparative efficiency of conventional and bulged belly fish trawls was studied by Varghese *et al.* (1968). In their study, they made net with bulged belly and compared with a conventional design under actual fishing conditions. Design aspects of 12.77 m two seam improved trawl was described by Vijayan *et al.* (1990) in Valappu area of Vypeen Island. Advantage of large meshes in 10.3 m mid water trawl was studied by Vijayan *et al.* (1992) by representing its design and specification. Comparative study on design and fishing efficiency of large meshed four seam trawl and high opening bottom two seam trawl off Mangalore was conducted by Nayak and Sheshappa, (1993). In Ratnagiri it was seen that for catching fish *Disco Dol* a two seam fish trawl net without side panel was commonly used.

Rao and Narayanappa, (1994) studied performance of 25 m rope trawl in inshore waters off Kakinada, Andhra Pradesh and design detail was described. The design and construction aspect of the *Disco Dol* was studied during this research work. Similarly design features of fish trawls of Thoothukkudi coast was studied by Neethiselvan and Brucelee, (2003). The design details, rigging and functional characteristics of semi-pelagic trawl were studied by Vijayan *et al.* (2003). Design and operational efficiency of mini trawl net for capturing demersal fishes and prawns in Netravati-Gurpur estuary at Manglore has been described by Sheshappa, (1978), in Kasargod district by Remesan and Ramachandran, (2005) and off Cochin by Boopendranath and Hameed, (2013). Design and technical specifications of demersal trawl used in the Turkish coast of the Aegean Sea was presented by Tosunoglu and Aydin, (2007).

Disco Dol net costs around Rs. 20,000/- to 30,000/-. The nets are generally fabricated by local net braiders. No standard designs or specifications are followed while fabricating them, which largely depend on individual experience, local practices, and demands of owner coupled with new trends or designs in vogue etc.

The documented information on the technical specifications and operation of fish trawl (137 m) or *Disco Dol* (125 *Angali*) net of Ratnagiri, would serve as a base line information for the technological modifications the net may undergo to increase its efficiency in the coming years.

REFERENCES

Akerman, S.E., (1986). The Coastal Set Bag net Fishery of Bangladesh Trials and Investigations Bay of Bengal Programme, BOBP/REP/34 (FAO), GCP/RAS/040/AWS, 1-25.

Boopendranath, M.R. and Hameed, M.S. (2013). Energy Analysis of Mini-trawl Operations, off Cochin, Kerala, India. *Fishery Technology*. 50: 289-293.

Deshpande, S.D., (1960). On the Comparative Catch Efficiency of Hand Operated and Winch Operated Trawls. *Indian Journal of Fisheries*. 7: 458-470.

Mohite, A.S., (1999). Stock Assessment of *Trichiurus Lepturus* (Linnaeus, 1758) and Study of gears Employed in its Fishery of Maharashtra Coast. Ph.D. Thesis, Central Institute of Fisheries Education, Mumbai. 129 pp.

Neethiselvan, N. and Brucelee, G., (2003). Analysis of Design Features of Fish Trawls and Shrimp Trawls of Thoothukkudi Coast. *Fishery Technology*. 40 (1): 18-23.

Nayak, B.B. and Sheshappa, D.S., (1993). Effect of Large Meshes on the Body of Trawl Net in Energy Conservation. *Fishery Technology*, 30: 1-5.

Parrish, B.B., (1959). Discussion on Relative Efficiency of Nets Made of Different Materials. In: Fishing Gear of the World. H. Kristijonsson (Ed). Fishing News (Books) Ltd., London: 164-165.

Rao, S.V.S. and Narayanappa, G. (1994). Performance of 25 m Rope Trawl in Inshore Waters. *Fishery Technology*. 31 (2): 118-121.

Remesan, M.P. and Ramchandran, A., (2005). Mini-trawls for Estuarine Fishing in Kasargod District. *Fishery Technology*. 42 (1): 41-46.

Sheshappa, D.S. (1978). The Design and Operational Efficiency of a mini trawl net for Capturing Demersal Fishes and Prawns in Estuaries. Mysore *Journal of Agriculture Science*. 12: 618-621.

Sreekrishna, Y. and Shenoy, L., (2001). Fishing gear and craft Technology Directorate of Information and Publications of Agriculture Indian Council of Agricultural research Krishi Anusandhan Bhavan, New Delhi, 342 pp.

Takayama, S. and Koyama, T., (1959). Increasing the Opening Height of a Trawl net by Means of A Kite. In: Modern Fishing Gear of the World, Kristjonsson, H. (Ed), Fishing News (Books) Ltd., London, 1: 185-195.

Tosunoglu, Z. and Aydin, C. (2007). Technical Characteristics of Demersal Trawl Nets Recently used in the Turkish Coast of the Aegean Sea. *Journal of Fisheries Science*. 1 (4): 184-187.

Varghese, C.P., Vijayan, V. and Kuriyan, G K., (1968). On the Comparative Efficiency of Conventional and Bulged Belly Fish Trawls. *Fishery Technology*, 5 (1): 9-14.

Vijayan, V., Varghese, M.D., George V.C. and Unnithan, G.R., (1990). Evolution of an Improved Trawl for Traditional Motorised Craft. *Fishery Technology*. 27: 1-4.

Page 63-67

PLANKTON AND FISHERIES
Edited by **: V.B. Sakhare; H.K. Jadhav and S.S. Jadhav**
Edition **: 2017**
ISBN : 978-93-5056-811-8
Published by **: Discovery Publishing House Pvt. Ltd., New Delhi (India)**

4

A Comparative Study on Economic Efficacy and Probable Viability between Natural Breeding and Ovaprim Induced Breeding in Goldfish, *Carassius auratus* (Cypriniformes: Cyprinidae) in Aquarium

Indranil Ghosh, Satyendranath Maitra[1], Bidhan Chandra Patra[2] & Tapas Kumar Dutta[3]

West Bengal University of Animal and Fishery Sciences, Kolkata - 700 037.
Acharya Prafulla Chandra College, New Barrackpore - 700 131.[1]
Vidyasagar University, Mednipur - 721 102 [2]
Bankura Sammilani College, Bankura - 722 101.[3]

ABSTRACT

We had carried out a series of comprehensive experiments with Goldfish ***(Carassius auratus)*** *to compare and contrast the economy of breeding experiments between natural (non-induced; in aquarium) and induced ones (also in aquarium) to scan its outcome using standard sized aquaria, maintaining all the protocols of aquaria management norms (maintaining 5.6 to 7.1 ppm of dissolved oxygen; pH 6.5 to 7.1; hardness 35-40 ppm and 22 to 23°C temperature among other parameters). With all the three sets of parallel experiments conducted for natural breeding and the ovaprim induced breeding; working fecundity (number of eggs spawned) and the per cent of fertilization were always about 15-20 per cent lower for natural ones as compared to those of ovaprim induced ones ($p < 0.05$). However, coming to hatching and month wise survival percent, followed for consecutive 3 months, yielded about 10 per cent (average) more for 'Natural breeding' as compared to those of 'Induced breeding'. The economic efficacy and its probable viability as regard to the Natural and ovaprim induced breeding in Goldfish have been discussed.*

INTRODUCTION

Most of the ornamental fishes breed naturally in captive environment. Except, a few, 'so-called difficult to breed' species like: Red-tailed black shark (Labeo *bicolor*), Briddle-shark (*Labeo frennatus*), Red-line Torpedo barb/Rose-line silver shark (*Puntius denisonii*) etc., need hormonal inducement as they refuse to breed in confined water or in aquarium naturally.

Goldfish (*Carassius auratus*) stands in the 'first row' of the aquarium fish-keeping history of the world. Unlike its 'so-called other partners of the family Cyprinidae (*e.g., Labeo rohita, Catla catla* etc.), it breeds naturally in captive environment. They have been successfully and commercially bred in ponds, ornamental garden pools, cement cisterns, glass aquaria and even in earthen pot (locally called as *'majla'* by the local breeders in West Bengal) by the aquarists. They also response to induced breeding technique which is a common practice in Indian Major Carp hatchery. So many scientists (Yamamot *et al.* 1966; Yamamoto and Yakazaki, 1967; Ortega-Salas and Reyes-Bustamante, 2006; Rahaman *et al.* 2011, Amin *et al.* 2013) got success in inducing goldfish in captivity with spawning hormones. The present paper is an attempt to compare the results between natural breeding and induced breeding in captivity.

Materials and Methods

- *Experimental species*: Red Oranda variety of gold fish–healthy and free from any sign of distress.
- *Instruments used*: Thermometer, thermostat, water heater (for aquarium use) portable pH meter (Hanna; sensitivity ± 0.02), Air pump with wooden diffuser, nylon spawning mop (properly disinfected), 1 ml. sterile insulin syringe (40 divisions; 1 division = 0.025 ml, all-glass aquaria (of desired sizes), Soft nylon scoop net, 'Power filter', petridish, magnifying glass.
- *Chemicals used:* Methylene blue (2% aqueous solution), Ovaprim, Common salt (for cleaning purpose).
- *Brood-stock conditioning:* Matured and healthy male and female gold fishes of 2+ years group and nearly equal in size (approximate total length of 21±1.7 cm.) were selected and kept for 15 days in glass aquaria for conditioning the brood fishes. Separate aquaria were used for males and females; and they were well fed with live *Daphnia magna*, brine-shrimp nauplii, hard-boiled egg yolk suspension and 'wheat-bread' (a very common home-made Indian food, very thinly made), three times a day with periodical siphoning of water from the bottom to remove faecal masses, surplus feed and other debris. Power filtration was provided in each aquarium twice daily (5 minutes duration each). 2 per cent aqueous solution of Methylene blue was added (@ 2-4 drops/5L of

water) as prophylaxis. Micro-environment manipulation was done to maintain the water quality parameters like dissolved oxygen pH, temperature, hardness, nitrate, nitrite and free ammonia (Table 4.1). All the parameters were observed as prescribed by (APHA, 2008).

- *Spawning aquaria:* Separate aquaria were used for natural and induced breeding (@0.5 ml of ovaprim/kg body weight, recommended dose by the manufacturer) where the breeding pairs were kept in water of almost same composition as maintained in conditioning tank, with nylon spawning mops for adhesion of their eggs after spawning. Number of eggs spawned (Working Fecundity), per cent of fertilization and per cent of hatching were also estimated (Table 4.2 and 4.3). Statistical analysis (t-test) was done to find the level of significance using softwares MS-Excel, Statplus.
- *Rearing:* Offsprings were reared in aquaria, maintaining good hygienic condition and fed with suitable good quality live feed and per cent of survival for three consecutive months was also calculated (Table 4.2 and 4.3). No artificial color enhancer was used in the feed. Color variations were also observed.

Observations are depicted in the following Tables 4.1 to 4.3.

Results

Table 4.1: Water Quality Parameters Maintained Throughout the Experiment

Parameters	Value
Dissolved oxygen	5.6-7.1 ppm
pH	6.5-6.8
Hardness	35-40 ppm
Temperature	22ºC-23ºC
Nitrate	Nil
Free ammonia	Nil
Nitrite	Nil

Table 4.2: Results of Three Sets of Experiments

Criteria	First	Set	Second	Set	Third	Set
	Non-induced	Induced	Non-induced	Induced	Non-induced	Induced
Working Fecundity	18,000	21,000	18,700	23,600	20,300	23,000
% of fertilization	87	90	88	91	89	92
% of hatching	84	76	83	77	85	79
% of survival after 1 month	90	79	89.5	81	90	80
% of survival after 2 months	87	77	89	77	88	79
% of survival after 3 months	87	67	86	65	88	70

Table 4.3: Comparative Data between Naturally Bred and Induced Bred Fishes (mean values)

Criteria	Naturally Bred	Induced Bred
Working Fecundity	19000	22533.33
% of fertilization	88%	91%
% of hatching	84%	77.33%
% of survival after 1 month	89.83%	80%
% of survival after 2 months	88%	77.66%
% of survival after 3 months	87.66%	67.33%

Discussion

Both Natural and Induced breeding of Goldfish (*Carassius auratus*) in captive water system was designed to monitor a sustainable economic viability for this group of ornamental fish breeding. Since there is some existing notion that induced breeding yields better quality of hatchlings as compared to those of naturally bred hatchlings, we were very much eager to accept or reject this very notion to guide the entrepreneurs in this field to support the economic growth. However, after analyzing the data obtained from three sets of parallel experiments we are convinced that at least in this Goldfish (*Carassius auratus*) strain the naturally bred hatchlings assure more economic viability to those of ovaprim induced hatchlings. The experimental data reveal glaringly that though the working fecundity ($P<0.05$) and fertilized egg percentage ($P<0.01$) were significantly high in induced bred hatchlings (18,000 to 20,300 and 20,000 to 23,000 as fecundity, 87 per cent to 89 per cent and 90 per cent to 92 per cent fertilized eggs in case of naturally bred and the induced bred Goldfish respectively (from a single brood) in comparison to those of naturally bred ones. However, when other developmental steps were considered such as: the hatching percentage and the viability percentage month wise for consecutive 3 months an unambiguous significant better off was observed for naturally bred hatchlings (Percentage of hatching was 83 to 85 per cent in naturally bred and 76 to 79 per cent in induced bred hatchlings). While so far as month wise survival rate is concerned again induced bred hatchlings clearly demonstrated (statistically significant) decreasing order of survival after each month of development observed for consecutive 3 months ($P<0.01$) in all cases. Ultimately after 3 months of hatching there were about 9732 and about 6633 marketable gold fishes survived from natural bred and induced bred goldfishes respectively.

In addition to that, fishes obtained from natural bred, exhibit better, attractive and more gorgeous coloration fetching better market value compared to those obtained from ovaprim induced bred. Thus it can be concluded that at least in Goldfish (*Carassius auratus*) the natural breeding technique should be encouraged as compared to the induced breeding technique as the earlier one is much more economy generating and attractive.

Finally we may envisage, in addition, genetic programming emerged in all the organisms according to the species specific mode of adaptation in respect of definite environmental endurance evolved through the millions of years interactive reactions with the then existing Natural Selection and the particular species making genomic DNA. Thus it appears that the adaptive mode of any species should be given priority for conducting this type of experiment. For the reason the naturally bred ones, in this series of experiments, could express gorgeousness both in colour and in other phenotypic expressions as compared to those in hormone induced bred fishes where the ovaprim acted as epigenetic factor and interfered the very adaptive co-operation between the genomic DNA and the environment.

REFERENCES

Amin Ruhul, Mazumder Farida, Nargis Akhtar, Khatun Mahmuda and Talukder Debashish. (2013). Reproductive Periodicity, Fecundity and Sex Ratio of Goldfish *Carassius auratus* (Cyprinidae) Under Laboratory Condition. *IOSR Journal of Agriculture and Veterinary Science*, 3(1): 36-41.

APHA. (2008). Standard Methods for Examination of Water and Wastewater. Clescerl, L, S. (Editor), Greenberg, A, E. (Editor), Eaton, A, D. (Editor) (21st ed.), *American Public Health Association, Washington, DC.*

Ortega-Salas A.A. and Reyes-Bustamante H. (2006). Initial Sexual Maturity and Fecundity of the Goldfish *Carassius auratus* (Cyprynidae) under Semi-controlled Conditions. *Rev. Biol. Trop. (Int. J. Trop. Biol.* ISSN-0034-7744), 54 (4): 1113-1116.

Rahaman Bazlur S.M., Mahmud Zakaria, Ahmed Faysal, Ghosh, Alokesh Kumar and Sabbir Wasim. (2011). Induced Breeding, Embryonic and Larval Development of Comet Gold Fish (*Carassius auratus*). *Electronic Journal of Biology*, Vol. 7(2): 32-39.

Yamamoto, K. and Yakazaki, F. (1967). Hormonal Control of Spermiation and Ovulation in Goldfish. *Gunma. Symp. Endocrinol*. 4, 131-145.

Yamamoto, K., Nagahama, Y., and Yakazaki, F. (1966). A Method to Induced Artificial Spawning of Goldfish all Through the Year. *Bull. Jpn. Soc. Sci. Fish.* 32, 977.

PLANKTON AND FISHERIES
Edited by : **V.B. Sakhare; H.K. Jadhav and S.S. Jadhav**
Edition : **2017**
ISBN : 978-93-5056-811-8
Published by : **Discovery Publishing House Pvt. Ltd., New Delhi (India)**

5 Study on Fecundity of Rosy barb, *Puntius conchonius*

R.K. Sadawarte, S.L. Bhandkoli, & V.R. Sadawarte[1]
College of Fisheries, Shirgaon, Ratnagiri - 415 629.
Marine Biological Research Station, Zadgaon, Ratnagiri - 415 612.[1]

ABSTRACT

In their natural habitat like rivers Rosy Barb may reach a length of 150 mm (Coffey, 1977), however in captivity they seldom exceed 85 mm (Axelrod, 1967). In wild, the males can be distinguished by their brilliant red body colour, dorsal fin with its upper half blackish and they are slimmer than the females which have shiny silvery yellow shade. The highest numbers of eggs laid by the female was during its 2nd spawn i.e. 263 and lowest number of eggs laid was during the 7th spawn i.e. 118.

Keywords: Eggs, Adhesive, Fry, Cladocerans, Artificial food.

INTRODUCTION

Rosy Barb, *Puntius conchonius* (Family - cyprinidae) is one of the most popular used as an ornamental fish and is a native fish of India. The original natural distribution of the Rosy Barb is considered to be in the North Eastern regions of India (Mills, 1988). The states in which they are originally found are namely: Assam, Bengal, Bihar, Punjab, Maharashtra (Chhapgar, 1982). The rivers in which they are originally found are namely: Ganga, Brahmaputra and Mahanadi in North India. In South India they are also found in the Cauvery river system (Hamilton – Buchanan, 1822). They have been exported from India well over 50 years ago (Chhapgar, 1982). Rosy Barb (*Puntius conchonius*) is an attractive aquarium and attracted attention of aquarists due to the following characters.

1. Hardy nature.
2. Very active.
3. Prolific breeder.

In their natural habitat like rivers they may reach a length of 150 mm (Coffey, 1977), however in captivity they seldom exceed 85 mm (Axelrod, 1967). They accept any type of artificial food. They are continuously hungry, perhaps because they are very active and untiring swimmers. When you pass their aquarium you will notice them constantly racing back and forth in groups of six or more. Their tank should be long and low with plenty of swimming area and numerous plants (Axelrod, 1967). Temperature should be kept around in the range of 25°C to 29°C. They grow very well in water which is slightly alkaline in the pH range of 8 to 8.5. Well water is extremely good for rearing of Rosy barb.

In wild, the males can be distinguished by their brilliant red body colour, dorsal fin with its upper half blackish and they are slimmer than the females which have shiny silvery yellow shade. Both the male and female bear a dark black spot on the caudal peduncles. Body is short to moderately elongate, deep laterally compressed. In the case of female abdomen is rounded. They have a short head, snout obtuse, conical or pointed, moderate eyes to dorso-lateral, not visible from below ventral surface (Jayram, 1981).

Fig. 5.1: **Male and Female of Rosy Barb**

Materials and Methods

In the present study, the experiments was conducted to study the spawning frequency of rosy barb. Two males and one female were used for the experiment.

Rosy Barb (*Puntius conchonius*) of the golden strain, was obtained from the local market. They were reared in the laboratory in 38 × 20 × 30 cm size glass aquaria. As a source of live feed, fresh water zooplankton was mass cultured using phased fertilization method (Shirgur, 1971) in plastic pool throughout the experimental period.

Rosy Barb attains maturity in four months. It is an oviparous fish in which female expel's out unfertilized eggs. After the eggs are expelled out, they are fertilized by the male externally. They lay eggs which are adhesive in nature. This type of fertilization is called external fertilization. These fertilized eggs hatch out within 33 to 54 hours. The temperature and pH noted during this period was 26°C to 29°C and 8.5 respectively. Rosy Barb, two males and one female were kept in an acrylic trap having a bottom of nylon mosquito net with a mesh size just large enough for the eggs to pass through them. Repeated spawning was carried out several times. The number of eggs released during each spawning period was counted to calculate the fecundity.

During the experiment, the Rosy Barb being a voracious feeder were fed with live feed twice daily with mosquito larvae, zooplankton like: cladocerans and chopped clam meat.

Result and Discussion

It is observed that *Puntius conchonius,* is a prolific breeder and attains maturity at about 37 mm and breeds almost throughout the year. The larvae metamorphose to the free swimming stage within 96 to 126 hours.

Table 5.1:

Sr. No.	Spawning Time	Period of Spawning	Total Eggs (Nos.)	Unfertilized Eggs (Nos.)	Hatchlings Size (4mm) (Nos.)	Temperature	P_H
1.	1st spawn	1st spawn	143	20	123	26	8.5
2.	2nd spawn	7 days	263	99	168	26	8.5
3.	3rd spawn	18 days	147	28	119	27	8.5
4.	4th spawn	26 days	192	39	153	26	8.5
5.	5th spawn	29 days	176	84	92	27	8.5
6.	6th spawn	36 days	208	77	131	27	8.5
7.	7th spawn	42 days	118	69	49	27	8.5
8.	8th spawn	56 days	152	85	67	26	8.5
9	9th spawn	79 days	187	93	94	27	8.5

Infusoria culture was used as feed for the newly hatched larvae after 33 to 96 hours. Afterwards they fed with freshwater zooplankton and then fed with artificial feed experiment.

Size of the eggs :- Approximately 1 mm.

Size of the newborn fry :- About 4.00 mm.

The highest numbers of eggs laid by the female was during its 2nd spawn *i.e.* 263 and lowest number of eggs laid was during the 7th spawn *i.e.* 118 (Table 5.1).

REFERENCES

Axelrod, H.R., (1967). Breeding Aquarium Fishes, *Book Ist by Dr. Herbert R. Axelrod Assisted by Susan R. Shaw*, pp. 321-325.

Chappgar, B.F., (1982). Species-wise Distribution of Indian Aquarium Fishes. Seminar on *"Prospects of Aquarium Fish Export from India"* Bombay. pp. 37-40.

Coffey, D.J., (1977). The Encyclopedia of Aquarium Fishes by *Rainbird Publishing Group Limited, London for Pelham Books Ltd.*, pp. 59.

Jayaram, K.C., (1981). The Fresh Water Fishes of India. *Published by the Director, Zoological Survey of India, Calcutta.* pp. 97-98.

Mills, D. (1988). Tropical Aquarium Fishes, *Chancellor Press, London.* pp. 84-91.

Shirgur, G.A., (1971). Observations on Rapid Production of Zooplankton in the Fish Nurseries by Intensive Phased Manuring. *Ind. J. Fish.*, 1 (2): 25-34.

Page 72-75

PLANKTON AND FISHERIES

Edited by: V.B. Sakhare; H.K. Jadhav and S.S. Jadhav

Edition: 2017

ISBN : 978-93-5056-811-8

Published by: Discovery Publishing House Pvt. Ltd., New Delhi (India)

6 Effect of Natural Feed on the Growth of Rosy Barb

R.K. Sadawarte, S.L. Bhandkoli & V.R. Sadawarte[1]

College of Fisheries, Shirgaon, Ratnagiri - 415 629.

Marine Biological Research Station, Zadgaon, Ratnagiri - 415 612.[1]

ABSTRACT

The use of live feed is essential for the maintenance of breeding stock and for rearing the larval stages, but the inadequate supply of live feed is a major problem in the maintenance of aquarium fishes. Therefore mass culture of live feeds has become necessary for large scale production of ornamental fishes.

A highly significant growth was observed in the body weight after 105 days. After 120 days, a highly significant growth was recorded in the body length of the fish.

Keywords: Length, Weight, Aquaria, Brood stock, Control.

INTRODUCTION

In the maintenance of aquarium fish, feeding constitutes a major factor. Good health and normal behaviour depend mainly upon the quality of diet. Although some of the formulated feeds are richer in protein than the live feeds, they can create unhygienic conditions in the aquarium. Therefore it is advisible to maintain a regular supply of live food. Newly spawned fish will accept live feed initially.

Live feed organisms serve as living capsules of nutrition. They consists of proteins, carbohydrates and fats and often contain different types of vitamins. The vitamins in the tissues of live feed organisms do not dissipate in water as in case of prepared feeds (Dwivedi *et al.* 1982).

Live feed is essential for the maintenance of breeding stock and for rearing the larval stages, but the inadequate supply of live feed is a major problem in the maintenance of aquarium fishes. Therefore mass culture of live feeds has become necessary for large scale production of ornamental fishes.

In the present study rearing of fry of rosy barb to adults stages were carried out by feeding live cladocerans *i.e.,* moina, daphnia and freshly chopped clam meat to observe their effect on growth and maturation.

Ten days old fry were used and reared for the period of 120 days. The live feed used was collected from mass culture tanks at Marine Biological Research Station, Ratnagiri. The observations for growth were recorded for every 15 days.

Materials and Methods

Ten days old fry of Rosy barb were obtained from the local aquarium fish dealers of Ratnagiri and reared in the laboratory conditions in 90 × 20 × 30 cm size glass aquaria. The average length of fry were 08.00 mm and average weight were 9.00 mg. The new born fry were initially fed with freshwater zooplankton and acclimated to test diet 4 days prior to the commencement of experiment. As a source of live feed, freshwater zooplankton was mass cultured using phased fertilization method (Shirgur, 1971) in plastic pool.

Fortnightly record of total length and weight of each fish from experimental group were kept from 1st day to 120 days. The average length and weight for experimental group of fishes were recorded. For the experiment 20 fry was used for experimental group and fed with live feed twice a day.

Results

The observations on body length and body weight are summarized (Table 6.1). The graphical representation of length and weight is given (Fig. 6.1).

Table 6.1: Effect of Natural Feed on the Growth of *P. conchonius*

Sr. No.	Observation	L (mm)	W (mg)
1.	0 Days	08.00 + 0.00	09.00 + 0.00
2.	15 Days	10.50 + 0.45	15.70 + 1.57
3.	30 Days	16.40 + 0.60	61.30 +6.45
4.	45 Days	22.60 + 0.63	138.10 + 9.99
5.	60 Days	29.20 + 0.44	334.70 + 21.28
6.	75 Days	35.30 + 0.51	552.20 + 23.71
7.	90 Days	37.00 + 0.33	672.60 + 17.81
8.	105 Days	38.20 + 0.29	780.90 + 17.55
9.	120 Days	42.30 + 0.74	850.00 + 25.58

Abbreviations -→+ Standard error of mean

* $P < 0.05$

** $P < 0.01$

*** $P < 0.001$

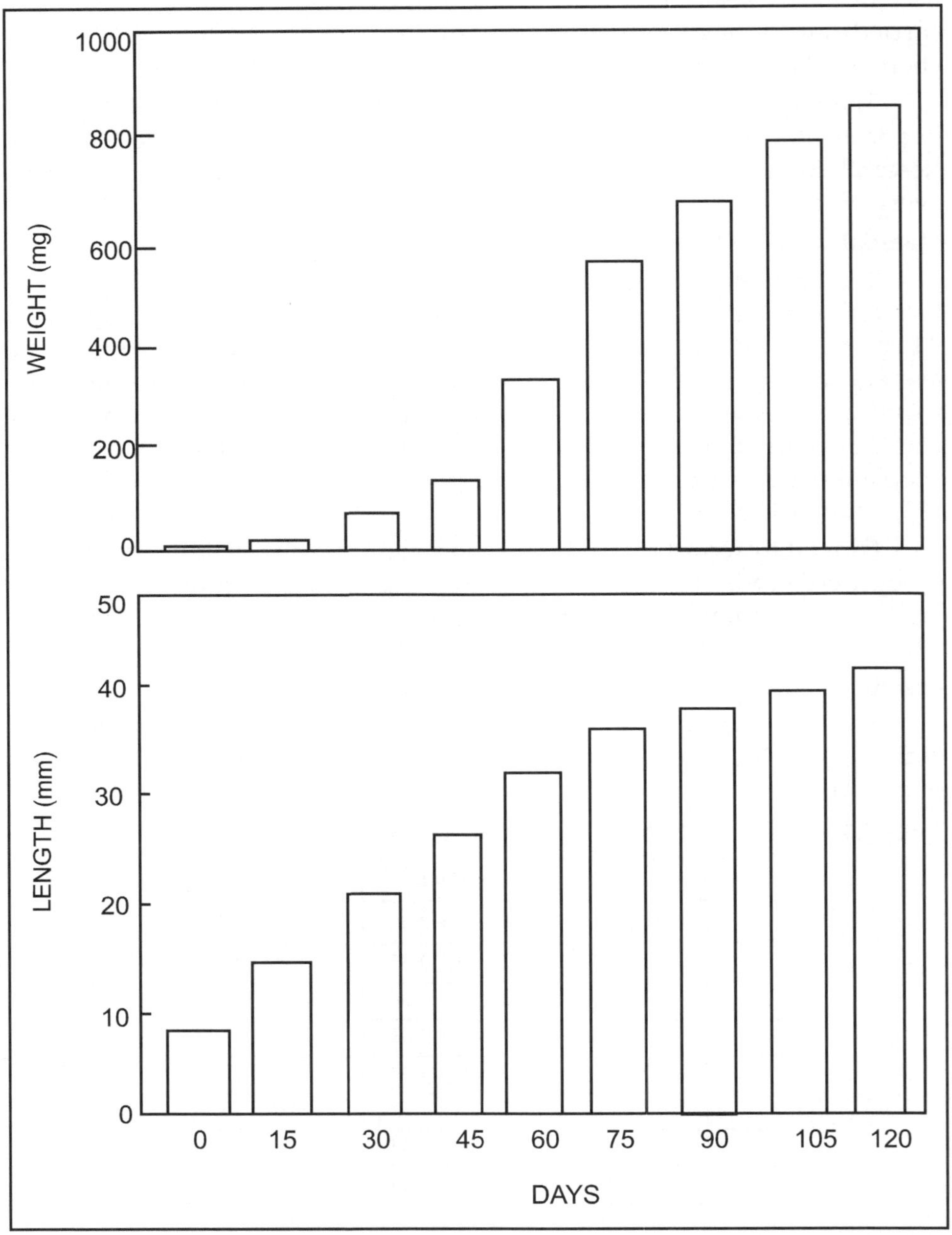

Fig. 6.1: **Effect of natural feed on the growth of *P. conchonius***

The observations are compared with the previous observations of 15 days interval of the same experiment. In the first 15 days there was no significant improvement in the body length and body weight of the fry. After 30 days, there was a highly significant increment in growth in the body length ($p < 0.001$) and body weight ($p < 0.001$) as compared to that of 15 days. There was a continuous highly significant growth recorded after 45, 60 and 75 days in body length and body weight as compared to 30, 45 and 60 days respectively. A highly significant growth was observed in the body weight after 105 days. After 120 days, a highly significant growth was recorded in the body length of the fish.

Discussion

Live feeds are found to be readily acceptable and are a good source of nutrition for aquarium fishes and they do not readily foul water hence are very suitable for small aquaria. In the present study, live feed was found to be very useful in increasing the growth of fish.

There was increase in the growth of fishes significantly. Rearing period of 75 days was found to be the best since a highly significant improvement was observed in the length and weight of Rosy Barb as compared to that of 60 days. There after the increase in length was lesser significant till 105 days. After 120 days, the body length showed a significant increase as compared to 105 days.

REFERENCES

Dwivedi, S.N., (1982). Methodology for Live Feed Culture and Pathology in Respect of Aquariculture. Seminar on "Prospects of Aquarium Fish Export from India." Bombay. pp. 81-88.

Shirgur, G.A., (1971). Observations on Rapid Production of zooplankton in the Fish Nurseries by Intensive Phased Manuring. *Ind. J. Fish.*, 1 (2): 25-34.

Page 76-82

PLANKTON AND FISHERIES
Edited by : **V.B. Sakhare; H.K. Jadhav** and **S.S. Jadhav**
Edition : **2017**
ISBN : 978-93-5056-811-8
Published by : **Discovery Publishing House Pvt. Ltd., New Delhi (India)**

7 Studies on Transportation of Live Ornamental Fish

Indranil Ghosh & Satyendranath Maitra[1]

West Bengal University of Animal and Fishery Sciences, Kolkata - 700 037.
Acharya Prafulla Chandra College, New Barrackpore - 700 131.[1]

ABSTRACT

Global ornamental fish trading has attained a huge momentum requiring multimillion workforces that transacts around billion dollars now days. But even now-a-day's intercontinental transportation in particular and the intra continental Fish transportation, in general, demands more 'Biosecurity' and maintenance of freshness during transportation needing 48 to 72 hours and 24-48 hours respectively and after transportation especially followed by healthy and stress tolerant by DA7 that essentially generates more rural urban economic growth remarkably. A modern experimental technique, however, can ensure the better Biosecurity, retention of freshness with stress tolerant capacity along with remarkably reduced mortality rate being within 1 to 3 per cent approximately after transportation. This modern technique of transportation demands reduced metabolism during transportation achieved by the addition of some antimicrobial agents and some Bio-preservatives (in a very low dose) and reducing water quantity within the polythene bags meant for transportation with some modulation of fish loading density. Overall expected implication has been discussed.

INTRODUCTION

The aqua-business of ornamental fish is an ever increasing activity both nationally as well as globally considering a large number of species involved in the aquarium trade with huge potentiality and demand in the market (Ghosh, 2006). Now-a-days, the status of aquarium and ornamental fish has been raised up to one of the standard consumer products (Ghosh, 2011), and supports thousands of rural people in developing countries (Felix *et al.* 2012) for their livelihood.

Successful termination of the end products of all aquariculture activities depends on fruitful marketing which is preceded by careful handling, packaging and good transportation of live ornamental fishes. Packaging is the integral part of live ornamental fish transportation, which contains and protects the product during its life cycle, as well as all elements intended for its use. Water quality, like the 'blood-life' of all aquatic cultural activities, is the most important for transportation. Hence, much importance should be given for transport water.

Ornamental fishes are usually packed in polythene bags of different sizes where they have to stay for a long period. In domestic transport, 18-48 hours of journey may be sufficient to reach any destination, but in export consignment, fishes may have to withstand comparatively longer period (48-72 hours) as they are compelled to be bottlenecked within very small containers till the bags are opened. This produces the stress, which creates a lot of problems, even leads to the ultimate fate-death very often, making the trade unprofitable. Maximum mortality of fish occur during '7 days post-shipment' or 'DA7 '- death after 7 days (Lim *et al.* 2003), and this period is very crucial and a serious threat to "Biosecurity' of fish. Modern 'HPT' system (Handling, Packaging and Transportation) not only maximizes the number of fishes to be transported with smaller quantity of water, but also ensure its 'Biosecurity', making the business profitable for both the 'sellers' and 'buyers' reducing the cost per 'unit freight'. The showy fishes must not only be charming to look at but also robust enough to withstand the long journey by road, by air or by railway the market with good return, before being sold at. Hence, 'HPT' needs skillful, necessary scientific knowledge and relevant infrastructural facilities. Realizing the above facts, the present paper was an attempt to observe the mortality percentage after 7 days of packaging, with high fish loading density with notionally consideration that the condition of packaged fish would be as like as if they were transported to a distance of 48-72 hours of journey.

Materials and Methods

Pre-Packaging Handling and Conditioning of Fish

- Fishes were collected from cisterns with the help of a very soft cloth-net to avoid unwanted injury.
- They were kept in small bare-bottom all-glass aquaria of 24´´ X 12´´ X 12´´ and then 12´´ X 8´´ X 8´´ dimensions gradually, to condition or acclimatize them to survive in a restricted place, much smaller than the place wherefrom they were picked up.
- Temperature was gradually lowered to 17-18°C, as low temperature reduces the rate of oxygen consumption and also restrict their movement; because the fishes will get a very little space in the polythene bag.

- Visual examination for any external parasites, or any sign of distress like: erratic swimming, clamped-fins, abnormal opercular movement etc., was done carefully.
- No feed were given since 48 hours before packing the fishes for complete defecation, as faecal matters can quickly contaminates the water during transport in a closed container; and no aeration was provided to increase the stress resistance.
- Necessary health prophylaxis was provided using chemicals (Table 7.1); these chemicals are commonly used by the 'fish-packers' (Herwig, 1979).

Table 7.1: Health Prophylactic Chemicals, Dosage and Treatment Protocols

Name of the Chemicals	Dosage	Treatment Protocols
Formalin	10-20 ppm	Bath/Dip
Neutral Acriflavin	1-2 ppm	Bath, 45-60 minutes
Metronidazole	4-8 ppm	Bath, 6-12 hrs
Malachite green	0.1 ppm	Bath, 30-60 minutes
Common salt	2-3%	1 hr or more
$KMnO_4$	0.1–0.5 ppm	Bath/Dip
Methylene Blue (2% aqueous solution)	2-5 drops/5L of water	Bath for long time
Chloramphenicol	9-10 ppm	Bath, 24 hrs

NaCl (0.5%) was added to the water as it was found to stabilize osmoregulatory mechanism and helps in reducing physiological responses to transport-stress; Na^+ tends to harden the fish and reduce slime formation and reduce the chance of foaming, thereby reduce mortality (Herwig, 1979). MS-222 (40 mg /L) was used as sedative to reduce aggressiveness and metabolic activities within polythene bags, as previous investigators proved the efficacy of this sedative (Pramod *et al.* 2010). MS-222 is the most widely used, very mild tranquilizer and fish easily recover from its effects, even after a long stupor (Berka, 1986). Zeolite (20g/L) was added in water as it effectively binds NH_3 in transport water (Herwig, 1979).

pH of the water was measured with a portable pH meter; DO meter was used to detect dissolved oxygen; and other parameters were estimated following standard method (APHA, 1999).

The sealed card-board boxes were kept aside as they are kept during actual shipment period, with occasional mechanical displacement and shaking.

Polythene bags were opened after 72 hours and fishes were released in glass aquaria for observation after proper acclimatization. Per cent of mortality in each packet was calculated (within 7 days after opening, Table 7.2).

Packaging the Fishes

Polythene bags of different sizes filled with water were used for packaging

↓

The bottom of the bag has a seam, and the two bottom corners were tied separately with rubber bands to round off the corners so that no fish is trapped and squashed at the corners

↓

Polythene bags were filled with clean, filtered, unpolluted, well oxygenated water (13.5-15.3 ppm)

↓

Sedatives and additives were added

↓

Fishes were loaded in polythene bags (Loading density is depicted in Table 7.2)

↓

The polythene bag was put within another bag

↓

A black paper was inserted between the two polythene bags

↓

Water: oxygen gas ratio maintained at 35%: 65% in polythene bags

↓

The upper portion of the bags were folded together and twisted and tightened with rubber bands to prevent leaking of oxygen

↓

The bags with fish were then placed in Styrofoam box meant for thermal insulation

↓

Small ice-packs were kept inside the box, between polythene bags to lower down the temperature

↓

Styrofoam box was covered with lid and all the edges were sealed with adhesive tape

↓

The sealed box was then placed in card-board box and all the edges were sealed with adhesive tape again

↓

The sealed card-board box is then properly marked with 'arrow' sign indicating the upper side

Table 7.2: Water Quality Parameters in Polythene Bags Before Fish Loading

Water Parameters	Concentration
Dissolved Oxygen	13.5-15.3 ppm
Carbon Dioxide	1.2-1.6 ppm
pH	6.5-9.5
Total NH_3- N	0 ppm
Unionized NH_3	0 ppm
Nitrite	0 ppm
Total Alkalinity	50-250 ppm
Total Hardness	20-250 ppm

Results and Discussion

Table 7.3: Loading Densities of Selective Ornamental Fishes (Number of Fish/ L) Packed for 48-72 Hours and per cent of Mortality (average value) within 7 days after Opening

Fish Group	Approximate Total Length of Fish (inches)	Loading Density (Fish/L)	% of Mortality (Average Value)
1	2	3	4
Guppy (common, normal tail & fin))	1.0	200- 130	02
,, (fancy variety)	1.25	55-35	02
Common Molly (small)	1.5	35-30	2.1
,, (medium)	2.0	25-20	02
,, (large)	2.5	20-15	2.1
Molly (sail fin)	2.5-3.0	05-03	00
,, (balloon)	2.5	09-05	01
Swordtail (common, small)	1.0	55-35	2.3
,, (medium)	1.5	35-25	2.1
,, (large)	2.5	20-15	2
,, (lyre-tail variety)	3.0	14-09	1.5
Swordtail (Hi-fin variety)	3.0	04-02	00
Platy (maculatus group), small	0.5-0.6	55- 40	01
,, (medium)	1.0	40-30	01
,, (large)	1.5	35-20	01
Platy (variatus group), small	0.5	55-35	01
,, (medium)	1.0	40-30	00
,, (large)	1.5	35-20	01
Platy (Hi-fin variety)	1.5-2.0	13-09	01

Contd...

1	2	3	4
Goldfish (single tail)	1.0	20-15	02
,, ,,	2.0	10-06	02
Goldfish (fan-tail)	2.0	07-04	00-1.0
Goldfish (veil tail/veil fin)	2.0	05-03	00-1.0
Rosy barb (normal fin)	1.5	20-14	01
Rosy barb (veil form)	1.5	17-10	01
Tiger barb (small)	1.0	40-30	01
,, (medium)	1.25	25-20	01
,, (large)	1.5	16-12	1.5
Zebra Danio (small)	1.0	50-35	01
,, (medium)	1.25	35-30	02
Zebra Danio (veil fin/long fin)	1.5	25-15	03
Cosby Gourami (Blue & Yellow)	2.0	17-12	0.5
,, ,,	2.5	10-07	0.5
Kissing gourami	2.0	15 10	01
,, ,,	3.0	07-05	02
Dwarf Gourami	1.25-1.75	20-14	00
Pearl Gourami	2.0	15-10	02
,, ,,	3.0	07-05	01
Widow Tetra	1.0-1.25	28-20	01
Serpae Tetra	1.0	35-20	03
,, ,,	1.5	25-15	03
Neon Tetra	1.0	35-25	04
Cardinal Tetra	1.25	25-20	05
Buenos Aires Tetra	1.5	25-20	03
,, ,, ,,	2.0	20-14	02
Angel (normal fin), small	1.0	21- 15	01
,, medium	1.5	08-05	01
,, big	2.0	03-02	0.5
Cichlids-Fire-mouth, Remirez' Dwarf cichlid, (small)	1.5	21-15	0.5
,, (medium)	1.75	14-10	0.5
,, (big)	2.0	03-02	0.5
Sharks (Labeo spp), small	1.5	28-21	02
,, medium	2.0	20-14	02
,, large	2.5	14-10	03
,, large	3.0	10-07	01
,, large	3.5-4.0	07-04	01
Cat fish *(Corydoras spp.)*	1.0	30-24	01
,, ,,	2.0	20-15	01
Tiger Loach *(Botia lohachata)*	2.0	18-10	01

The mortality per cent was low, as observed; and the fishes those survived performed well with respect to their swimming behaviour and acceptance to food in glass aquaria, as well as displayed ornamental characteristics. Although, the per cent of mortality might vary, if the fishes were actually shipped to the destination of 72 hours' journey. However, by adopting these procedural systems for ornamental fish handling, packaging, we have been able to reduce mortality rate remarkably to ensure enhanced and new economic direction at one hand and huge engagement of workforce on the other hand.

REFERENCES

APHA. (1999). Standard Methods for the Examination of Water and Wastewater. American Public Health Association; 20th edition.

Berka, R. (1986). The Transport of Live Fish. A Review. *European Inland Fisheries Advisory Commission (EIFAC) Technical Paper*, 48, pp. 1-52. ftp://ftp.fao.org/docrep/fao/009/af000e/af000e.pdf.

Felix, N., J.D. Jameson and R. Alan Brindo. (2012). Ornamental Fish Farming - A Successful Cottage Industry in Rural and Urban India. *Aquaculture Asia (Sustainable Aquaculture)*. Volume XVII No. 3, July-September, pp. 14-18.

Ghosh, Indranil. (2006). The Ornamental Fish Sector in India and the West Bengal Scenario. *INFOFISH International*, No. 4 (July/August), pp. 28-31.

Ghosh, Indranil. (2011). Aquariculture of Living Jewels: An Opportunity for Aqua Business. In: Limnology: Current Perspective-Proceedings of National Conference on Current Perspectives in Limnology 25th-26th December 2009 (Sakhare, V.B. Ed.), 96-101, Daya Publishing House, New Delhi.

Herwig, N. (1979). Handbook of Drugs and Chemicals used in the Treatment of Fish Diseases. Charles Thomas Publishers, Springfield, IL. pp. 272.

Lim, L. C., Dhert, P. and Sorgeloos, P. (2003). Recent Developments and Improvements in Ornamental Fish Packaging Systems for Air Transport. *Aquaculture Research*, 34, pp. 923-935. doi: 10.1046/j.1365-2109.2003.00946.x

Pramod P.K, A. Ramachandran, T.P. Sajeevan, S. Thampy and S.S. Pai. (2010). Comparative Efficacy of MS-222 and benzocaine as anaesthetics under Simulated Transport Conditions of a Tropical Ornamental Fish *Puntius filamentosus* (Valenciennes). *Aquaculture Research*, 41:309-314.

Page 83-107

PLANKTON AND FISHERIES

Edited by : **V.B. Sakhare; H.K. Jadhav** and **S.S. Jadhav**

Edition : **2017**

ISBN : 978-93-5056-811-8

Published by : **Discovery Publishing House Pvt. Ltd., New Delhi (India)**

8

Zooplankton Diversity in Jawalban Reservoir, Maharashtra

Vishwas Balasaheb Sakhare

Post Graduate Department of Zoology

Yogeshwari Mahavidyalaya, Ambajogai - 431 517.

INTRODUCTION

Zooplankton are microscopic, free swimming, heterogenous assemblage of tiny plants and animals which are represented by wide array of taxonomic groups *i.e.*, protozoa, rotifera, cladocera, ostracoda and copepoda. They found in fresh, brackish as well as marine habitats. Most of them depend to a large extent, on various bacterioplankton and phytoplankton for food. Many of the larger forms feed on smaller zooplankton, forming secondary consumers. Some of them are detritivore feeders, browsing and feeding on the substrate attached organic matter, phytoplankton or concentrating on the freely suspended organic matter particles or those lying on the bottom sediment.

Zooplankton communities play an important role in the aquatic food chain and also contribute significantly to the secondary productivity of freshwater ecosystem (Saikia and Das, 2003). Zooplankton by their heterotrophic activity plays a key role in the cycling of organic materials in aquatic ecosystems and used as bioindicators, which are evaluated through presence/absence, condition, relative abundance, reproductive success, community structure (*i.e.*, composition and diversity), community function (*i.e.*, trophic structure), or any combination thereof (Hellawell, 1986).

Zooplankton constitute important food item of many omnivorous and carnivorous fishes. The larvae of carps mainly feed on zooplankton (Dewan *et al.* 1977) because zooplankton provides the necessary amount of protein for the fast growth and specially that of gonad.

Zooplankton supports the commercially important fish population. They are the major mode of energy transfer between phytoplankton compositions, abundance and seasonal variations is helpful in planning and successful fishery management of particular aquatic ecosystem. Zooplankton can also play an important role in indicating the presence or absence of certain species of fishes or in determining the population densities.

Zooplankton diversity is an important aspect in study of aquatic ecosystem. It provides ways of predicting productivity and it is one of the principle links in the aquatic food chain. Knowledge on zooplankton diversity is also helpful in knowing the health of aquatic ecosystem. Zooplankton community distribution largely depends on some of the complex factors like change of climatic conditions, physical and chemical parameters and vegetation present in area. Zooplankton are the central trophic link between primary producers and higher trophic levels.

Generally zooplankton community in freshwater ecosystems ranges in size from a few tens of microns (protozoa) to >2 mm (macroplankton).

The diversity of zooplankton of India is considerably rich as compared to world fauna (Khan, 2003). As per a rough estimate, the rotifera (330 species), cladocera (110 species) and copepoda (88 species) of the country, comprise nearly 13.20 per cent, 25.88 per cent and 17.60 per cent respectively of the world fauna.

An appreciable research work has been done in India on qualitative and quantitative analysis of zooplankton (Negi and Pant 1983; Pant *et al.* 1985; Chauhan 1988; Mishra and Saksena 1990; Sinha and Sinha 1993; Pandey *et al.* 1994; Singh and Sinha 1995; Choudhary and Singh 1999; Kumar 2001; Sharma and Hussain 2001; Sinha and Islam 2002; Khan 2002; Maruthanayagam *et al.* 2003; Kar and Barbhuiya 2004; Pathak and Mudgal 2004; Khare 2005; Mishra 2005; Sharma 2005; Wanganeo and Wanganeo 2006; Kiran *et al.* 2007; Bath 2008; Kudari and Kanamadi 2008; Sharma and Sharma 2008; Chattopadhyay and Barik 2009; Purushothama *et al.* 2011; Balakrishna 2012; Goswami and Mandkodi 2012; Sharma *et al.* 2012; Balakrishna *et al.* 2013, Das and Kar 2013; Kar and Kar 2013; Srivastava 2013; Tamot and Awasthi 2013; Dubey *et al.* 2014; Gyatri *et al.* 2014; Tyor *et al.* 2014, Mahesh *et al.* 2015; Sanyal *et al.* 2015 etc. Such studies from Maharashtra state have been very recently initiated and the only contributions on this aspect are those of Pathak 1999; Quadri 2004; Sakhare 2007; Harney *et al.* 2008; Jetithor 2010; Mohite 2010; Dhembare 2011; Ingole *et al.* 2011; Joshi 2011; Kolhe 2011; Ingole 2013; Jadhav *et al.* 2013; Malthane 2013; Patil 2013; Chalak 2014; Buktar 2015; Korgaonkar and Bharamal 2016).

Fig. 8.1: **Jawalban Reservoir**

Materials and Methods

The zooplankton samples were collected on monthly basis for the period of June 2013 to May 2015. Zooplanktons were collected by filtering 100 liters of water through plankton net made up of bolting silk. The zooplanktonic samples were preserved in 5 per cent formalin. The preserved samples were brought to the Research Laboratory of Department of Zoology, Yogeshwari Mahavidyalaya, Ambajogai (Maharashtra) for qualitative and quantitative analysis and the identification was done with the help of standard keys described by Pennak (1978), Battish (1992), Dhanapathi (2000), Lynne (2004) and Kumar (2015).

Results

Microscopic examination of zooplanktons revealed that there were four groups consisting of 27 species of zooplankton in order rotifers (12 species), cladocerans (6 species), copepods (5 species) and ostracods (4 species) (Table 8.1). The species observed were *Brachionus calyciflorus, Brachionus bidentata, Brachionus falcatus, Brachionus angularis, Brachionus diversicornis, Keratella tropica, Keratella quadrata, Lecane (monostyla) bulla, Trichocera porcellus, Monostyla quadridenta, Asplanchna priodonta,* and *Filina longiseta* (Rotifers); *Diphanosoma sarsi, Ceriodaphnia cornuta, Moina micrura, Alona rectangular, Alona nana, Indialana ganapati* (cladocerans);

Heliodiaptomus contortus, Phyllodiaptomous annae, Diaptomous orientalis, Mesocyclops hyalinus, Mesocyclops leuckarti (Copepoda); Stenocypris major, Cypris obensa Cyclocypris globosa and *Candocypria osborni* (Ostracoda).

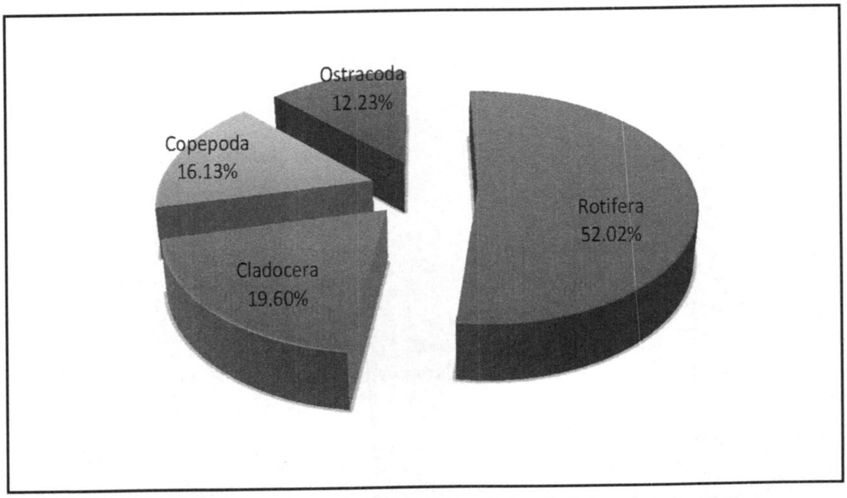

Fig. 8.2: **Percentage composition of available zooplankton groups in Jawalban Reservoir (Year 2013-14)**

Table 8.1: Zooplankton Diversity of Jawalban Reservoir

Cladocera	
1.	*Diphanosoma sarsi*
2.	*Ceriodaphnia cornuta*
3.	*Moina micrura*
4.	*Alonella nana*
5.	*Alona rectangular*
6.	*Indialona ganapati*
Rotifera	
1.	*Brachionus calyciflorus*
2.	*Brachionus bidentata*
3.	*Brachionus falcatus*
4.	*Brachionus angularis*
5.	*Brachionus diversicornis*
6.	*Keratella quadrata*
7.	*Keratella tropica*

Contd...

8.	*Monostyla quadridentata*
9.	*Lecane (Monostyla) bulla*
10.	*Trichocera porcellus*
11.	*Asplanchna priodonta*
12.	*Filinia longiseta*
	Copepods
1.	*Heliodiaptomus contortus*
2.	*Phyllodiaptomus annae*
3.	*Diaptomus orientalis*
4.	*Mesocyclops hyalinus*
5.	*Mesocyclops leuckarti*
	Ostracods
1.	*Stenocypris major*
2.	*Cypris obensa*
3.	*Cyclocypris globosa*
4.	*Candocypria osborni*

During 2013-14, rotifer dominated the zooplankton population (52.02%), followed by cladocera (19.60%), copepoda (16.13%) and ostracoda (12.23%) are presented in Fig. 8.2. The flourishing of zooplankton groups at high temperatures producing a distinct peak in summer season explains the positive correlations with temperature. Summer months exhibited higher population of zooplankton. Cladocerans, rotifers, copepods as well as ostracods showed the summer maxima and minima in monsoon season.

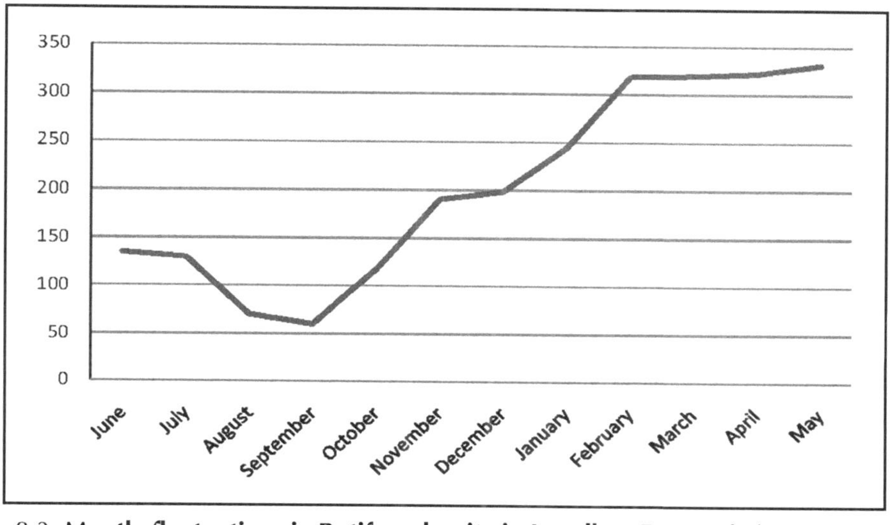

Fig. 8.3: **Montly fluctuations in Rotifera density in Jawalban Reservoir (Year 2013-14)**

Table 8.2: Species Composition of Rotifera (density: organisms/liter) during year 2013-14

Species/Month	Jun	Jul	Aug	Sep	Oct	Nov	Dec	Jan	Feb	Mar	Apr	May
Brachionus calyciflorus	20	10	15	10	25	20	20	25	25	35	30	35
Brachionus bidentata	15	10	15	05	10	15	20	35	40	25	30	35
Brachionus falcatus	15	15	05	05	10	15	15	20	25	15	15	20
Brachionus angularis	15	20	15	00	10	20	15	25	30	20	25	30
Brachionus diversicornis	10	05	05	20	20	20	18	25	32	35	35	28
Keratella tropica	15	10	05	00	10	15	10	10	15	15	20	15
Keratella quadrata	10	05	10	15	17	20	25	25	28	27	30	28
Lecane (monostyla) bulla	05	10	00	00	10	15	10	15	15	20	15	24
Trichocera porcellus	10	15	00	00	00	15	15	15	25	30	25	25
Monostyla quadridenta	05	05	00	00	00	05	10	10	23	32	27	24
Asplanchna priodonta	05	20	00	05	05	15	20	24	35	30	40	30
Filina longiseta	10	05	00	00	00	15	20	15	25	35	30	37
Total	135	130	70	60	117	190	198	244	318	319	322	331

Rotifers were represented by 12 species. During present investigation, 5 species of *Brachionus* were recorded which contributed highest amount of rotifer population (Table 8.2). Among the rotifers, *Brachinous angularis* and *Keratella tropica* were absent in September 2013, while *Lecane (Monostyla) bulla* was not seen in two months (August and September), and *Trichocera porecellus*, *Monostyla quadrata* and *Filinia logiseta* were absent in three months (August, September and October). *Asplanchna priodonta* was absent in August 2013. The maximum rotifer population was recorded in May 2014 (33 organisms/liter) and minimum population in September 2013 (60 organisms/liter).

Cladocerans were represented by 6 species (Table 8.3). The peak period of cladocerans was observed in the month of May 2014 (147 organisms/liter) and it was minimum in the month of July 2013 (11 organisms/liter) (Table 8.3 and Fig. 8.4). *Ceriodaphnia cornuta* was absent in entire rainy season *i.e.*, June to September, while *Alona rectangular* was not seen in August 2013 and *Indialona ganapati* in July and August. *Alona nana* was absent in three months of rainy season *i.e.*, July, August and September.

Copepods were represented by 5 species (Table 8.4). Its maxima was 115 organisms/liter in the month of May 2014 and minima was 05 organisms/liter in the month of August 2013 (Fig. 8.5). *Diaptomous orientalis* was recorded only in seven months. It showed presence mostly in summer season. *Phyllodiaptomous annae* was absent in three months of rainy season *i.e.* July, August and September, while *Mesocyclops hyalinus* and *Mesocyclops leuckarti* were absent in August 2013.

Table 8.3: Species Composition of Cladocera (density: organisms/liter) during year 2013-14

Species/Month	Jun	Jul	Aug	Sep	Oct	Nov	Dec	Jan	Feb	Mar	Apr	May
Diphanosoma sarsi	02	05	05	02	05	07	10	10	20	28	25	30
Ceriodaphnia cornuta	00	00	00	00	10	10	15	12	15	25	25	20
Moina micrura	04	02	10	02	10	15	17	17	20	25	15	30
Alona rectangular	08	04	00	02	05	05	10	14	25	30	20	30
Alonella nana	04	00	00	00	10	10	10	15	30	20	30	15
Indialona ganapati	10	00	00	08	15	12	15	20	32	18	20	22
Total	28	11	15	14	55	59	77	88	142	146	135	147

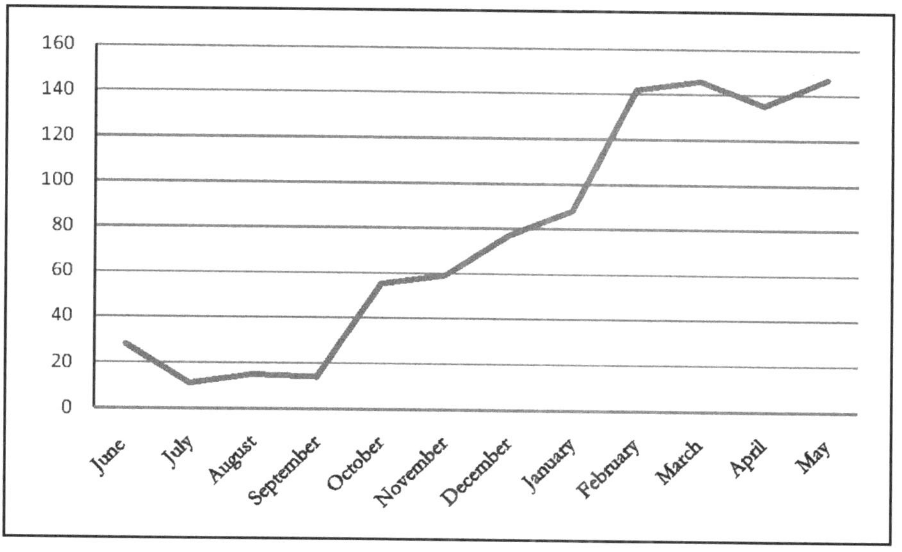

Fig. 8.4: **Monthly fluctuations in cladocera density in Reservoir (2013-14)**

Table 8.4: Species Composition of Copepoda (density: organisms/liter) during year 2013-14

Species/Month	Jun	Jul	Aug	Sep	Oct	Nov	Dec	Jan	Feb	Mar	Apr	May
Heliodiaptomus contortus	04	10	05	10	12	15	10	15	15	20	15	18
Phyllodiaptomous Annae	15	00	00	00	18	20	27	25	15	20	30	32
Diaptomous orientalis	00	00	00	00	00	00	00	02	04	02	05	10
Mesocyclops hyalinus	02	02	00	04	10	17	15	10	10	20	16	27
Mesocyclops leuckarti	10	05	00	20	20	18	25	25	25	30	32	28
Total	31	17	05	34	60	70	77	77	79	92	98	115

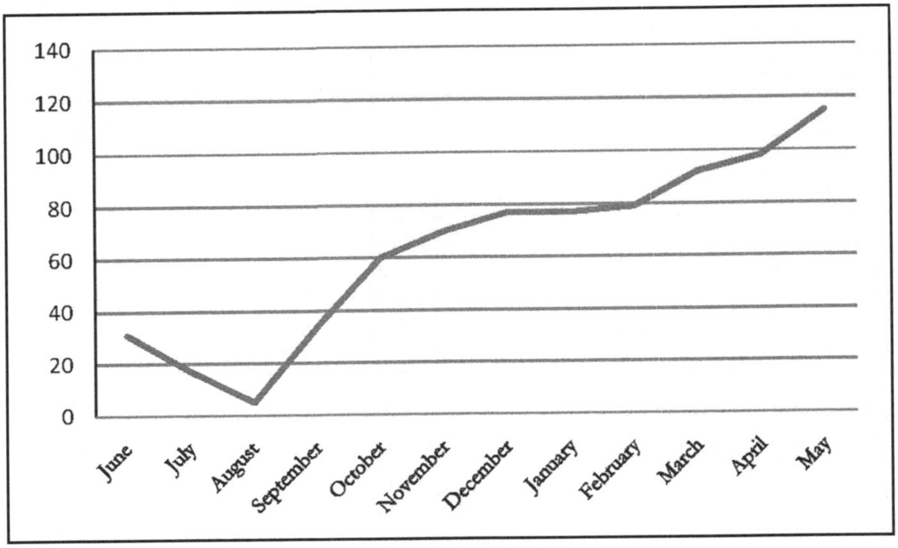

Fig. 8.5: **Monthly fluctuations in copepoda density in Jawalban Reservoir (2013-14)**

Ostracods were represented by 4 species (Table 8.5). *Stenocypris major* was not recorded in September 2013. *Cyclocypris globosa* was absent in July and August, while *Candocypria osborni* was not seen in three months of rainy season *i.e.* July, August and September. The highest density of ostracods was observed in May 2014 (91organisms/liter), while lowest density was recorded in August 2013 (07 organisms/liter) (Fig. 8.6).

Table 8.5: Species Composition of Ostracoda (density: organisms/liter) during year 2013-14

Species/Month	Jun	Jul	Aug	Sep	Oct	Nov	Dec	Jan	Feb	Mar	Apr	May
Stenocypris major	04	10	05	00	18	17	12	10	19	20	30	29
Cypris obensa	02	10	02	02	12	14	18	20	25	22	20	27
Cyclocypris globosa	05	00	00	07	05	05	04	10	12	08	15	10
Candocypria osborni	05	00	00	00	10	10	18	18	20	20	18	25
Total	16	20	07	09	45	46	52	58	76	70	83	91

During second year of investigation (2014-15), zooplanktons were represented by rotifer, cladocera, copepoda and ostracoda. The percentage composition of zooplankton in Jawalban reservoir is shown in Fig. 8.7. Among zooplankton, rotifers dominated (61.72%), followed by cladocera (19.78%), copepoda (12.78%) and ostracoda (5.72%).

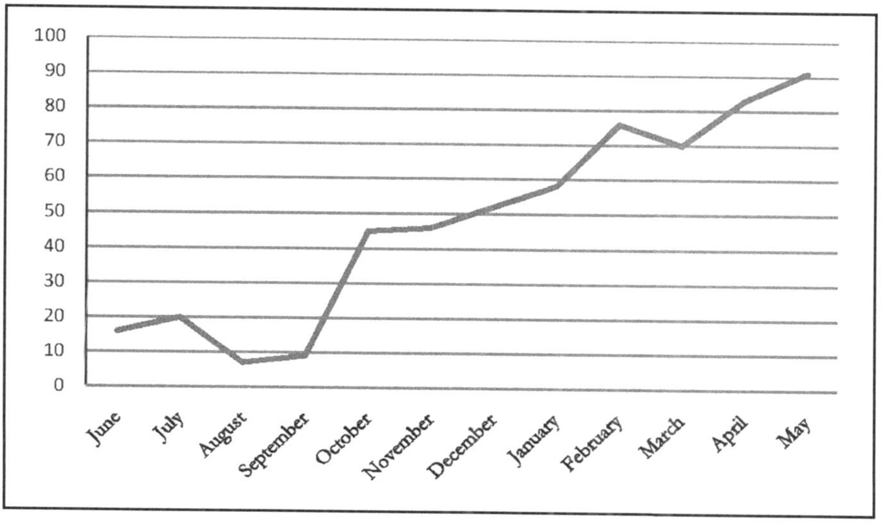

Fig. 8.6: **Monthly fluctuation in ostracoda density in Jawalban Reservoir (Year 2013-14)**

Rotifers accounted for about 61.72 per cent during year 2014-15, and were represented by 12 species (Table 8.6). The highest density of rotifers was observed in the month of May 2015 (367 organisms/liter) and lowest in August 2014 (50 organisms/liter). Throughout the summer months, rotifer population was maximum. However, during rainy season, the rotifer population was less (Fig. 8.8). The species *Brachinous angularis* and *Trichocera porcellus* were absent in two months *i.e.* July and August. *Brachionus bidentata* was not seen in rainy season, while *Brachionus diversicornis* also absent in three months of rainy season.

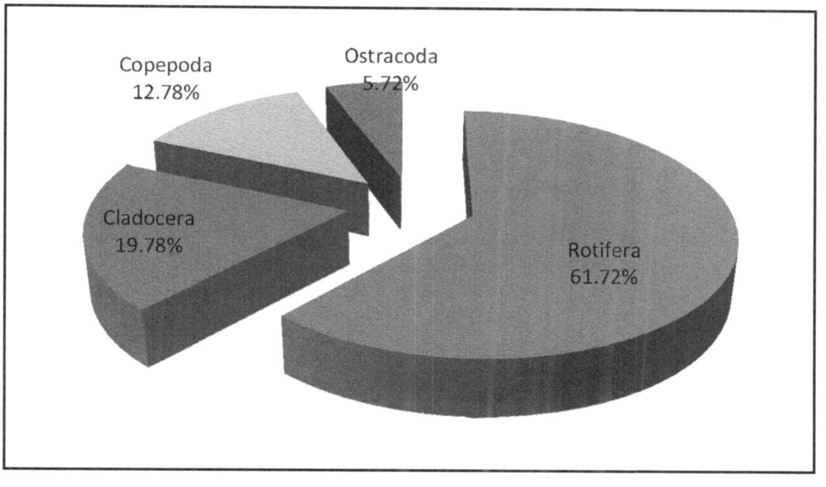

Fig. 8.7: **Percentage composition of available zooplankton groups in Jawalban Reservoir (Year 2014-15)**

Table 8.6: Species Composition of Rotifera (density: organisms/liter) during year 2014-15

Species/Month	Jun	Jul	Aug	Sep	Oct	Nov	Dec	Jan	Feb	Mar	Apr	May
Brachionus calyciflorus	20	14	05	05	10	15	18	20	20	30	24	35
Brachionus bidentata	00	00	00	00	22	20	25	23	30	35	42	34
Brachionus falcatus	05	07	05	10	10	12	15	20	32	38	30	33
Brachionus angularis	02	00	00	05	10	08	10	15	18	20	20	25
Brachionus diversicornis	05	00	00	00	15	10	20	15	15	18	25	22
Keratella tropica	10	10	05	5	15	15	18	20	25	28	35	40
Keratella quadrata	15	05	15	15	20	25	25	28	30	28	28	30
Lecane (monostyla) bulla	10	15	10	05	10	16	19	27	35	30	35	40
Trichocera porcellus	04	00	00	10	15	20	22	23	38	30	30	25
Monostyla quadridenta	10	05	05	15	10	15	20	22	25	28	30	42
Asplanchna priodonta	02	04	00	02	02	05	05	10	10	25	15	15
Filina longiseta	02	05	05	05	15	10	10	18	15	18	20	26
Total	85	65	50	77	154	171	207	241	293	328	334	367

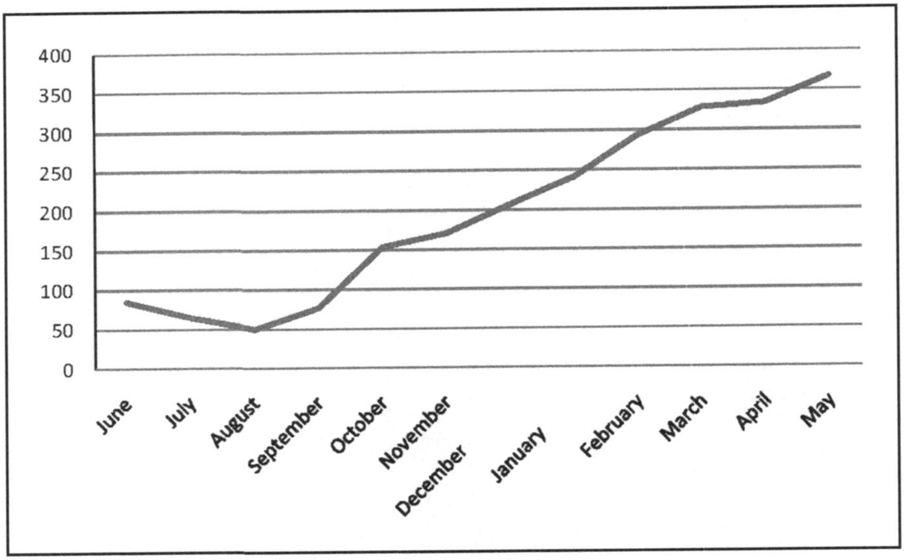

Fig.8.8: **Monthly fluctuations in Rotifera in Jawalban Reservoir (2014-15)**

Table 8.7: Species Composition of Cladocera (density: organisms/liter) during year 2014-15

Species/Month	Jun	Jul	Aug	Sep	Oct	Nov	Dec	Jan	Feb	Mar	Apr	May
Diphanosoma sarsi	05	02	02	05	08	06	08	10	15	10	20	15
Ceriodaphnia cornuta	10	05	00	00	12	10	15	10	25	18	15	20
Moina micrura	05	00	00	00	00	00	00	00	28	23	20	27
Alona rectangular	10	05	05	04	12	14	12	14	22	20	15	15
Alonella nana	05	00	00	00	00	00	00	00	20	25	25	20
Indialona ganapati	10	05	02	08	10	14	12	14	28	25	15	25
Total	45	17	09	17	42	44	47	48	138	121	110	122

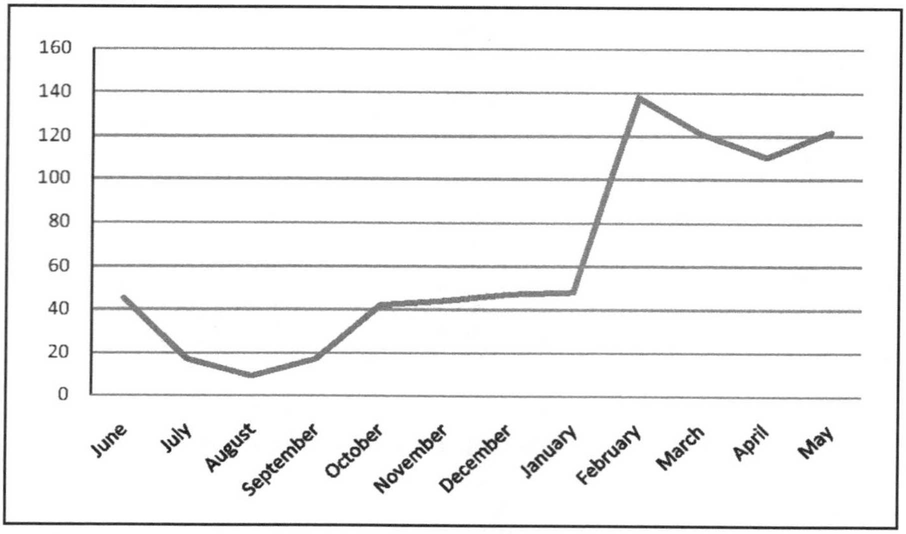

Fig. 8.9: **Monthly fulctuation in cladocera in Jawalban Reservoir (2014-15)**

Cladocerans were represented by 6 species and accounted for about 19.78 per cent. The peak period of cladocerans was observed in the month of February 2015 (158 organisms/liter) and it was minimum in the month of August 2014 (14 organisms/liter) (Fig. 8.9). The species *Moina micrura* and *Alona nana* were absent for seven months (from July 2014 to January 2015), while *Ceriodaphnia cornuta* was absent in two months *i.e.* August and September (Table 8.7).

Table 8.8: Species Composition of Copepoda (density: organisms/liter) during year 2014-15

Species/Month	Jun	Jul	Aug	Sep	Oct	Nov	Dec	Jan	Feb	Mar	Apr	May
Heliodiaptomus contortus	05	10	10	05	12	12	10	17	15	15	18	15
Phyllodiaptomous annae	05	02	02	04	07	04	04	10	10	10	08	10
Diaptomous orientalis	00	00	00	00	05	05	04	05	15	10	18	15
Mesocyclops hyalinus	05	02	05	00	00	05	06	06	15	15	07	10
Mesocyclops leuckarti	05	05	07	05	07	10	10	10	15	15	14	15
Total	20	19	24	14	31	36	34	48	70	65	65	65

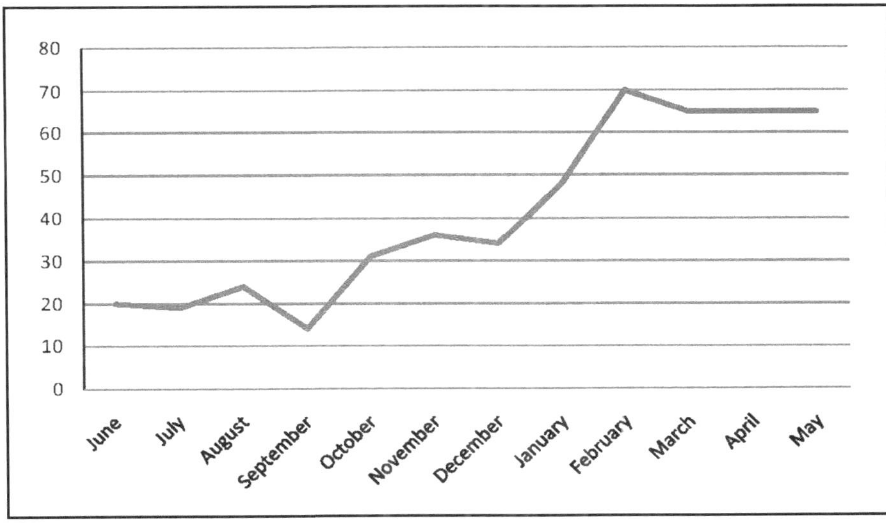

Fig. 8.10: **Monthly fluctuatons in Copepoda in Jawalban Reservoir (2014-15)**

Copepods accounted for about 12.78 per cent and were represented by 5 species (Table 8.8). The population was more during summer and least during rainy season. The maximum density was observed in February (70 organisms/liter) and minimum in September (14 organisms/liter) (Fig. 8.10). *Mesocyclops hyalinus* was not observed in two months (September and October). *Diaptomous orientalis* was totally absent in rainy season.

Ostracoda come 4th in the order of occurrences, and were represented by 4 species. The population was more during summer and least during rainy season (Fig. 8.11). The maximum density was 44 organisms/liter in March 2015 and ostracods were totally absent in September 2014 (Table 8.9). *Cyclopcypris globosa* was showed absence in six months *i.e.*, from June 2014 to November 2014. *Stenocypris major* and *Cypris obensa* were absent in September 2014 and *Candocypria osborni* was not seen in three months of rainy season *i.e.* July to September.

Table 8.9: Species Composition of Ostracoda (density: organisms/liter) during year 2014-15

Species/Month	Jun	Jul	Aug	Sep	Oct	Nov	Dec	Jan	Feb	Mar	Apr	May
Stenocypris major	05	04	02	00	05	06	05	08	08	12	10	08
Cypris obensa	02	02	02	00	04	05	05	05	06	10	08	07
Cyclocyprisglobosa	00	00	00	00	00	00	05	05	10	12	07	10
Candocypria osborni	02	00	00	00	04	02	04	05	05	10	05	05
Total	09	06	04	00	13	13	19	23	29	44	30	30

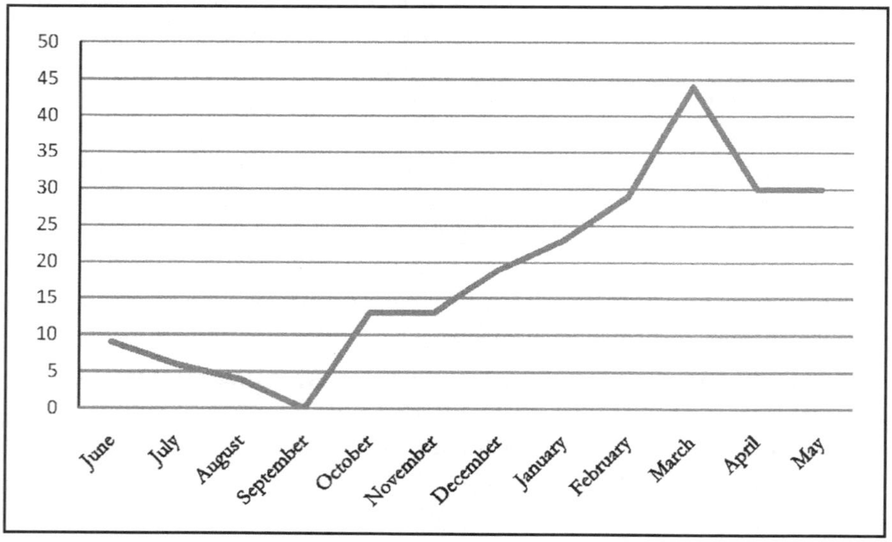

Fig. 8.11: **Monthly fluctuation in Ostracoda in Jawalban Reservoir (2014-15)**

Discussion

A total of 27 species of zooplankton belonging to rotifers (12 species, cladocerans (6 species), copepods (5 species) and ostracods (4 species) were recorded from Jawalban reservoir. The zooplankton density in different season was in order of summer> winter> monsoon. Increase in temperature and high evaporation during summer season enhances the rate of decomposition due to which the water becomes nutrient rich resulting in increase in population density of zooplankton. Low population density during monsoon may be due to the dilution effect by rain water and high water level (Akbulut, 2004 and Mulani *et al.* 2009).

In the present investigation the peak of zooplankton was found during summer season. Summer peak of zooplankton has been also reported by George, (1966), Selot, (1977), Sukhija, (2010), Alone *et al.* (2012) and Pandey

et al. (2013). Presence of maximum zooplankton in summer might be due to presence of higher population of bacteria. According to Singh (1991) and Pandey *et al.* (1995) optimal thermal and nutritional condition and higher concentration of oxygen might be responsible for higher zooplankton population.

Sadanand and Yamakanamardi (2014) observed maximum abundance of zooplankton during summer season and least during rainy season.

Joshi (2011) observed summer maxima of zooplankton in Rajura Lake of Buldhana district of Maharashtra. The summer population maxima of zooplankton were co-related with high temperatures and a high standing crop of primary producers leading to greater availability of food.

On similar lines, Bhadane (2015) identified 32 species of zooplankton from Ramkund of Godavari river, Nashik district, Maharashtra. Zooplankton were represented by four groups, *i.e.* *(i)* rotifera; *(ii)* cladocera; *(iii)* copepoda and *(iv)* ostracoda. Rotifera and cladocera were represented by 11 and 9 species respectively, while copepoda and ostracoda were represented by 8 and 4 species respectively. During summer seasons a higher population of zooplankton was recorded. All the groups of zooplankton showed maxima in summer and minima in winter.

Patel *et al.* (2013) and Suganthi *et al.* (2014) also reported maximum occurrence of zooplankton in summer.

Shivanshanakar and Venkataramana (2013) reported 23 species from Bhadra reservoir of Karnataka. They recorded 23 species of zooplankton, out of which rotifers comprise of 8 species, cladocera 5 species, copepods 3 species, ostracods 2 species and protozoans 5 species. The season-wise zooplankton analysis showed maximum occurrence in summer due to the different environmental and inflow characteristics of the water body.

Balakrishna *et al.* (2013) studied physico-chemical parameters and plankton diversity of Ghanpur Lake, Warangal (Andhra Pradesh). They identified 13 species of zooplanktons. Out of 13, rotifers were represented by 7 species of rotifers, 3 species of copepods, 2 species of cladocera and 1 species of ostracoda. Rotifera, cladocera and copepoda populations were high during summer season and low in rainy season, while the ostracod species were recorded high in rainy season and low in winter season.

The lower density of zooplankton during rainy season might be due to flood and fast water current. Normally, the monsoon is associated with lower population densities due to its dilution effect and decrease in photosynthetic activity by primary producers. Similar results have been shown by Baker (1979) and Ude *et al.* (2011).

According to Sharma (2010) the rotifer communities exhibit higher species diversity, higher evenness, lower dominance and lack of quantitative dominance of any individual species. The rotifers comprise the dominant

qualitative component of zooplankton (171 species) of Deeper Beel of Assam. Vanjare and Pai (2010) reported 13 rotifer species from a pond in Pune (Maharashtra).

Rotifers were the dominant group among zooplankton community constituting 52.02 per cent and 61.72 per cent of the total zooplankton population during year 2013-14 and 2014-15 respectively. In the present study, 5 species of *Brachionus* were recorded which contributed highest among rotifer population. The population density of rotifers was maximum in summer and minimum in monsoon season. The study shows similarities with Sakhare (2007) and Balakrishna *et al.* (2013) in occurrence of highest density in summer and lowest in monsoon.

Kanagasabapathi and Rajan (2010) recorded 12 genera of rotifers from Irrukkangudi reservoir of Tamil Nadu. Khan (2003) reported 43 species of rotifers belonging to 12 families which constituted nearly 29 per cent of the species reported from West Bengal and 13 per cent of the India's rotifer fauna. Ingole (2013) reported 11 genera of rotifers from Majalgaon reservoir and observed *Brachionus angularis, B. longiseta, F. opoliensis, Kelliocottia* sp., *Notholocaocum minota* and *Rotaria* sp., as dominant species. Karuthapandi *et al.* (2013) reported 114 species of freshwater rotifers from Andhra Pradesh.

Sontakke and Mokashe (2014) reported zooplankton diversity of Dekhu reservoir from Aurangabad and reported maximum rotifer diversity and population density in all the seasons. The dominance of rotifers in the lake was due to the continuous supply of food material. They also reported maximum zooplankton density in summer and minimum in monsoon.

Datta (2011) studied zooplankton diversity of two wetlands of Jalpaiguri district of West Bengal and observed rich zooplankton diversity in both the wetlands. Rotifer was the richest group with 48 species, which accounts for 63 per cent of total zooplankton population.

The cladocerans are micro-crustaceans usually inhabit every type of habitat in the littoral, limnetic or benthic zones of freshwater ecosystems. Of the 11 families listed under the order cladocera, nine are known from Indian waters (Michael and Sharma, 1988). Uma *et al.* (2014) reported eight varieties of ostracods from Ambattur Lake of Tamil Nadu.

Cladocerans occupy the second trophic level *i.e.*, primary consumer level in an aquatic ecosystem. Besides this, cladocerans also serve as diet for fishes. There are many published reports on seasonal occurrences of different cladoceran species (Michael and Sharma 1988; Sharma and Kotwal 2011; Gupta 2002; Raghunathan 1989; Raghunathan and Kumar 2003; Sharma and Chanderkiran 2011; Sharma *et al.* 2005; Thakur *et al.* 2013; Shah and Pandit 2014; Siraj *et al.* 2007).

Sharma and Kotwal (2011) accounted diversity and dynamics of cladocera in a subtropical pond at Sungal (J&K) in which cladocera was represented by eight species. The population of cladoceran passed through two minimas and maximas.

Sakhare (2007) reported plankton population dynamics of Yeldari reservoir (Maharashtra) in which cladocera was represented by 7 species. The group showed maxima in summer and minima in winter. In Jawalban reservoir, the cladoceran occurred more during summer months and least during monsoon months.

Jalizadeh and Yamakanamardi (2012) studied the seasonal fluctuation of cladocera abundance with special reference to seasonal changes in physico-chemical parameters in lentic ecosystem of Mysore. The physico-chemical variables influencing the abundance of cladocera were dissolved oxygen, NO_3, BOD and conductivity in Bannur Lake; COD, turbidity and water temperature in Lingambudi Lake. No physico-chemical variables revealed correlation with the abundance of cladocera in Hebbal Lake.

Hutchinson (1967) pointed out that water temperature increases the development of cladocera while Patalas (1972) stated that temperature is the primary factor influencing the zooplankton abundance. Quadri and Yousuf (1980) also recorded the significance of temperature in occurrence and the distribution of cladocera in Kashmir Lake. The present investigation corroborate with the findings of Hutchinson (1967).

Copepods are the most important food items in freshwater aquaculture, and their nauplii are especially valuable for fish fry (Szlauer and Szlauer, 1980). In Central Europe, efforts have been made to use copepods and other components of zooplankton for feeding fish in aquaculture (Szlauer and Szlauer, 1980; 1982).

Copepods prefer a more stable environment and are generally considered as water pollution-sensitive taxa as they disappear in severely contaminated waters *(Das et al. 1996)*. On the contrary, a change in the number of copepods with seasonal occurrence in the different Indian lakes and reservoirs has been reported (Thakur *et al.* 2013; Jadhav *et al.* 2013; Tijare and Thosar 2010; Sakhare 2007; Alfred and Thapa 1996).

Ostracods look like seed, hence calles 'seed shrimps'. Patil and Talmale (2005) stated that in freshwaters of Maharashtra there are 38 species of ostracods under 15 genera. Patil (2002) reported 7 ostracod species from Ujani wetland. Shinde *et al.* (2014) revealed the presence of 17 species of ostracods from different localities of Northern Western Ghats. Of the 17 species of ostracods, 13 were recorded in the pools on the basaltic mesa.

Ostracods are small bivalve crustaceans. They are very common in the most inland waters, where they abound in the benthic and periphytic animal communities, but they also occur in marine interstitial and even semi-terrestrial environments. They are of great interest as a model group in various ecological and evolutionary studies. This is because the calcified valves of non-marine ostracod can be very common in lake sediments and this adds a real-time frame to the evolution of ostracod lineages as well as of their biological traits (Jalizadeh and Yamakanamardi, 2012).

Of the 11 families listed under the order cladocera, nine are known from Indian waters (Michael and Sharma, 1988). Uma *et al.* (2014) reported eight varieties of ostracods from Ambattur Lake of Tamil Nadu.

Sakhare (2012) studied seasonal variation of zooplankton community in Udyan sarovar tank of Ambajogai and reported 4 species of ostracods *viz; Stenocypris spp., Cypris obensa, Cyclocypris globosa* and *Candocypria osborni*. In Bhavthana reservoir also same species were recorded. In the present study, higher density of ostracods was recorded during summer season. This is in confirmation with the findings of Deshmukh (2001) and Sakhare (2007).

Patra *et al.* (2011) studied ecology and diversity of zooplankton in relation to physico-chemcial characteristics of water of Santragachi Jheel, West Bengal. A total of 18 species belonging to 12 families and 15 genera were recorded. The population density of total zooplankton showed summer maxima in the Jheel. Maximum abundance of rotifer fauna was recorded during summer season in sewage sites whereas cladocera population showed maximum density at non-sewage sites. Copepods showed post monsoon maxima in sewage sites in the Jheels.

Sehgal *et al.* (2013) studied zooplankton diversity in Dimbhe reservoir of Maharashtra and reported seven species of zooplankton. In Dimbhe, zooplankton diversity followed the order of copepoda > ostracoda > rotifera > cladocera.

Sivakami *et al.* (2015) carried out an analysis of zooplankton in lake from Pudukkotai district of Tamil Nadu. They reported 40 species belonging to 5 groups. Out of 40 species, two each belonged to protozoa and ostracoda, 27 to rotifera, 5 to cladocera, 3 to copepoda and 1 to anostraca. A percentage composition revelaled that rotifera represented 66.03 per cent, cladocera 12.23 per cent, protozoans 9.56 per cent, copepods 7.11 per cent and ostracods 3.51 per cent respectively.

Kadam *et al.* (2014) studied zooplankton diversity in Pillowa reservoir in Morena district of Madhya Pradesh. They reported 27 species, out of which 4 species belonged to protozoa, 10 species to rotifera, 6 species to cladocera, 5 species to copepoda and 2 species to ostracoda. The abundance of zooplankton in Pillowa reservoir followed a sequence as rotifera> copepoda>cladocera>protozoa>ostracoda. The zooplanktonic forms exhibited were protozons (9.50%), rotifers (54.84%), cladocerans (14.43%), copepods (15.70%) and ostracods (5.54%).

Balai *et al.* (2014) studied diversity and seasonal variations in zooplankton in Jaismand Lake of Udaipur (Rajasthan) and reported 51 species of zooplankton,out of which 17 species belonged to rotifera, 18 species to cladocera, 5 species to ostracoda and 4 species to copepoda. Among zooplankton, rotifera was observed as the dominant group and the highest count was recorded in the summer.

REFERENCES

Akbulut, E.N. (2004). The Determination of Relationship between Zooplankton and Abiotic Factors using Canonical Correspondence Analysis (CCA) in the ova Stream (Ankara/ Turkey), *Acta Hydrochimica Hydrobiologica*, 32(6): 434-441.

Alfred, J.R.B. ad Thapa, M.P. (1996). Limnological Investigation on Ward's Lake-A wetland in Shillong, Meghalaya, N.E. India. Rec. Zool. Surv. India. Occ. Paper No. 169:1-125 (Published by the Director, Zool. Surv. India, Kolkata).

Alone, M., Alone, A. and Bhagel, A. (2012). Water Quality of Man River in Relation to Physico-chemical Characteristics of Zooplanktons. *Flora and Fauna*, 18(1): 81-84.

Baker, R.L. (1979). Specific Status of *Keratella cochlearis* (Goose) and *K. eurlinare ahlao* from (Rotifera and Brachionidae) morphological and Ecological Consideration .*Canadian Journal of Zoology*, 57: 1719-1722.

Balai, Vijay Kumar, Sharma, L.L. and Ujjania, N.C. (2014). Diversity and Seasonal Variations of zooplankton in Jaismand Lake, Udaipur, India, *Indian J. Anim. Res.*, 48 (5):432-437.

Balakrishna, Dhatrika, (2012). Ecological Studies and zooplankton Diversity in Three Different Lentic Water Bodies of Warangal District, A.P. Ph.D Thesis, Kakatiya University, Warangal.

Balakrishna. D., Mahesh.T., Laxmiprasad. K. and Ravinder Reddy. T. (2013). A Study of Physico-chemical Properties and Zooplankton Diversity of Laknavaram Lake, Andhra Pradesh, *International J. on Chemical Sci.*, 4 (1): 33-39.

Balakrishna, D., Reddy, T.R., Reddy, K.V. and Samatha, D. (2013). Physico-chemical Parameters and Plankton Diversity of Ghanpur Lake, Warangal, A.P., India. *International Journal of Zoology Research*; 3(1): 44-48.

Bath, K.S. (2008). Ecology of Kansli Wetland with Reference to the Invertebrate Fauna. In: Ecobiology of Aquatic Insects (Eds. Arvind Kumar and Harbhajan Kaur), pp. 86-90, Daya Publishing House, Delhi.

Battish, S.K. (1992). Freshwater zooplankton of India. Oxford and IBH Publishing Co., New Delhi.

Bhadane, R.S. (2015). Zooplankton Diversity in Ramkund of Godavari River, Nashik District, Maharashtra. *Bionano Frontier*, 8(3):128-130.

Buktar, P.P. (2015). Studies on some Aspects of Ecology and Fisheries of Two Reservoirs in Beed district of Maharashtra, Ph.D. thesis, Dr. Babasaheb Ambedkar Marathwada University, Aurangabad.

Chalak, A.D. (2014). Studies on some Aspects of Fish and Fisheries of Bhavthana Reservoir in Beed District, Maharashtra, Ph.D. thesis, Dr. Babasaheb Ambedkar Marathwada University, Aurangabad.

Chattopadhyay, C. and Barik, A. (2009). The Composition and Diversity of net Zooplankton Species in A Tropical Freshwater Lake. *International Journal of Lakes and Rivers*. 2 (1): 21-30.

Chauhan, R. (1988). Seasonal Abundance of zooplankton in Rewalsar Lake, H.P. *Geobios New Report*, 7(2):117-121.

Choudhary, S. And Singh, D.K. (1999). Zooplankton Populations of Boosra Lake at Muzaffarpur, Bihar. *Environment and Ecology*. 17(2):444-448.

Das, P. and Kar, D. (2013). Studies on Zooplankton Diversity and physico-chemical Parameters of Ramnagar anua, Cachar, Assam. *International Journal of Current Research*. 5:3058-3062.

Datta, Tanmay. (2011). Zooplankton Diversity and Physico-chemical Conditions of Two Wetlands of Jalpaiguri District, India. *International Journal of Applied Biology and Pharmaceutical Technology*, 2(3):576-583. Journal available online at www.ijabpt.com.

Deshmukh, U.S. (2001). Ecological Studies of Chhatri lake, Amravati; with Special Reference to Planktons and Productivity. Ph.D. thesis, Amravathi University, Amravathi.

Dewan, S., Ali, M. and Islam, M.A. (1977). Study on the Size and Pattern of Feeding of Fries and Fingerlings of Three Major Carps, *e.g. Labeo rohita* (Ham), *Catla catla* and *Cirrhina mrigala*. *Bangladesh J. Agri*. 2(2):223-228.

Dhanapathi, M.V.S.S.S. (2000). Taxonomic Notes on the rotifers from India (from 1889-2000) IAAB, Hyderabad Publ.10, 1-178.

Dhembare, A.J. (2011). Diversity and Its Indices in Zooplankton with Physico-chemical Properties of Mula Dam Water Ahmednagar, Maharashtra India. *Eur. J. Exp. Biol.*, 1(4): 98 103.

Dubey, Monika, Anju Kumar Tiwari, Susan Manohar and Nemi Chand Ujjania. (2014). Plankton Diversity in Kaliasote Reservoir, Bhopal (India). *Ecology Enviornment and Conservation*. 20(4):1889-1893.

Gayathri, S., Latha, N., Mohan, M.R. (2014). Studies on Population Dynamics and Seasonal Abundance of Zooplankton Community in Doddavoderahalli lake, Bangalore. *Int. J. Emerg. Trends Eng. Dev.*, 4(1): 50 55.

George, M.G. (1966). Diurnal Variations in Physico-chemical Factors and Zooplankton in Surface Layer of three Fresh Water Ponds. *Indian Journal of Fisheries*, 13: 48-82.

Goswami, A.P., Mankodi, P.C. (2012). Study on Zooplankton of Freshwater Reservoir Nyari-II Rajkot Dist, Gujarat, India, ISCA. *J. Biol. Sci.*, 1(1): 30 34.

Gupta, S. (2002). Studies on the Diversity of cladocerans in the lake Mansar, Jammu. M. Phil. Dissertation, University of Jammu, Jammu.

Harney, N.V., Sitre, S.R., Wadhave, N.S. and Nasare, P.N. (2008). Zooplankton Diversity in a Anthropologically Affected Freshwater lake of Bhadrawati town in Chandrapur district of Maharashtra, *Ecology and Fisheries*, 1(1):27-34.

Hellawell J.M. (1986). Biological Indicators of Freshwater Pollution and Environmental Management. In Pollution Monitoring Series. Elsevier Applied Science Publishers, London, UK (p. 546).

Hutchinson, G.E. (1967). A Treatise on Limnology. Introduction to Lake Biology and the Limnoplankton. John Wiley and Sons, New York London, pp. 115.

Ingole, S.B. (2013). Correlation of rotifers with Physico-chemical Factors at Majalgaon Reservoir, Maharashtra. In: Emerging Trends in Fisheries and Aquaculture (Eds. V.B.Sakhare and B.Vasanthkumar), pp. 225-231, Astral International Pvt. Ltd., New Delhi.

Ingole S.B., Kadam G.A, Naik S.B. and Kulkarni, G.K. (2011). Water Quality of Majalgaon Dam with Special Reference to Zooplankton. In: Limnology Current Perspective (Edited by. V.B. Sakhare, Daya Publishing House, New Delhi, 248-263.

Jadhav, R.N; Pimpliskar Mukesh and Handa Shruti. (2013). Zooplankton Diversity of Nirmal Lake, Vasai, Dist. Thane (M.S.) India. *J. Aqua. Biol.* 27(1): 1-6.

Jalilzadeh, Koorosh and Yamakanamard, S.M. (2012). Abundance of cladocera in Three Contrasting Lentic Ecosystems of Mysore, Karnataka In: Perspectives in Ecology (Eds. V.B. Sakhare and J.S. Mohite), 134-143, Oxford Book Company, Jaipur.

Jalilzadeh, Koorosh and Yamakanamard, S.M. (2012). Total zooplankton Abundance and Biomass in Three Contrasting Lentic Ecosystems of Mysore, Karnataka State, In: Advances in Aquatic Ecology (Vol. 6) (Eds. V.B.Sakhare. and Patricio Rene De los Rios Escalante), pp. 34-49. Daya Publishing House, New Delhi.

Jetithor, S.G. (2010). Studies on some Aspects of Ecology and Fisheries of Harni (Katgaon) Reservoir in Osmanabad district, Maharashtra, Ph.D. thesis, Dr. Babasaheb Ambedkar Marathwada University, Aurangabad.

Joshi, Prasanna. (2011). Studies on Zooplankton of Rajura Lake of Buldhana district, Maharashtra, India. *Science Research Reporter*, 1(3):132-137.

Kadam, C.P., Dandolia, H.S., Kausik, S., Saksena, D.N. and Shrotriy, V.P. (2014). Biodiversity of Zooplankton in Pillowa Reservoir district Morena, Madhya Pradesh, India. *Int. J. of Life Sciences*, 2(3): 263-267.

Kanagasabapathi, V. and Rajan, M.K. (2010). A Pre-liminary Survey of Plankton in Irrukkangudi Reservoir, Virudhunagar district, Tamil Nadu, India. *J. Phytol.* 2(3): 63-72.

Kar, D. and Barbhuiya, M.H. (2004). Abundance and Diversity of zooplankton in Chatla Haor, A Floodplain Wetland in Cachar district of Assam. *Environment and Ecology*, 22 (1): 247-248.

Kar, S. and Kar, D. (2013). Studies on zooplankton Diversity of an Oxbow Lake of South Assam, India. *International Journal of Current Research*, 5(12):3652-3655.

Karuthapandi, M; Rao, D.V. and Xavier Innocent. (2013). Freshwater rotifers of Andhra Pradesh - Checklist, *International Journal of Life Science and Educational Research* 1(1): 1-13. Paper available online at http://www.ijlser.com.

Khan, R.A. (2002). Freshwater Zooplankton and their Role in Aquatic Productivity. In: Proc. 89th Ind. Sci. Cong. Part III, 100-101.

Khan, R.A. (2003). Faunal Diversity of Zooplankton in Freshwater Wetlands of Southeastern West Bengal, Zoological Survey of India, Kolkata, Occasional Paper No. 204, pp. 107.

Khare, P.K. (2005). Physico-chemical Characteristics in Relation to Abundance of Plankton of Jagat Sagar Pond, Chhatarpur, India. In: Advances in Limnology (Ed. S.R. Mishra), 162-174, Daya Publishing House, Delhi.

Kiran, B.R., Puttaiah, E.T. and Devidas Kamath. (2007). Diversity and Seasonal Fluctuation of zooplankton in Fish Pond of Bhadra Fish Farm, Karnataka. *Zoos' Print Journal*. 22(2):2935-2936.

Kolhe, B.G. (2011). Ecological Studies of Zooplankton with Reference to Water Quality of Godavari River from Nashik district, Ph.D. thesis, Dr. Babasaheb Ambedkar Marathwada University, Aurangabad.

Korgaonkar, D.S., and Bharamal, D.L. (2016). Seasonal Variation in Plankton Diversity of Dhamapur Lake (Malvan) of Sindhudurg District (MS), India. *Int. J. Curr. Microbiol. App. Sci.*5(3): 884-889. doi: http://dx.doi.org/10.20546/ijcmas.2016.503.102.

Kudari, V.A. and Kanamadi, R.D. (2008). Impact of Changed Trophic Status on the Zooplankton Composition in Six Water Bodies of Dharwad District, Karnataka State. *Environmental Monitoring and Assessment*. 144(1-3):301-313.

Kumar, Arvind. (2015). Freshwater Plankton and Macrophytes of India, Astral International Pvt.Ltd., New Delhi.

Kumar, K.S. (2001). The Fresh Water zooplankton of some Lakes in Dharmapuri District Tamilnadu. *J. Aqua. Biol.*, 16:5-10.

Lynne M. Witty. (2004). Practical Guide to Identify Freshwater Crustacean zooplankton, Co-operative Freshwater Ecology Unit, Department of Biology, Laurentian University, Sudbury, Ontario, Canada.

Mahesh, T., Balakrishn, D., Surender Reddy, K. and Ravindra Reddy, T. (2015). A Study of Zooplankton Diversity and their Seasonal Variation in Kandlapally Lake, Jagtial, Telangana. *International Journal of Science and Engineering*, 1(1):27-36.

Malthane, G.A. (2013). Diversity of Zooplanktons of Nalganga Reservoir Nalgangapur, Buldana District, Maharahstra. *Ecology and Fisheries*, 6(2):113-116.

Maruthanayagam, C., Sasikumar, M., and Senthilkumar, C. (2003). Studies on Zooplankton Population in Thirukulam Pond during Summer and Rainy Seasons. *Nature Environ. Poullut. Technol.* 2:13-19.

Michael, R.G. and Sharma, B.K. (1988). Fauna of India and Adjacent Countries, Indian Cladocera (Crustacea: Branchiopoda: Cladocera), Zoological Survey of India, Calcutta, pp. 262.

Mishra, S.R. (2005). Zooplankton and their Seasonal Variations in a Sewage Collecting River at Gwalior, Madhya Pradesh. In: Advances in Limnology (Ed.S.R.Mishra), 1-44, Daya Publishing House, Delhi.

Mishra, S.R. and Saksena, D.N. (1990). Seasonal Abundance of the Zooplankton of Waste Water from the Industrial Complex at Birla Nagar (Gwalior) India. *Acta Hydrochim. Hydrobiol.*, 18:215-220.

Mohite, J.S. (2010). Studies on some Aspects of Ecology of Ramdara Reservoir, Tuljapur (Dist. Osmanabad, Maharahstra), Ph.D. thesis, Swami Ramanad Teerth Marathwada University, Nanded.

Mulani, S.K., M.B. Mule, and S.U. Patil. (2009). Studies on Water Quality and Zooplankton Community of the Panchganga River in Kolhapur city. *Journal of Environmental Biology*. 30: 455-459.

Negi, V. and Pant, M.C. (1983). Analysis of Zooplankton Community of Lake Khurpa Tal (Kumaun Himalaya). *Tropical Ecology*, 24(2): 271-282.

Pandey, B.N., Jha, A.K., Das, P.K.L. and Pandey, K. (1994). Zooplanktonic Community in Relation to Certain physico-chemical Factors of Koshi swamps, Purnia (Bihar). *Env. and Ecol.* 12 (3):563-567.

Pandey, B.N., Mishra, A.K., Das, P.K.L. and Jha, A.K. (1995). Studies on Hydrological Condition of River Saura in Relation to its Impact on Biological Health. In: Recent Researches in Aquatic Environment (Eds. Ashutosh Gautam and N.K. Agarwal), pp. 57-65, Narendra Publishing House, New Delhi.

Pandey, B.N., Siddhartha, R., Tanti, K.D. and Thaku, A.K. (2013). Seasonal Variation in zooplanktonic Community in Swamp of Purnia (Bihar), India. *Aquatic Biology Research* 1(1):1-9.

Pant, M.C., Joshi, A. and Sharma, P.C. (1985). Species Composition, Temporal Abundance and Community Structure of zooplankton in lake Sat Tal (U.P.), India. *Arch. Hydrobiol.,* 102 (4):519-602.

Patalas, K. (1972). Crustacea Plankton and the eutrophication of st. Lawrence Great Lakes. *J. Fish. Res. Bd. Can;* 29: 1451-1462.

Patel, Vima, Shukla, S.N. and Patel,Vijay Kumar. (2013). Studies on the Diversity of Zooplankton and their Seasonal Variations in Govindgarh Lake at Rewa (M.P.), India. *Indian Journal of Applied Research,* 3(11):544-546.

Pathak S.K. and Mudgal L.K. (2002). A Pre-liminary Survey of zooplankton of Virla Reservoir of Khargaon. (Madhya Pradesh) India. Indian, *J. Env. and Ecoplan.,* 6(2):297-300.

Pathak, S.K. and Mudgal, L.K. (2004). Biodiversity of zooplankton of Virla Reservoir Khargone (M.P.) India. In: Biodiversity and Environment (Edited By Arvind Kumar), 317-321, A.P.H. Publishing Corporation, New Delhi.

Pathak, V.M. (1999). Ecobiology of Freshwater zooplankton, Ph.D. thesis, Dr. Babasaheb Ambedkar Marathwada University, Aurangabad, pp. 193.

Patil, B.V. (2013). Zooplankton Composition in Reservoirs of Buldhana District, Maharashtra. *Ecology and Fisheries,* 6(2):99-112.

Patil, S.G. (2002). Freshwater ostracoda. Wetland Ecosystem Services No. 3, Fauna of Ujani, pp. 87-90, Zoological Survey of India, Kolkata, 196 pp.

Patil, S.G. and Talmale, S.S. (2005). A Checklist of Freshwater ostracods (ostracoda: crustacea) of Maharashtra, India. *Zoo's Print Journal,* 20(5): 1872-1873.

Patra, Ashish, Kalyan Brata Santra and Chanchal Kumar Manna. (2011). Ecology and Diversity of zooplankton in Relation to physcio-chemical Characheristics of Water of Santragachi Jheel, West Bengal, India. *J.Wet. Eco.,* 5:20-39.

Pennak, R.W. (1978). Freshwater Invertebrates of United States, 2nd edition, John Wiley and Sons Inc. Lnodon-Chapman and Hall Ltd., New York, USA, 803.

Purushothama, R., H.A. Sayeshwara, Mahesh Anand Guodar and K. Harish Kumar. (2011). Physico-chemical Profile and Zooplankton Community Composition in Brahmana Kalashi tank, Sagara, Karnataka, India. *The Ecoscan.* 5 (1 and 2): 43-48.

Qadri, M.Y. and Yousuf, A.R. (1980). Influence of the Physico-chemical Factors on the Seasonality of Cladocera in Lake Manasbal. *Geobios.* 7: 273-276.

Quadri, S.A. (2004). Studies of Biodiversity of zooplankton from Aurangabad district, Ph.D. thesis, Dr. Babasaheb Ambedkar Marathwada University, Aurangabad, pp. 101.

Raghunathan, M.B. (1989). Indian Cladocera (Crustacea). *Indian Review of Life Sciences.* 9: 137-152.

Raghunathan, M.B. and Kumar, S. (2003). A Checklist of Indian cladocera (Crustacea). *Zoo's. Print. J.* 18: 1180-1182.

Sadanand, D.S. and Yamakanamardi, M. (2014). Water Quality Index and Abundance of Total zooplankton in Varuna, Madappa and Giribettethe Lakes of Mysore, Karanataka State, India. *International Journal of Environmental Sciences*, 4(5): 683-693.

Saikia, S.K. and Das, D.N. (2003). Diversity Indices of zooplankton and Water Quality in two Freshwater Ponds of Arunachal Pradesh, India. *Geobios*. 30 (2-3):113-116.

Sakhare, V.B. (2007). Reservoir Fisheries and Limnology, Narendra Publishing House, Delhi.

Sakhare, V.B. (2012). Zooplankton Diversity in Udyan Sarovar Tank in Ambajogai, Maharashtra. In: Perspectives in Ecology (Eds. V.B. Sakhare and J.S. Mohite), pp. 152-158, Oxford Book Company, Jaipur.

Sanyal, P., Bhattacharya, N. and Chakraborty, S.K. (2015). Biomonitoring of Four Contrasting Wetlands of Kolkata, West Bengal based on zooplankton Eco-dynamics and biotic indices. *Journal of Environmental Protection*, 6:683-699. http:// dx.doi.org/10.4236/ jep.2015.67062.

Sehgal, K., Phadke, G.G., Chakraborty, S.K. and S. Vijay Kumar Reddy. (2013). Studies on zooplankton Diversity in Dimbhe Reservoir, Maharashtra, India. *Advances in Applied Science Research*, 4(1):417-420.

Selot, M. (1977). Ecological Study of Dulhara tank with Special Reference to Plankton Population and Physico-chemical Properties of Water. Ph.D. Thesis, Ravishankar University, Raipur.

Shah, Javaid Ahmad and Pandit, Ashok Kumar. (2014). Taxonomic Survey of crustacean zooplankton in Wular Lake of Kashmir, Himalaya. *J. Evol. Biol. Res.* 6(1): 1-4.

Sharma, B.K. (2005). Rotifer Communities of Floodplain Lakes of the Brahmaputra basin of Lower Assam (N.E. India): Biodiversity, Distribution and Ecology. *Hydrobiologia*. 533:209-221.

Sharma, B.K. (2010). Rotifer Communities of Deeper Beel, Assam, India: Richness, Abundance and Ecology. *Journal of Threatened Taxa*. 2(8): 1077-1086.

Sharma, B.K. and Sharma, S. (2008). Zooplankton Diversity in Floodplain Lakes of Assam. Records of Zoological Survey of India. Occasional paper no 290: 1-307.

Sharma, B.K. and Hussain, M. (2001). Abundance and Ecology of zooplankton in a Tropical Flood Plain Lake, Assam. *Ecology, Environment and Conservation*. 7(4):397-403.

Sharma, K.K. and Chanderkiran. (2011). Comparative Analysis of cladoceran Communities from three Subtropical Freshwater Ponds of Jammu. Patterns, Composition and Diversity. *The Bioscan*. 6(2): 233-237.

Sharma, K.K; Kaur, S. and Gupta, S. (2005). Distributional Pattern of cladoceran in Subtropical Lake, Mansar, *J. and K. Nat. J. Life Sci*. 2(1-2): 23-26.

Sharma, K.K. and Kotwal, Sanjay (2011). Studies on Diversity and Dynamics of Cladocera in a Sub-tropical Sungal Pond, Akhnoor (J&K). *The Bioscan*, 6(4):623-625.

Sharma V., Bhoopendra Kumar V., and Madhu Sudan Sharma. (2012). Zooplankton Fauna in Relation to physico-chemical Characteristics in Madar Tank, Udaipur, Rajasthan, India, *I. Res. J. Environment Sci.* 1(3): 5-10.

Shinde, Y.S; Reginald Victor and Pai, Kalpana. (2014). Freshwater ostracods (Crustacea: Ostracoda) of the Plateaus of the Northern Western Ghats, India. *Journal of Threatened Taxa*, 6(4): 5667-5670.

Shivashankar, P. and Venkataramana, G.V. (2013). Zooplankton Diversity and their Seasonal Variations of Bhadra Reservoir, Karnataka, India. *Int. Res. J. Enviornment Sci.*, 2(5):87-91.

Singh, R. (1991). Rotifer Fauna of Jamalpur, Munger, Bihar. *Journal of Current Biological Sciences.*, 8: 45-46.

Sinha B. and Islam M.R. (2002). Seasonal Variation in zooplankton Population of two Lentic Bodies and Assam State Zoo cum Botanical Garden, Guwahati, Assam. *Ecology, Environment and Conservation*, 8:273-278.

Sinha, K.K. and Sinha, D.K. (1993). Seasonal Trends in Physico-chemical Factors and Zooplankton in a Freshwater Pond of Munger, Bihar. *J. Ecobiol.*, 5(4): 299-302.

Singh, Meena and Sinha, R.K. (1995). Diel Variation of Water Quality and Zooplankton Community in A Freshwater Pond of Patna, Bihar, *Ecology, Environment and Conservation*, 1(1-4):57-64.

Siraj, S; Yousuf, A.R. and Parveen, M. (2007). Cladoceran Community in Sheshbug Wetland, Kashmir. *J. Res. Dev.* 7: 67-74.

Sivakami, R., Arumugam, V. and Premkishore, G. (2015). An Analysis of Zooplankton in a Lake Pudukkottai district, Tamil Nadu, India. *Int. J. Curr. Micrbiol. App. Sci.*, 4(5):377-389.

Sontakke, Gajanan and Mokashe, Satish. (2014). Diversity of Zooplankton in Dekhu Reservoir from Aurangabad, Maharashtra. *Journal of Applied and Natural Science*, 6(1):131-133.

Srivastava, S.K. (2013). Monthly Variation in the Occurance of Zooplankton in a Freshwater Body, Ramgarh Lake, Gorakhpur, U.P. *International Journal of Applied Biosciences*. 1(2): 23-27.

Suganthi, A., Ezhumalai, P. and Chezhian, Y. (2014). Zooplankton Diversity in Certain Ponds of Cuddalore district of Tamil Nadu, India. *Biolife*. 2(4): 1316-1319. Online available on www.biolifejournal.com.

Sukhija, L. (2010). Hydrobiological Studies of Foy Sagar lake, Ajmer. *Nature Environment and Pollution Technology*, 9(3): 601-604.

Szlauer, B., and Szlauer, L. (1980). The use of Lake Zooplankton as Feed for carp (*Cyprinus carpio* L.) Fry in Pond Culture. *Acta Ichthyol. Piscat*. 10(1): 79-102.

Szlauer, L. and Szlauer, B. (1982). Utilization of Autumn zooplankton in Carp fry Rearing. *Acta Ichthyol. Piscat*. 12(2):71-81.

Tamot, Praveen and Ashu Awasthi. (2013). Limnology and Fish Diversity of eutrophicated Tropical Wetlands (Motia pond and Jawahar Bal Udhyan pond) Bhopal, India. *Ecology, Environment and Conservartion.*, 19(1):189-194.

Thakur, R.K; Jindal, R; Singh Uday Bhan and Ahluwalia, A.S. (2013). Plankton Diversity and Water Quality Assessment of Three Freshwater Lakes of Mandi (Himachal Pradesh, India) with Special Reference to Planktonic Indicators. *Environ. Monit. Assess*. 185: 8355-8373.

Thirupathaiah, M., Sammatha, C.H., Sammaiah, C.H. (2011). Diversity of zooplankton in Freshwater Lake of Kamalapur, Karimnagar District (A.P) India. *Ecoscan*, 5(1 2): 85 87.

Tijare, R.V. and Thosar, M.R. (2010). Studies on Ecology of Zooplankton Found in Freshwater Lake of Gadchiroli City, Maharashtra. *J. Aqua. Biol*. 25(1): 20-23.

Tyor, A.K., Chopra, G. and Kumari, S. (2014). Zooplankton Diversity in Shallow Lake of Sultanpur National Park, Gurgaon (Haryana). *International Journal of Applied Biology and Pharmaceutical Technology*, 5(1): 35-40.

Ude, E.F., Ugwu, L.L.C. and Mgbenka, B.O. (2011). Evaluation of zooplankton Diversity in Echara River, Nigeria. Conti. *J. Biol. Sci.* 4 (1):1-5.

Uma Chandra, N., Revathi, K. and Rekha,V. (2014). Biodiversity of ostracods in Ambattur Lake, Tamil Nadu, India. *Ecology Environment and Conservation*. 20(1):167-174.

Vanjare, A.I. and Pai, Kalpana. (2010). Rotifers from a Pond in Pune (India), with the Record of *Ptygura pedunculata* (Edmondson, 1939) (Rotifera : Monogononta) from the Oriental Region, *Turk. J. Zool.* 34:417-419.

Wanganeo, A. and Wanganeo, R. (2006). Variation in Zooplankton Population in two Morphologically Dissimilar Rural Lakes of Kashmir Himalayas. Proc. Nat. Acad. Sci. India. 76 (B) III.

Page 108-135

PLANKTON AND FISHERIES
Edited by : V.B. Sakhare; H.K. Jadhav and S.S. Jadhav
Edition : 2017
ISBN : 978-93-5056-811-8
Published by : Discovery Publishing House Pvt. Ltd., New Delhi (India)

9 Plankton Diversity in Harni (Katgoan) Reservoir of Osmanabad District Maharashtra

S.G. Jetithor and V.B. Sakhare[1]

Department of Fishery Science, Arts,
Science and Commerce College, Naldurg - 413 602.
Post Graduate Department of Zoology
Yogeshwari Mahavidyalaya, Ambajogai - 431 517.[1]

INTRODUCTION

The plankton community is a hetergenous group of tiny plants (phytoplankton) and animals (zooplankton) adapted to suspension in the sea and freshwaters. The first use of the term 'plankton' is attributed to the German marine biologist, Victor Hensen. According to Hensen's (1887) terminology 'plankton' included all organic particles 'which float and involuntarily in the open water, independent of shores and bottom'. The dependence of plankton upon water movements for maintenance and transport is accurately implied in this definition (Greek planktos meaning wandering).

The ability of water to produce plankton depends on many factors, but the most important is usually the availability of inorganic nutrients for phytoplankton growth. Essential elements for phytoplankton growth include C, O, P, N, S, K, Na, Ca, Mg, Fe, Mn, Cu, Zn, B, Co, Cl and possibly few others. Phoshprous is the most often element regulating phytoplankton growth.

To monitor the aquatic ecosystems and integrity of water, plankton has been used recently as bioindicator (Beaugrand *et al.* 2000). Bioindicators and biotic indexes are being used by Europeans to assess water quality of water bodies (Sousa *et al.* 2008) for last 100 years.

Phytoplankton community comprises of a heterogeneous group of tiny plants adapted to various aquatic environments. Their nature and distribution varies considerably with respect to seasons and water quality. Their dominance also leads to qualitative changes of aquatic ecosystems. Information pertaining to the nature, type and distribution of these organisms provide clue regarding the environmental conditions prevailing in their habit.

Phytoplankton constitutes the base of the ecological pyramid providing food energy for the higher trophic levels of the aquatic ecosystems. In view of this relationship, attempts have been made to correlate primary productivity and fish yields (*e.g.*, Sreenivasan 1964, 1968; Melack 1979). In addition, phytoplankton is also important as an index of the trophic status of a water body. Thunmark and Nygaard (in Wetzel, 1975) have developed a number of phytoplankton indices to quantify algal species as indicators of aquatic enrichment. Relationship between algal associations and lake fertility is also discussed in detail by Hutchinson (1967).

Various ecological aspects of phytoplankton have been a subject of study in India by several workers (Singh 1979, Agarwal 1980, Hosmani and Bharathi 1980, Nandan and Patel 1985a, 1986, Zafar 1986, Velecha and bhatnagar 1988, Anjana *et al.* 1998, Nandan and Ansari 1999, Khare 1999, Sukumaran and Das 2001, 2002, Nandan and Jain 2005, Begum and Narayana 2006, Nandan and Mahajan 2006, Ranjan *et al.* 2007 Sivakumar and Karuppasamy 2008, Dhavale *et al.* 2009, Mohite and Joshi 2009, Nasare *et al.* 2009).

Zooplankton communities play an important role in the aquatic food chain and also contribute significantly to the secondary productivity of freshwater ecosystem (Saikia and Das, 2003). It also helps in biomonitoring the freshwater ecosystems (Sinha, 2002). The diversity indices for zooplankton can be used for monitoring freshwater pollution by adopting appropriate diversity measures of species (Saikia and Das, 2003).

Zooplankton by their heterotrophic activity plays a key role in the cycling of organic materials in aquatic ecosystems and used as bioindicators. The biondicators are evaluated through presence/absence, condition, relative abundance, reproductive success, community structure (*i.e.*, composition and diversity), community function (*i.e.*, trophic structure), or any combination thereof (Hellawell, 1986).

Zooplankton supports the economically important fish population. They are the major mode of energy transfer between phytoplankton compositions, abundance and seasonal variations is helpful in planning and successful fishery management (Jhingran, 1974).

Zooplankton can also play an important role in indicating the presence or absence of certain species of fishes or in determining the population densities.

Potentiality of zooplankton as bioindicator is very high because their growth and distribution are dependent on some abiotic (*e.g.*, temperature, salinity, stratification, pollutants) and biotic parameters (*e.g.*, food limitation, predation, competition). Pandey and Verma (2004) revealed that abiotic parameters (*e.g.*, pH, transparency, temperature, dissolved oxygen and some micronutrients) in relation to seasonal fluctuation influence zooplankton abundance.

Protozoa are thought to be the first animals to have evolved. Though they depict remarkable diversity in form and structure, yet they have a simple body consisting only of one cell. All the multicellular organisms are believed to have originated from them. Planktonic protozoans are limited to ciliates and flagellates. Among the unicellular protozoa, the heterotrophic nanoflagellates are the major consumers of free-living bacteria and other smaller heterotrophic nanoflagellates. The abundant heterotrophic nanoflagellates (105 to 108 /L in highly eutrophic lentic ecosystems) range in size from about 1.0 to about 20 Lm. They include non-pigmented species that structurally have very closely related pigmented species in the phytoplankton. The ciliates are larger in size (8 Lm to 300 Lm) but are less abundant (102 to 104/l). While the smallest planktonic ciliates feed on the picoplankton, the larger ciliates feed on the heterotrophic nanoflagellates and small nanophytoplankton. Among the ciliates, those containing captured chloroplasts from the ingested algae or those containing more permanent symbiotic green algae (zoochlorellae) are common. Among the protozoans are two orders of amoebae that are primarily associated with the sediments and littoral aquatic vegetation and large numbers of meroplanktonic species (Edmondson, 1959; Battish, 1992).

Rotifers occur in an endless variety of aquatic and semi-aquatic habitats. These fascinating creatures were first studied and described by Leeuwenhoek as early as 1703. In the twentieth century Jennings (1903, 1928), De Beauchamp (1928, 1932), Myers (1931, 1933, 1941), Pennak (1940,1953) ND Hyman (1940, 1951) made valuable contributions to our knowledge of rotifera. The occurrence and distribution of the rotifers in India has been worked out by several limnologists (Santhanam and Murthy 1985, Anderson 1889, Arora 1962, 1963a, 1964, 1965, 1966a, Nayar 1964, 1965a, 1965b, 1968, Dhanapathi 1973, 1974, 1975b, 1976a, 1976b, 2000; Chowdhary *et al.* 1978 and Battish 1968, Pradhan *et al.* 2006).

The cladocerans commonly known as 'waterfleas' form a primitive group of micro crustaceans. They invariably constitute a dominant component of freshwater zooplankton, play an important role in the aquatic food chain and also contribute significantly to zooplankton dynamics and secondary productivity in freshwater ecosystems.

Cladocera have been reported from all over the world. While it is true that several genera and some species are cosmopolitan, certain species are endemic. In view of the cosmopolitan nature of this group particularly at the higher taxonomic categories, treatises from the different parts of the world are of importance for any detailed work. In this context, general compilations of Baird (1850), Keilhack (1909), Henry (1822), Manuilova (1964) and Flossner (1972) are relevant. In the Indian context the studies on cladocera usually form part of general limnological investigations in lakes, ponds and reservoirs, wherefrom several genera and species are reported from time to time. For want of treatises on the Indian species based on well illustrated figures and keys, many errors have crept in. The indiscriminate and uncritical use of monographs from other parts of the world has led to reports of the occurrence of several species that have no place in our fauna. While there are occasional papers on the taxonomy of freshwater cladocera in India, no comprehensive treatment of this group exists for country.

Of the 11 families listed under the order cladocera, nine are known from Indian waters (Michael and Sharma, 1988). The systematic studies on cladocera were initiated as early as 1860, when Baird described a new species of Genus Daphnia from the material collected by Rev. Hislop from Nagpur, Central India.

Cladocerans are a crucial group among zooplankton and form the most useful and nutritive group of crustaceans for higher members of fishes in the food chain.

Copepods are minute (0.3 to 2.5mm) crustacean lacking a distinct shell fold and having a simple median eye. In their free living forms the body is elongated and segmented, distinguished into a broad appendage-bearing part called the metasoma and posterior urosome separated by a major articulation. The urosome ends in a caudal furca. Of the antennae, the first are often longer and uniramous. The maxillipeds are the first thoracic appendages, followed by four biramous swimming legs with the fifth leg reduced and uniramous. Gravid females carry their eggs in one or two egg sacs. Copepods pass through a series of naupliar and copepoid stages during their development. The copepods comprise of calanoids, cyclopoids and harpacticoids.

Copepods are much hardier and strongly motile than all other zooplankton with their tougher exoskeleton and longer and stronger appendages. They have long developmental time and a complex life history with early larval stages difficult to distinguish. They are almost wholly carnivorous on the smaller zooplankton for their food needs. Among the three orders of copepods, cyclopoid copepods are generally predatory on (carnivorous) on other zooplankton, and fish larvae. The cyclopoid copepods also feed on algae, bacteria and detritus. The second group of copepods, calanoid copepods change their diet with age, sex, season, and food availability. The calanoid copepods are omnivorous feeding on ciliates, rotifers, algae, bacteria and detritus. The third group harpacticoid copepods are primarily benthic.

The Ostracods are bivalved organisms and belong to phylum Arthropoda. They mainly inhabit the lake bottom and among macrophytes and feed on detritus and dead plankton. Ostracods are in turn consumed by fishes and benthic macro invertebrates (Chakrapani *et al.* 1996). There are over 1700 species of known ostracods of which about one-third are freshwater forms. They inhibit a wide variety of freshwaters likes: lakes, pools, swamps, streams and heavily polluted areas (Edmondson, 1959).

Multi-lake studies have been used to explore variations in the zooplankton community along a number of limnological gradients. For example, zooplankton community size structure has been used as an indicator of lake trophic status (Bays and Crisman, 1983, Beaver and Crisman, 1990, Canfield and Jones, 1996 and Pace, 1986). Studies have compared the abundance and biomass of micro - and macro zooplankton (Bays and Crisman, 1983, Pace, 1986 and Sprules *et al.* 1988) to algal chlorophylls (Canfield and Jones, 1996), Carlson's Trophic State Index (Bays and Crisman, 1983), and nutrients (Pace, 1986 and Sprules, 1977). Zooplankton indicator species have been used to determine shifts in trophic state (*e.g.,* Fuller *et al.* 1977 and Sprules, 1977). Several studies have examined differences in rotifer communities in lakes of various trophic states (Beaver and Crisman, 1990, Fuller *et al.* 1977 and Gannon and Stemberger, 1978). Abundance of selected major zooplankton groups (*e.g.* Rotifera, Copepoda) has also been used to show changes in trophic state (Gannon and Stemberger, 1978 and Pace, 1986).

The zooplankton study has been a fascinating subject for a long time. Enough literature exists on the zooplankton of various water bodies (Arora 1966, Victor and Fernando *et al.* 1982, Chauhan 1988, Birasal *et al.* 1989, Kulshrestha *et al.* 1989, Fasihuddin and Kumari 1990, Chauhan 1993, Sinha and Sinha 1993, Kumar 1995, Bais and Agarwal 1995, Singh and Sinha 1995, Choudhary and Singh 1999, Balmurugan *et al.* 2001, Patil and Mudgal 2002, Prakash *et al.* 2002, Sinha and Islam 2002, Maruthanayagam *et al.* 2003, Aziz and Ezz 2004, Sahib 2004, Sunkad and Patil 2004, Mishra 2005, Chandrasekhar 2006, Kesharwarni *et al.* (2006), Thirumathal 2006, Mukherji and Nandi 2006, Renuga and Ramnibai 2006, Kiran *et al.* 2007, Pathak 2009. Rawat and Sharma 2010). Such studies from state of Maharashtra have been very recently initiated and the only contributions on this aspect are those of Goel *et al.* (1968), Deshmukh (2001), Pawar *et al.* (2003), Sakhare and Joshi (2002, 2006), Chavan *et al.* 2006, Walujkar and Hiware (2006), Bhagat and Meshram 2007, Pandit *et al.* (2007), Sakhare (2007), Harney *et al.* (2008) and Telkhade *et al.* (2008).

- *About the Reservoir:* Harni (Katgaon) reservoir is situated near Katgaon village in Tuijapur tahsil of Osmanabad district and is connected by an approach road of the length of 6.5 km., from Solapur-Hyderabad-National Highway No. 9. This approach road takes off near the Khanapur stage on the National High-way. The project is constructed across Harni river, a tributary of river Bori, having catchment area of 190.624 km^2 (73.60 sq. miles) at the project site. The head works of the project were started in June 1961 and completed in June 1964. This project envisages construction of an earthen dam and includes other works such as: ogee spillway with its appurtenant works, head regulator on right flank and canals on left and right flanks taking off from the same head sluice.

Table 9.1: The Salient Features of Harni (Katgaon) Reservoir

1.	Name of River	Harni
2.	Location	Katgaon village
3.	Sub basin number	19
4.	Water Spread Area (ha)	239
5.	Year of Construction	1964
6.	Length of earthen dam	2,163.975 meters
7.	Length of ogee spillway	276.025 meters
8.	Maximum flood discharge	58,490 cusecs
9.	Maximum height of dam in river bed	17.080 meters
10.	Gross storage capacity (Mcum)	12.580
11.	Live storage capacity (Mcum)	11.170
12.	Carry Over capacity (Mcum)	1.410
13.	Catchment Area (km^2)	190.624
14.	Length of irrigation channel Left flank canal (km) Right flank canal (km)	27.35514.481
15.	Irrigation potential (ha)	1,660

No village was submerged under this reservoir. The villages such as: Katgaon, Khanapur and Darshnal of Tuljapur and Tandulwadi and Musti of Solapur taluka receive benefit due to the irrigation facilities under this reservoir. The salient features of Harni (Katgaon) reservoir are depicted in Table 9.1.

The climate of reservoir area is primarily dry. The rainy season starts from mid-June and remains till end of September. With onset of the rainy season there is an appreciable drop in temperature. From October to November the climate is humid. From mid-November to January it is winter. From February to March the climate is dry and from April to June it is summer. May is the hottest month. The average rainfall of area is 730 mm.

Materials and Methods

Standard methodology after Welch (1948) and Jhingran *et al.* (1969), with suitable modifications to suit local availability was used. Procedure adopted is briefly described below:

Fig. 9.1: **A panoramic view of Harni (Katgaon) reservoir**

(a) Collection.

(b) Preservation and transportation.

(c) Washing.

(d) Qualitative analysis.

(e) Quantitative analysis.

(a) *Collection*: Collection of planktons was done by using a plankton net with 38 cm diameter of the mouth and a bolting silk No. 20 (173 meshes/ inch). An inron tube was firmly tied to the tapering end of the net and the open end of the plankton collecting tube was covered by a piece of bolting silk, securely tied with cotton thread so that plankton collected through the net could be easily transferred into separate plastic bottles.

(b) *Preservation and transportation*: Initial study for taxonomic identification and general behaviour was carried out on live plankton. Subsequently; quantitative estimations were made on plankton preserved in 5 per cent formalin. An ice container was used for live transportation to the laboratory.

(c) *Washing*: Samples collected from Harni (Katgaon) reservoir were easily washed with formalin water. For this purpose a glass funnel and a piece of bolting silk were used. But, washing was rather difficult for samples collected from few sites. It is because these samples contained lot of debris, micro - and macro-phytes. By using a wash bottle containing formalin water, washing was carried out in the following manner:

The whole plankton sample was measured (used for quantitative estimation) and diluted to a desirable concentration depending upon the density of plaktonic population in such a way that they could be easily counted individually under light binocular microscope. For dilution a polson plankton splitter was used. Generally one fourth of the total biomass in a sample was used for washing to minimize error. This small fraction of collected plankton material was transferred on a set of different mesh size sieves and shaken gently. By this procedure, it was possible to remove easily the fine debris and soil particles. After that, the whole plankton material was collected in Petri-plate containing formalin water. At this stage, the sample containing some plant material and some other foreign particles were easily removed with the help of different size brushes. Finally, the remaining plankton material was transferred to fresh formalin solution and the whole plankton concentration was measured and multiplied with the dilution factor, already made by splitter.

(*d*) *Qualitative Analysis*: For qualitative analysis, a light binocular and an inverted plankton micro-scope are used. As far as possible, the animals were identified up to species level.

Preliminary identification was made by using Pennak (1978), Battish (1992), Michael (1973) and Dhanapathi (2000) as basic references.

The rotifers were ordinarily distinguished at species level by trophic characteristics in whole animal. Although in some difficult cases animals were crushed with the help of 2 micro-needles to force animal out.

Generally, the cladocerans were identified by carapace characteristics, although in a number of cases a minor dissection of post abdominal segment with the help of 2 mico-needles was carried out. After dissection, these abdominal segments were observed under high power in a glycerine mount.

Copepods were generally identified with the help of body appendages and for species identification a minor dissection on the 5th leg was carried out in a glycerine mount. Animal or dissected apart as observed under high power.

For identification of ostracods, body shell was removed to study detailed structure. These animals also required a minor dissection of furca. After dissection, furca was observed under high power in glycerine.

(*e*) *Quantitative Estimation*: For quantitative estimation of plankton, a Sedgwick-Rafter counting cell of mm 2 and micropipette of glass van grade I of 1, 2 and 5 ml capacity were used. For this purpose, 1 ml of plankton sample was drawn and transferred to the Sedgwick-Rafter counting cell. Observations were made under the binoculars and counting was done up to genetic level. For the sake of convenience, blood cell counter make was used for accurate and quick counting. The procedure was repeated 5 times to get an average. The total population of individual plankton genera in a reservoir was calculated by the following formula:

N = n x1/w

Where,

N = Number of individuals of a species per cubic meter

n = Number of individuals of a species in 1 ml.

1 = Dilution factor

w = Amount of water hauled

When the plankton were collected by filtration the pollution of a species was calculated as follows:

N = nxdx10/w

Where,

N = Number of individuals of a species in cubic meter

n = Average number of individual of a species in one ml

d = Dilution factor

w = Amount of water filtered

Results

- *Zooplankton Diversity:* During 2007-08, rotifer dominated the zooplankton population (40.80%), followed by copepoda (23.74%), cladocera and ostracoda (12.92% each) and protozoa (9.7%). The percentage composition of zooplankton during year 2007-08 is presented in Fig. 9.2. Total 34 different species of zooplankton were identified (Table 9.2). The maximum zooplankton population was observed during summer and minimum during winter season (Fig. 9.3).

Protozoans were high in rainy season. Rotifers, cladocerans, copepods as well as ostracods showed the summer maxima. The protozoans, ostracods, rotifers and copepods showed minima in winter season, while cladocerans were observed less in rainy season.

Table 9.2: List of Zooplankton in Harni (Katgaon) Resevoir

Protozoans:	*Diffugia spp., Arcella spp., Vorticella spp., Opercularia spp., Paramecium caudatum Colpidium sp.*
Rotifera:	*Branchionus flacatus Brachionus calyciflorus Brachionus diversicornis Filina longiseta Keratella tropica Keretella quadrata Lecane bulla Trichocera porecelus Trichocera longiseta.*
Cladocera:	*Indialona ganapati Moina micrura Diaphanosma sarsi Alona rectangular Biapertura karna Ceriodaphnia cornuta Diaphanosoma excisum.*
Copepoda:	*Diaptomus marshianus Phylladiaptomus anus annae Nedodiaptomus linddbergi Nauplius larva Mesocyclops leukarti Mesocyclops hyalinus Cyclops viridis.*
Ostracoda:	*Stenocypris sp., Cypris obensa Stenocypris sp., Cyclocypria globosa Candocypria osborni Cyprinotus sps.*

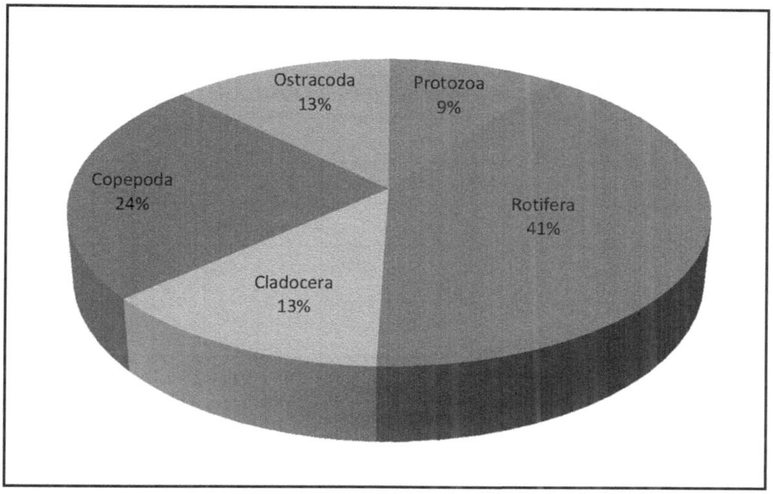

Fig. 9.2: **The percentage of composition of zooplankton in Harni (Katgaon) reservoir during 2007-08**

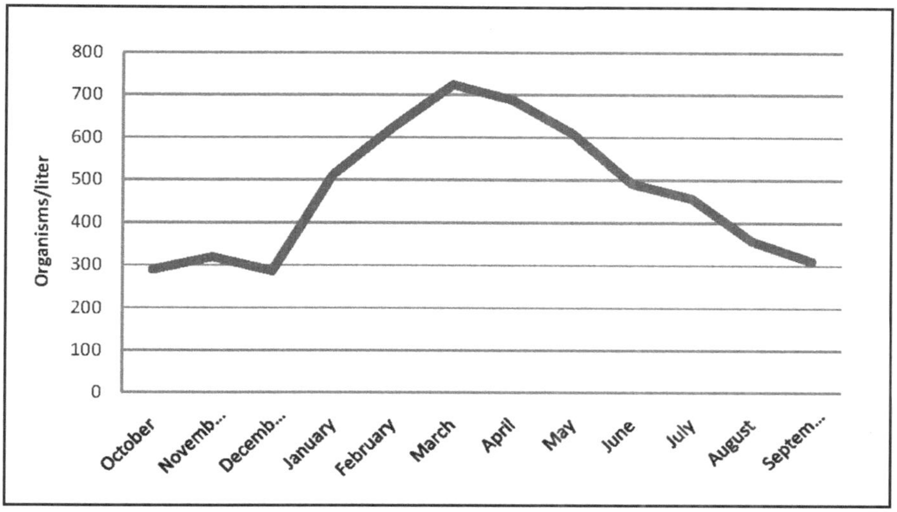

Fig. 9.3: **Monthly fluctuations in zooplankton in Harni (Katgaon) reservoir during year 2007-08**

Protozoans were represented by 6 species (Table 9.3). The species *Paramecium caudatum* and *Colpidium sps* were observed in 10 months, while *Opercularia sps.,* and *Arcella sps.,* were absent in rainy summer season respectively. *Difflugia* and *Vortocella sps* were absent for the months of summer (February and March). The maximum protozoan population was recorded in August 2008 (73 organisms/liter) and minimum population in the month of November 2007 (17 organisms/liter).

Table 9.3: Composition of Protozoans (density: organisms/liter) during year 2007-08

	Oct	Nov	Dec	Jan	Feb	Mar	Apr	May	Jun	Jul	Aug	Sept
Difflugia sps.	20	03	09	03	-	-	05	02	03	18	30	21
Arcella sps.	12	05	07	06	-	-	-	-	10	15	16	12
Voritcella sps.	08	02	02	04	-	-	04	-	05	13	12	13
Opercularia sps.	09	-	03	13	02	06	10	16	-	-	-	-
Paramecium, caudatum	07	03	02	20	18	30	16	18	11	18	13	03
Colpidium sps.	06	04	04	08	04	09	05	07	08	04	02	05

Rotifers were represented by 9 species (Table 9.4) and species *Brachionus flacatus, Brachionus diversicornis* and *Keratella tropica* recorded throughout the study period, while *Lecane bulla* was accounted for 8 months only. The peak of rotifers was observed during months of May 2008 (264 organisms/liter) and it was minimum in the month of October (100 organisms/liter).

Table 9.4: Composition of Rotifera (density: organisms/liter) during year 2007-08

	Oct	Nov	Dec	Jan	Feb	Mar	Apr	May	Jun	Jul	Aug	Sept
Brachionus falcatus	24	23	32	38	51	46	60	70	63	50	42	38
Brachionus calyciflorus	12	38	-	22	16	21	18	26	30	25	14	24
Brachionus diversicornis	22	22	16	29	38	49	50	40	17	26	15	22
Filinia longiseta	-	19	19	12	19	18	23	20	15	-	05	-
Keratella tropica	21	16	12	10	22	30	24	21	34	27	16	25
Keratella quadrata	11	12	14	16	14	12	22	30	21	22	-	-
Lecane bulla	-	18	18	21	32	29	22	-	19	13	-	-
Trichocera porcelus	10	-	13	24	20	24	22	29	28	20	-	-
Trichocera longiseta	-	14	19	20	21	27	20	28	25	19	20	24

Cladocera were represented by 6 species (Table 9.5). The species *Indialona ganapati, Diaphanosoma sarsi, Ceriodaphnia cornuta* and *Diaphanosoma excisum* were recorded throughout the investigation, while *Alona rectanguila* was totally absent in rainy season. *Moina micrura* and *Biapertura karna* were absent in two months of winter season. The maximum cladoceran population (126 organisms/liter) was recorded during March and minimum population (32 organisms/liter) during November.

Table 9.5: Composition of Cladocera (density: organisms/liter) during year 2007-08

	Oct	Nov	Dec	Jan	Feb	Mar	Apr	May	Jun	Jul	Aug	Sept
Indialona ganapati	07	02	07	16	12	19	22	07	07	06	10	07
Moina micrura	06	-	-	18	22	28	18	08	09	09	11	10
Diaphanosoma excisum	09	04	03	14	15	10	04	07	08	04	01	02
Diaphanosoma sarsi	08	09	09	10	14	20	16	05	02	04	06	04
Alona rectangular	04	08	06	17	21	18	13	10	-	-	-	-
Biapertura karna	-	-	07	15	18	22	08	06	06	13	07	06
Ceriodaphnia cornuta	07	09	02	09	16	09	09	04	03	03	02	05

Copepoda was represented by 7 species (Table 9.6). The maxima was 207 organisms/liter during March and minima was 54 organisms/liter during December. *Mesocyclops sps.,* and *Neodiaptomus lindbergi* were accounted throughout the year while *Diaptomus marshianus* was absent in three months of rainy season (July to September). *Nauplius larva* and *Cyclops viridis* were absent in October and December 2007.

Table 9.6: Composition of Copepoda (density: organisms/liter) during year 2007-08

	Oct	Nov	Dec	Jan	Feb	Mar	Apr	May	Jun	Jul	Aug	Sept
Diaptomus marshianus	13	15	09	12	18	21	30	22	14	-	-	-
Phyllodiaptomus annae	-	08	05	08	17	20	23	26	16	16	18	-
Neodiaptomus lindbergi	20	12	13	13	27	27	40	22	13	13	08	14
Nauplius larva	-	07	-	15	18	30	25	28	28	11	17	07
Mesocyclops leukarti	11	26	14	20	25	41	31	21	15	23	12	12
Mesocyclops hyalinus	14	08	13	32	42	50	28	18	19	09	16	20
Cyclops viridis	-	11	-	07	11	18	08	29	10	08	07	06

Ostracoda was represented by 5 species (Table 9.7). The highest density of ostracods was observed in April (112 organisms/liter), while lowest density was recorded in November 2007 (21 organisms/liter).

Table 9.7: Composition of Ostracoda (density: organisms/liter) during year 2007-08

	Oct	Nov	Dec	Jan	Feb	Mar	Apr	May	Jun	Jul	Aug	Sept
Stenocypris sps.	-	-	-	12	20	16	27	21	10	15	20	28
Cypris obensa	10	06	10	07	19	18	30	19	09	10	14	03
Cyclocypris globosa	12	07	04	18	22	23	23	22	21	17	13	07
Candocypria osborni	-	03	08	13	19	20	17	17	10	12	-	05
Cyprinotus sps.	06	05	06	08	10	13	15	10	12	13	10	07

During second year of investigation (2008-09) zooplankton were represented by protozoa, rotifera, cladocera, copepod and ostracoda. The percentage composition of zooplankton during year 2008-09 is presented in Fig. 9.4. The monthly variation in total plankton population during year 2008-09 is shown in Fig. 9.5.

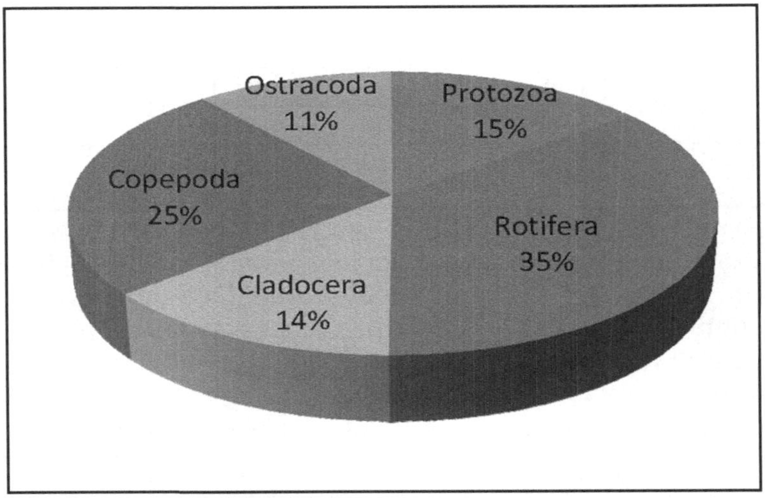

Fig. 9.4: **The percentage of composition of zooplankton in Harni (Katgaon) reservoir during 2008-09**

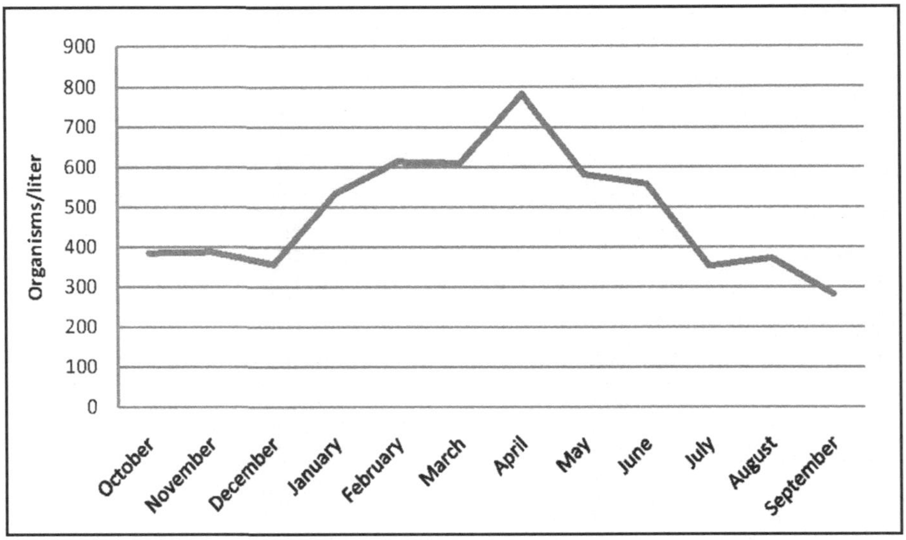

Fig. 9.5: **Monthly fluctuations in zooplankton in Harni (Katgaon) reservoir during year 2008-09**

Protozoa was represented by 6 species (Table 9.8). The maxima was 95 organisms/liter during October and minima was 54 organisms/liter during January 2009. *Vorticella* spp., were absent throughout the summer and *Cospidium* spp., were present only in 7 months. *Difflugia* spp and *Arcella* spp., were also absent in three months of summer.

Table 9.8: Composition of Protozoans (density: organisms/liter) during year 2008-09

	Oct	Nov	Dec	Jan	Feb	Mar	Apr	May	Jun	Jul	Aug	Sept
Difflugia sps.	23	12	08	09	-	-	-	15	20	24	28	20
Arcella sps.	20	08	20	10	13	-	-	-	13	21	17	30
Voritcella sps.	19	14	08	06	-	-	-	-	10	19	26	18
Opercularia sps.	12	11	12	03	14	09	27	20	18	-	-	-
Paramecium, caudatum	21	16	10	08	23	38	32	23	21	13	-	-
Colpidium sps.	-	-	-	08	13	15	06	16	-	-	06	04

Rotifera accounted for about 35 per cent during year 2008-09 and were represented by 9 species (Table 9.9). The highest density of rotifers (278 organisms/liter) was recorded in the month of April 2009 and minimum in September 2009 (102 organisms/liter). Throughout the summer months, rotifer population was maximum. It was minimum in rainy season.

Cladocerans accounted for about 14 per cent and were represented by 7 species (Table 9.10). The maximum population was recorded in March (131 organisms/liter) and minimum population in the month of November (37 organisms/liter). Cladocerans were maximum throughout the summer season. Out of 7 species, 5 were present throughout the year, while *Alona rectangular* was absent in rainy season. *Biapertura karna* was not seen in October 2008.

Table 9.9: Composition of Rotifera (density: organisms/liter) during year 2008-09

	Oct	Nov	Dec	Jan	Feb	Mar	Apr	May	Jun	Jul	Aug	Sept
Brachionus falcatus	28	24	13	35	33	42	56	34	17	21	30	29
Brachionus calyciflorus	-	-	15	17	30	19	26	30	32	15	26	18
Brachionus diversicornis	-	08	19	26	28	39	30	27	30	18	21	24
Filinia longiseta	-	20	-	23	10	08	17	11	16	22	-	-
Keratella tropica	26	25	17	29	25	27	33	25	26	17	25	20
Keratella quadrata	20	15	13	09	14	22	28	29	12	-	-	-
Lecane bulla	21	17	09	20	22	15	30	26	20	14	-	14
Trichocera porcelus	20	15	20	18	14	18	21	06	12	09	-	-
Trichocera longiseta	22	18	21	28	20	28	29	10	22	23	28	-

Table 9.10: Composition of Cladocera (density: organisms/liter) during year 2008-09

	Oct	Nov	Dec	Jan	Feb	Mar	Apr	May	Jun	Jul	Aug	Sept
Indialona ganapati	08	04	09	17	13	17	25	08	07	08	12	09
Moina micrura	09	10	09	19	20	30	21	14	10	08	13	14
Diaphanosoma excisum	08	03	03	16	18	10	03	04	10	05	02	03
Diaphanosoma sarsi	09	03	03	12	13	18	12	07	03	06	05	03
Alona rectangular	08	06	07	15	25	19	17	12	-	-	-	-
Biapertura karna	-	05	04	17	20	28	11	03	08	14	07	03
Ceriodaphnia cornuta	04	06	04	08	14	19	06	04	02	03	03	07

Copepoda was accounted for about 25 per cent and were represented by 7 species (Table 9.11), and *Neodiaptomus lindbergi* was absent throughout the study period. *Diaptomus marshianus* and *Mesoccyclops hyalinus* were present for 8 and 9 months respectively. *Cyclops viridis, Mesocyclops leukarti, Nauplius larva* and *Phylladiaptomus annae* were present in 11 months. The peak period of copepods was observed during month of April (255 organisms/liter) and it was minimum during the month of September 2009 (26 organisms/liter).

Table 9.11: Composition of Copepoda (density: organisms/liter) during year 2008-09

	Oct	Nov	Dec	Jan	Feb	Mar	Apr	May	Jun	Jul	Aug	Sept
Diaptomus marshianus	-	22	10	10	38	30	21	14	28	-	-	-
Phyllodiaptomus annae	-	14	10	21	18	08	20	10	30	12	15	18
Neodiaptomus lindbergi	20	10	20	18	10	20	35	28	26	20	18	08
Nauplius larva	08	08	14	13	19	12	22	15	18	08	20	-
Mesocyclops leukarti	16	12	06	18	32	42	70	40	27	16	22	-
Mesocyclops hyalinus	12	24	18	20	40	10	65	35	22	-	-	-
Cyclops viridis	06	09	15	16	16	15	22	20	20	11	11	-

Ostracoda was represented by 5 species (Table 9.12). *Cyclocypris globosa* and *Cyprinotus sps.*, were present for 12 months. *Stenocypris sps.*, were absent for 3 months of winter season and two months of rainy season. *Cypris obensa* and *Candocyprias osbornii* were absent in two months of rainy season. Throughout the summer month, ostracod population was maximum. It was minimum in rainy season.

- *Phytoplankton Diversity*: 10 species of chlorophyceae, 5 species of cyanophyceae, 6 species of bacillariophyceae and 3 species of euglenophyceae were recorded from the Harni (Katgaon) reservoir (Table 9.13).

Table 9.12: Composition of Ostracoda (density: organisms/liter) during year 2008-09

	Oct	Nov	Dec	Jan	Feb	Mar	Apr	May	Jun	Jul	Aug	Sept
Stenocypris sps.	-	-	-	06	12	13	30	25	18	10	-	-
Cypris obensa	07	11	05	10	14	16	22	16	22	-	-	11
Cyclocypris globosa	12	10	08	15	13	12	18	10	06	08	10	16
Candocypria osborni	13	09	09	13	11	10	13	28	20	-	08	-
Cyprinotus sps	12	08	11	12	08	10	15	16	12	06	04	08

Table 9.13: Phytoplankton Diversity in Harni (Katgaon) Reservoir

Chlorophyceae:	*Ulothrix zonata Zygnema sp., Pediastrum duplex, Pediastrum simplex, Scendesmus armatus, Oedogonium patulum, Ankistrodesmus falcatus, Chlorella valgoris, Cosmarium contractum, Closterium limneticum*
Cyanophyceae:	*Oscillatoria chlorine Oscillatoria limnosa Anabaena constricta Merismopedia punctata Microcystis aerugenose*
Bacillariophyceae:	*Navicula gracilis Navicula viridula Nitzschia subtilis Bacillaria paradoxa Diatoms vuloare Synedra affinis*
Euglenophyceae:	*Eugelna stellata, Euglena viridis Euglena pisciformis*

Table 9.14: Plankton Groups and their Composition in Harni (Katgaon) Reservoir during year 2007-09

Groups	Range (Units l^{-1})	Average (%)
Chlorophyceae	370 to 1360	1060(34.99)
Cyanophyceae	420 to 2010	910(30.04)
Bacillariophyceae	350 to 470	300(9.90)
Euglenophyceae	215 to 540	280(9.24)
Phytoplankton		2550(84.19)
Protozoans	17 to 95	58(1.91)
Rotifers	100 to 270	182(6.00)
Cladocerans	32 to 131	64(2.11)
Copepods	26 to 255	117(3.86)
Ostracods	21 to 112	58(1.91)
Zooplankton		479(15.81)
Total Zooplankton		3029

From chlorophyceae *Chlorella valgaris, Pediastrum spp.,* and *Scendesmus armatus* dominated the reservoir. The maximum population of chlorophyceae was recorded in April (1360 l^{-1}).

From cyanophyceae *Oscillatoria spp.,* and *Microcystis aeurogenose* dominated the reservoir. This group attained a highest peak in summer, with maxima in May at 2010 l^{-1}.

Among bacillariophyceae *Navicula spp., Synedra affinis* and *Bacillaria paradoxa* dominated the reservoir. Their population was maximum (470 l^{-1}) in July. The maximum population of bacillariophyceae in rainy season may be due to the inflow of water inside the reservoir.

Euglenophyceae was represented by 3 species. *Euglema spp.,* increased in number in winter season. The maximum population of euglenophyceae was recorded in December (540 l^{-1}).

Discussion

Present study has revealed 6 species of protozoans, 9 species of rotifers, 7 species of cladocera, 7 species of copepods and 6 species of ostracoda.

Renuga and Ramanibai (2010) studied the zooplanktonic community of Krishnagiri reservoir in Tamil Nadu. They recorded 23 species of zooplankton belonging to 4 groups *i.e.,* rotifer, cladocera, copepod and ostracoda. Rotifera represented by 8 species, cladocera represented by 5 species, copepod by 6 species and ostracoda by 4 species.

Rajashekhar *et al.* (2010) studied seasonal variation of zooplankton from Khaji kotnar reservoir in Gulbarga district of Karnataka. Out of 24 species, 10 species belongs to rotifer, 6 species belongs to cladocera, 5 species belongs to copepod and 3 species of ostracoda. Rotifera was the dominant group throughout the study period and highest count was recorded in the summer season while low incidence was observed in southwest monsoon season.

Moitra and Bhowmik (1968) observed members of three main zooplanktonic groups *i.e.,* rotifera, cladocera and copepoda, which dominate in freshwater fish pond in Kalyani, West Bengal.

In Ramauna reservoir four genera of rotifera and cladocera and two genera under copepod were observed by Agarwal (1980). However, Pathak and Mudgal (2004) observed five genera of rotifers, three genera of cladocerans and ostracodans and two genera each in respect of protozoans and copepodans in Visla reservoir of Madhya Pradesh.

The numerical variation in peak periods of different group of zooplankton might be due to different biological parameters. In Harni (Katgaon) reservoir rotifers were found dominant over the other groups. This findings is in agreement with Chakravarthy and Asthana (1989), Kohli *et al.* (1982) and Kiran *et al.* (2007).

Sakhare (2007) recorded 8 species of rotifers, 6 species of cladoerans, 7 species of copepods and 4 species of ostracods from Yeldari reservoir in Maharashtra.

Deshmukh (2001) and Sakhare (2007) reported maximum rotifers in summer season, which corroborate with the present investigation.

Cladocerans popularly known as 'water flea' prefer to live in deep water and constitute a major item of food for fish. Thus they hold key position in food chain and energy transformation (Uttangi, 2001). About 6000 species of freshwater cladocerans occur through the world (Korovchinsky, 1996) of which 110 species have been recorded from India (Patil and Goudar, 1989). Pandit *et al.* (2007) observed *Ceriodaphina cornuta, Bosminopsis dietersi, Biapertura karua* and *Alona pulchella* in Pravara river near Sangamner, Maharashtra. Population of cladocerans in different water bodies have been reported by Rao and Muley (1981), Kaushik and Sharma (1994), Murugan *et al.* (1998), Mathew (1985) and Battish and Kumari (1986).

Freshwater copepods constitute one of the major zooplankton communities occurring in all types of water bodies and ranging from free living to parasitic forms. They serve as food to several fishes and play a major role in ecological pyramids. About 120 species of the free living freshwater copepods are known from India (Uttangi, 2001).

In the present study, most abundant species of copepods were *Mesocyclops leukarti* and *Neodiaptomus lindbergi*. Chauhan (1993) has recorded maximum copepods in summer and minimum during winter. According to Das *et al.* (1996) copepods favour more stable environment and generally regarded as pollution sensitive taxa as they disappear once a water gets polluted.

Ostracods are small crustaceans having the bivalve carapace enclosing the laterally compressed body. They inhabit all kinds of freshwater and marine water environments. The freshwater ostracods occur in lakes, ponds, pools, swamps, streams and even polluted waters. Majority of them are free living and few are commensals on the gills of cray fishes and in the intestine of fishes and amphibians. Approximately 110 species are known from the inland water bodies of the Indian subcontinent (Patil and Gouder, 1989).

In the present study among ostracods *Stenocypris spp., Cypris obensa, Cyclocypris globosa, Candocypria osborni and Cyprinotus sps* were recorded.

Pandit *et al.* (2007) recorded *Hemicypris fossucula* and *Darwinula* sp from Paravara river. According to Harshey *et al.* (1987) ostracods grow well in hard water. Hujare (2005) reported absence of any seasonal trend in ostracods.

Distribution of phytoplankton and zooplankton in time and space, their composition and seasonal variations are essential pre-requisite for any successful fishery management. The plankton community structure represents the biological productivity of the system.

The phytoplankton in a reservoir is an important biological indicator of the water quality. While phytoplankton are important primary producers and the basis of the food chain in open water, some species on the other hand can be harmful to human and other vertebrates by releasing toxic substances (hepatotoxins or neurotoxins etc.,) into the water. Proliferation of harmful organisms, particularly species should be monitored. Phytoplankton studies and monitoring are useful for control of the physico-chemical and biological conditions of the water in any irrigation project. Therefore certain groups of phytoplankton, especially blue green algae, can degraded recreational value of surface water, particularly thick surface scum, which reduces the use of amenities for contact sports, or large concentrations, which cause deoxygenation of the water leading to fish death (Whitton and Patts, 2000). Over the last few decades, there has been much interest in the processes influencing the development of phytoplankton communities, primarily in relation to physico-chemical factors (Akbay *et al.* 1999; Peerapornpisal *et al.* 1999; Elliott *et al.* 2002).

In India, many hydrobiologists have carried out a considerable amount of research on seasonal succession, production ,phytoplankton abundance and the variations in the different freshwater ecosystems.

Govind (1963) worked on the phytoplankton functions with reference to environmental condition and factors regulating the production and succession of algae.

Hosmani and Bharthi (1980) carried out limnological studies of ponds and lakes of dharwad with reference to phytoplankton ecology of four water bodies.

Goel *et al.* (1986) studied the freshwater bodies with special reference to their chemistry and phytoplankton in Southern Maharashtra. Mahajan (2005) studied phytoplankton in a reservoir of Khargone, Madhya Pradesh.

Kant and Raina (1985) studied the qualitative and quantitative distribution of phytoplankton from two ponds of Jammu.

Sharma (2009) recorded 75 species of phytoplankton belonging to six groups from Loktak Lake in Manipur.

Sharma and Lyngdoh (2003) studied abundance and ecology of net and phytoplankton of a subtropical reservoir of Meghalaya (N.E. India).

Venu and Seshavatharam (1984) studied phytoplankton production in relation to physico-chemical conditions in lake Kondakarla.

The qualitative texture of phytoplankton community observed in Harni (Katgaon) reservoir indicated a sequence of chlorophyceae (10)> bacillariophyceae (6)>cyanophyceae (5) and euglenophyceae (3).

Kumar (1995) reported bacillariophyceae, chlorophyceae and cyanophyceae among phytoplankton. Phytoplankton community constituted 64.9 to 66.8 per cent of total zooplankton and showed its peak values in January and September. The members belong to bacillariophyceae (80.5%) and cyanophyceae (87.3%) dominated during January and September respectively.

Yousuf and Parveen (1990) recorded 84 taxa of phytoplankton from Dal lake. Of these 50 belonged to chlorophyceae, 16 each to cyanophyceae and bacillariophyceae and two to euglenophyceae. Chlorophyceae was the most dominant group among the phytoplankton population qualitatively as well as quantitatively. The group contributed on an average about 48.06 per cent of the total population, recording a range of 10.25 per cent to 93.43 per cent. Bacillariophyceae contributed 4.09 per cent to 87.09 per cent with a mean of 26.33 per cent. Eugelnophyceae was next in order contributing on an average 15.22 per cent of the total population. Cyanophyceae was the most scare group with a mean contribution of 10.38 per cent.

Verma and Shukla (1970) recorded 30 genera of phytoplankton from Kamla Nehru tank, Muzzafarnagar.

Similarly Hossain *et al.* (2006) recorded 38 genera of phytoplankton during three month study period in earthen fish ponds within the Mymen singh region of Bangladesh.

Harilal (2005) recorded 23 genera of phytoplankton from Neyyar and 20 from Karamana river of Kerala. Members of chlorophyceae were found to predominate in two rivers.

Ayoade *et al.* (2009) recorded 32 genera of phytoplankton from Tehri dam. Green algae which accounted for 69.5 per cent of the phytoplankton density were represented by 10 genera.

In present investigation the phytoplankton constituted 84.19 per cent of the total plankton, while the zooplankton was recorded at 15.81 per cent of the total plankton (Table 9.13). Sugunan and Yadava (1991b) reported 96.41 per cent of phytoplankton and 3.59 per cent of zooplankton in the Nongmahir reservoir of Meghalaya. In Yeldari reservoir Sakhare (2007) recorded 84.03 per cent phytoplankton and 15.97 per cent zooplankton.

Vyas and Kumar (1968) made a study on productivity and periodicity of phytoplankton of the Indrasagar tank, Udaipur in relation to physico-chemical characteristics. Green algae dominated the phytoplankton both as regards number of species and number of individuals. A definite phytoplankton periodicity has been observed. The green algae dominating in the rainy and winter seasons and the blue–green algae during the summer.

Hulyal and Kaliwal (2009) studied dynamics of phytoplankton in relation to physico-chemical factors in Almatti reservoir of Bijapur district, Karnataka.

Tiwari and Chauhan (2006) observed maximum population of chlorophyceae in winter season. As compared to other classes of phytoplankton, the members of euglenoid were recorded least in number. The maximum population of euglenoids was recorded in winter.

REFERENCES

Agarwal, S.S. (1980). Some Aspects of Limnology of Ramaua dam with Special Reference to Phytoplankton and Zooplankton. Ph.D. Thesis, Jiwaji University, Gwalior.

Akbay, N., Anul, N., Yerti, S., Soyupak, S. and Yurteri, C. (1999). Seasonal Distribution of Large Phytoplankton in Keban dam Reservoir. *Plank. Res.*, 21(4): 771-787.

Anjana, S; Gujarathi, S; and Kanhere, R.R. (1998). Seasonal Dyanamics of Phytoplankton Population in Relation to Abiotic Factors of a Fresh Water Pond at Barwani (M.P.). *Poll. Res.* 17: 133-136.

Anderson, H.H. (1989). Notes on Indian Rotifers. *J. Asiatic Soc.* Bengal, Calcutta. 58: 345-358.

Arora, H.C. (1962). Studies on Indian Rotifer. Part I. On A Small Collection of Illoricate Rotifer from Nagpur, India with Notes on their Bionomics. *J. Zool. Soc. India.* 14:33-44.

Arora, H.C. (1963a). Studies on Indian Rotifer. Part II. Some Species of the Genus *Brachionus* from Nagpur. *J. Zool. Soc. India.* 15:112-121.

Arora, H.C. (1964). Studies on Indian Rotifer. Part III. *J. Zool. Soc. India.* 16 (1-2):1-6.

Arora, H.C.(1965). Studies on Indian Rotifer. Part VI. On A Collection of Rotifer from Nagpur, India with Four New Species and a New Variety. *Hydrobiologia.* 26:444-456.

Arora, H.C. (1966). Responses of Rotifer to Variation in some Ecological Factors. *Proc. Indian Acad. Sci.* 63:57-66.

Arora, H.C. (1966a). Studies on Indian Rotifer. Part III. On *Brachionus calyciflorus* and some Varieties of the Species. *J. Zool. Soc. India.* 16:1-6.

Ayoade, A.A., Agarwal, N.K. and Chandda Saklani, A. (2009). Changes in Physico-chemical Features and Plankton of two Regulated High Altitude Rivers Garhwal Himalaya, India. European *Journal of Scientific Research.* 27(1):77-92.

Aziz, N.E.A and Ezz, A.S.M. (2004). The Structure of Zooplankton Community in Lake Maryout, Alexandria, Egypt. *Egptian J. Aquatic Res.*, 30 (A):160-170.

Baird, W. (1850). The Natural History of the British Entomostracous. Roy. Soc. London; 1-364.

Bais, V.S. and Agrawal, N.C. (1995). Comparative Study of the Zooplanktonic Spectrum in the Sagar Lake and Military Engineering lake. *J. Environ. Biol.*, 16 (1): 27-32.

Balmurugan, S., Arivazhagan, R. and Subramanian, P. (2001). Seasonal Variation of Zooplankton Population in Ayyampalayam Temple Tank, Tiruchirappali, Tamilnadu, India. *Journal of Advanced Zoology*, 22: 52-55.

Battish, S.K. (1968). A Study of the Taxonomy and Seasonal Variation of Rotifers and Crustaceans. M.Sc. (Hons.) Thesis, Punjab University, Chandigarh, 199pp.

Battish, S.K. (1992). Freshwater Zooplankton of India. Oxford and IBH Publishing Co. Pvt. Ltd. New Delhi.

Battish, S.K. and Parminder Kumari. (1986). Effect of Physico-chemical Factors on the Seasonal Abundance of Cladocera in Typical Pond at Village of Raqba, Ludhiana. *Indian Ecol.* 13 (1):146-151.

Bays J.S. and T.L. Crisman. (1983). Zooplankton and Trophic State Relationships in Florida Lakes. *Can. J. Fish. Aquat. Sci.* 40:1813-1819.

Beaver, J. R. and Crisman, T.L. (1990). Use of Microzooplankton as an Early Indicator of Advancing Cultural Eutrophication. *Verh. Internat. Verein. Limnol.* 24 :532-537.

Begum, N.B. and Narayana, J. (2006). Phytoplankton Diversity of Floor Lentic Water Bodies in and Around Davangarere City, Karnataka. *J. Aqua. Biol.* 21(2): 13-18.

Bhagat, V.B. and Meshram, C.B. (2007). Zooplankton Dynamics of Ambadi dam ear Akot, Ankola, Maharashtra. *J. Aqua. Biol.* 22(1):19-20.

Birasal, N.R; Nadkarni, V.B. and Gouder, B.Y.M. (1989). Ecology of Zooplankton of Sepa Reservoir of Kali River during the Filling Phase Western Ghats, *Karnataka. J. Freshwater Biol.* 1(1): 15-23.

Canfield , T.J. and Jones, J.R. (1996). Zooplankton Abundance, Biomass, and Size Distribution in Selected Midwestern Waterbodies and Relation with Trophic State, *J. Freshwat. Ecol.* 11: 171-181.

Chakrapani, B.K., Krishna, M.B. and Srinivasa, T.S. (1996). A Report on the Water Quality, Plankton and Bird Populations of the Lakes in and Around Bangalore and Maddur, Karnataka, India. Department of Ecology and Environment, Government of Karnataka. http://wgbis.ces.iisc.ernet.in/energy/water/paper/Tr-115/ref.htm

Chakravarthy, N.M. and Asthaana, A. (1989). Plankton Succession and Ecology of a Sewage Treated Pond in West Bengal. *Environment and Ecology*. 7:549-554.

Chauhan, R. (1993). Seasonal Fluctuation of Zooplankton in Renuka Lake, Himachal Pradesh. *Uttar Pradesh J. Zool.*, 111(1):17-20.

Chauhan, R. (1988). Seasonal Abundance of Zooplankton in Rewalsar Lake, H.P. *Geobios New Report*. 7 (2):117-121.

Chavan, R.J., Mohekar, A.D. and Hiware, C.J. (2006). Ecology and Behaviour of Zooplanktons in Manjara Project Reservoir in Maharashtra. In: Ecology of Lakes and Reservoirs (Dr. V.B. Sakhare, Ed.), Daya Publishing House, Delhi, pp. 151-162.

Choudhary, S. and Singh, D.K. (1999). Zooplankton Populations of Boosra Lake at Muzaffarpur, Bihar. *Environment and Ecology*. 17 (2):444-448.

Chowdhary, S.K., Sharma, J.P. and Srivastava, J.B. (1978). On the Rotifer Fauna of Jammu Ponds. *Proc. Indian Sci. Congr.* (Abstracts).

Das, P.K., Michael, R.G. and Gupta, A. (1996). Zooplankton Community in Lake Tasek a tectonic Lake in Garo Hills, India. *Trop. Ecol.* 37(2):257-263.

Das, R.K. (1996). Monitoring of Water Quality, its Importance in Disease Control. Paper Presented in Nat. Workshop on Fish and Prawn Disease, Epizootics and Quarantine Adoption in India. October 9, 1996. CICFRI. pp. 51-55.

Das, S.M. (1961). Hydrogen ion Concentration, Plankton and Fish in Freshwater Eutrophic Lakes of India. *Nature*. 191 (478): 511-512.

Das, S.M. and Srivastava, V.K. (1956). Some New Observations on Plankton from Freshwater Ponds and Tanks of Lucknow, India. *Sci. and Cult.* 21: 446-467.

Datta, N.C., Bandyopadhyay, B.K., Das, M.K. and Bandyopadhyay, S.B. (1982). Diurnal rhythm of some Physico-chemical Properties and Zooplankton in a Tropical Freshwater Pond in Calcutta, West Bengal. *Ind. J. Phy. Nat. Sc.* 2:22-27.

De Beauchamp, P.M. (1928). Cou d' oeil sur less Recherché Recentes Relative aux Rotifers et less mthodes qui leur sont Applicable. *Bull. Biol. France et de la Belgique*. 62:51-125.

De Beauchamp, P.M. (1932). Contribution a l'etude du genre Ascomorpha et des Processus Digestifs chez les rotifers. *Bull. Soc. Zool. France*. 57:428-449.

Deshmukh, U.S. (2001). Ecological Studies of Chhatri Lake, Amravati; with Special Reference to Planktons and Productivity, Ph.D. Thesis, Amaravati University, Amravati, pp. 175.

Dhanapathi, M.V.S.S.S. (1973). On the Occurrence of the Rare Rotifer Rotaria Neptunia (Ehrenberg) in India. *Curr. Sci.* 42:770.

Dhanapathi, M.V.S.S.S. (1974). A new Brachionid Rotifer Platyias Quadricornis andhraensis subsp. Nov. from India. Curr. Sci. 43:358.I. *Hydrobiologia*. 45: 357-372.

Dhanapathi, M.V.S.S.S. (1975b). Rotifers from Andhra Pradesh, India. *J. Linn. Soc. (Zool.)*, 57:85-94.

Dhanapathi, M.V.S.S.S. (1976a). Rotifers from Andhra Pradesh, India, III. Family Lecanidae Including Two New Species. *Hydrobiologia*. 48:9-16.

Dhanapathi, M.V.S.S.S (2000). Taxonomic Notes on the Rotifers from India (from 1889-2000). Pub. Indian Association of Aquatic Biologists, Hyderabad, pp. 178.

Dhavale, S.D., Lakde, H.M. and Lohare, S.D. (2009). Studies on Algal Flora and Physic-chemical Characteristics of Shikara Reservoir in Nanded District, Maharashtra. *Ecology and Fisheries*. 2 (2):69-72.

Edmondson, W.T. (1959). Rotifera, pp. 420-494. In: Freshwater Biology (eds. H.B. Ward and G.C. Whipple). (2nd edition, W. T. Edmondson ed.) John Wiley and sons. Inc. New York, 1248 pp.

Elliott, J.A., Irish, A.E. and Reynolds, C.S. (2002). Predicting the Spatial Dominance of Phytoplankton in Light Limited and Incompletely Mixed Eutrophic water Column using the PROTECH Model. *Fresh. Bio.* 47: 433-440.

Flossner, D. (1972). Krebstiere, crustacea. kiemen-und Blattfusser Branchipooda, Fishlause, Branchiura. Die Teirwelt Deutschlands. 60: 501 pp.

Fuller, D. R., Stemberger, R.S. and Gannon, J.E. (1977). Limnetic Rotifers as Indicators of Trophic Change. *J. Elisha Mitchell. Sci. Soc.* 93:104-113.

Gannon J.E. and R.S. Stemberger. (1978). Zooplankton (especially crustaceans and rotifers) as Indicators of Water Quality, Trans. Am. Micros. Soc. 97:16-35.

Goel, P.K., Kulkarni, A.Y. and Khatavkar, S.D. (1968). Species Diversity in Phytoplankton Communities in a Few Freshwater Bodies in Southern Maharashtra. *Geobios*. 15:150-156.

Goel, P.K., Khatavkar, S.D., Kulkarni, A.Y. and Trivedy, R.K. (1986). Studies on Freshwater in Southwestern Maharashtra with Special Reference to their Chemistry and Phytoplankton. *Poll. Res.* 5(2):79-84.

Govind, B.V. (1963). Pre-liminary Studies on Plankton of the Tungabhadra Reservoir. *Indian J. Fish.* 10 (1):148-158.

Harilal, C.C. (2005). Phytoplankton Diversity of Two Rivers of Kerala with Special Reference to Aquatic Nutrients. *Poll. Res.* 24 (4):773-776.

Harney, N.V., Sitre, S.R., N.S.Wadhave, N.S. and Nasare, P.N. (2008). Zooplankton Diversity in a Anthropologically Affected Freshwater Lake of Bhadrawati Town in Chandrapur District of Maharashtra. *Ecology and Fisheries*. 1 (1):27-34.

Harshey, D.K., Shrivastav, A.K. and Patil, S.G. (1987). Studies on the Ecology of Freshwater Ostracoda. Part II. Population Ecology in Balsagar Tank, Jabalpur, M.P., India. *J. Curr. Biosci.* 4 (4):127-134.

Hellawell J.M. (1986). Biological Indicators of Freshwater Pollution and Environmental Management. In Pollution Monitoring Series. Elsevier Applied Science Publishers, London, UK (p. 546).

Henry, M. (1822). A Monograph of the Freshwater Entomostraca of New South Wales. Proc. Linn. Soc. New South Wales. 47:26-52.

Hosmani, S.P. and Bharthi, S.G. (1980). Limnological Studies in Ponds and Lakes of Dharwar. Comparative Phytoplankton Ecology of Four Water Bodies. *Phycos*. 19 (1):27-43.

Hujare, M.S. (2005). Hydrobiological Studies on some Water Reservoirs of Hatkanangale tahsil (Maharashtra). Ph.D. Thesis, Shivaji University, Kolhapur.

Hulyal, S.B. and Kaliwal, B.B. (2009). Dynamics of Phytoplankton in Relation to Physic-chemical Factors of Almatti Reservoir of Bijapur District, Karnataka State. *Environmental Monitoring and Assessment*. 153 (1-4):45-59.

Hussain, M. (1977). Ecobiology of Freshwater Protozoa, Ph.D. Thesis, Osmania University, Hyderabad.

Jennings, H.S. (1903). Rotatoria of the United States, II. A Monograph of the Rattulidae. *Bull. U.S. Fish Comm.* (1902):273-352.

Kant, S. and Raina, A.K. (1985). Limnological Studies of Two Ponds in Jammu. 1. Qualitative and Quantitative Distribution of Phytoplankton. *Zoologica Orientalis*. 2:89-92.

Kaushik, S. and Sharma, N. (1994). Physico-chemical Characteristics and Zooplankton Population of A Perennial Tank, Matsya Sarowar, Gwalior. *Environment and Ecology*. 12 (2): 429-434.

Keilhack, L. (1909). Phyllopoda, In: A Brauers. Die Susswasserfauna Dautschlands. Jena; 10:1-112.

Kesharwani Sadhna, Mandloi, A.K. and Dube, K.K. (2006). Diversity of Zooplankton in Amkhera Pond of Jabalpur (M.P.) India. *Natural Journal of Life Sciences*, 3: 359-364.

Kiran, B.R., Puttaiah, E.T. and Kamath, Devidas. (2007). Diversity and Seasonal Fluctuation of Zooplankton in Fish Pond of Bhadra Fish Farm, Karnataka. *Zoos' Print Journal*. 22(2):2935-2936.

Korovchinsky, N.M. (1996). How Many Species of Cladocera are there? *Hydrobiologia*. 321:191-204.

Kumar, Arvind. (1995). Periodicity and Abundance of Plankton in Relation to Physic-chemical Characteristics of a Tropical Wetland of South Bihar. *Eco. Env. and Cons*. 1(1-4):47-51.

Manuilova, E.F. (1964). Cladocera of the Fauna of the USSR. Zool. Inst. Acad. Naukssar; 88:1-327

Maruthanayagam, C., Sasikumar, M. And Senthilkumar, C. (2003). Studies on Zooplankton Population in Thirukkulam Pond during Summer and Rainy Seasons. *Nature Environ. Pollut. Technol*. 2:13-19.

Mathew, P.M. (1985). Seasonal Trends in the Fluctuations of Plankton and Physic-chemical Factors in a Tropical lake (Govindgarh Lake, M.P.) and their Tnter-relationship. *J. Inland Fish. Soc. India*. 17 (1&2):11-24.

Melack, I.M. (1979). Photosynthetic Rates in four Tropical Freshwaters. *Freshwater Biology*. 9: 555-571.

Michael, D.S. (1969). The Ecology of Vascular Hydrophytes in Lake Kasiba. *Hydrobiol*. 34:448-464.

Michael, R., G. (1973). A Guide to the Study of Freshwater Organisms, *Madurai Univ. J. Suppl*. (Ed.) 1:186 pp.

Michael, R.G. and Sharma, B.K. (1988). Fauna of India, Indian cladocera (Crustacea: Branchiopda: Cladocera), Zoological Survey of India, Calcutta.

Michael, R.G. (1969). Seasonal Trends in Physico-chemical Factors and Plankton of Freshwater Fishponds and their Role in Fish Culture. *Hydrobiol*. 33(1):145-160.

Mishra, S.R. (2005). Zooplankton and their Seasonal Variations in a Sewage Collecting River at Gwalior, Madya Pradesh. In: Advances in Limnology (Ed. S.R. Mishra), Daya Publishing House, Delhi, pp. 1-44.

Mukherji, Manika and Nandi, N.C. (2006). Ecology, Biodiversity and Management of Rabindar Sarovar in Kolkata, West Bengal. In: Ecology of Lakes and Reservoirs (Dr. V.B. Sakhare), Daya Publishing House, Delhi, pp. 36-53.

Murugan, N., Murugavel, P. and Kodarkar, M.S. (1998). Cladocera (The Biology, Classification, Identification and Ecology), Publication No. 5, Indian Association of Aquatic Biologists, Hyderabad.

Myers, F.J. (1931). The Distribution of Rotifera on Mount Desert Island. *Amer. Mus. Novit.* 494:1-12.

Myers, F.J. (1933). A New Genus of Rotifers (Dorria). *Jour. Roy. Micros. Soc.* 53:118-121.

Myers, F.J. (1941). Lecane Curvicornis Var. miamiensis, New Variety of Rotatora, with Observations on the Feeding Habits of Rotifers. Notul. Nat. 75:1-8.

Nandan, S.N. and Ansari Ziya. (1999). Ecological Study of Algae from Mausam River flowing through Malegaon City (Maharashtra). BRI'S *JAST*. 11 (1):31-38.

Nandan, S.N. and Jain, D.S. (2005). Study of Algae Tolering Organic Pollution of Sonvad dam and Devbhane dam of Maharashtra. In: Advances in Limnology (Ed. S.R. Mishra, Daya Publishing House, Delhi, pp. 214-222.

Nandan, S.N. and Mahajan, S.R. (2006). Studies on Algae of Polluted Lakes of Jalgaon (Maharashtra): Role of Blue Green Algae. In: Ecology of Lakes and Reservoirs (Dr.V.B. Sakhare), pp. 54-62.

Nandan, S.N. and Patel, R.J. (1985a). Seasonal Variations of Phytoplankton in the Vishwamitri River, Baroda. In: Advances in Applied Phycology (Eds. A.C. Shukla and S.N. Pandey), pp. 262-269.

Nandan, S.N. and Patel, R.J. (1986). Assessment of Water Quality of Vishwamitri River by Algal Analysis. India. *J. Environ. Hlth.* 29 (2):160-161.

Nasare, P.N., Wadhave, N.S., Harney, N.V. and Sitre, S.R. (2009). Studies on Phytoplankton Diversity of Vinjasan Lake in Bhadrawati town of Chandrapur district, Maharashtra. *Ecology and Fisheries*. 2 (1):95-100.

Nayar, C.K.G. (1964). Morphometric Studies on the Rotifer *Brachionus calyciflorus* Pallas. *Curr. Sci.* 33:469-470.

Nayar, C.K.G. (1965a). Cyclomorphosis of *Brachionus calyciflorus* Pallas. *Hydrobiologia*. 25: 538-544.

Nayar, C.K.G. (1965b). Taxonomic Notes on the Indian Species of Keratella (Rotifera). *Hydrobiologia*. 26:457-462.

Pace M J. (1986). An Empirical Analysis of Zooplankton Community Size Structure Across Lake Trophic Gradients, *Limnol. Oceanogr.* 31: 45-55.

Pandit, S.V., Vaidya, V.V. and Joshi, P.P. (2007). Studies on Zooplankton Diversity of Pravara River, Near Sangamner Dist. Ahmednagar, M.S. *J. Aqua. Biol.* 22 (1):33-38.

Pathak, Janardan. (2009). Studies on Plankton Dynamics in a Fresh Water Pond Aquaculture System in Assam, Ph.D. thesis, Gauhati University, Guwahati, Assam.

Pathak S.K. and Mudgal L.K. (2002). A Pre-liminary Survey of Zooplankton of Virla Reservoir of Khargaon. (Madhya Pradesh). India. *Indian J. Env. and Ecoplan*. 6 (2): 297-30.

Patil, C.S. and Gouder, B.Y.M. (1985). Ecological Study of Freshwater Zooplankton of a Subtropical Pond (Karnataka, India). *Int. Revue Ges. Hydrobiol. 70:* 279-287.

Patil, C.S. and Gouder, B.Y.M. (1989). Freshwater Invertebrates of Dharwad, Prasaranga, Karnatak University, Dharwad.

Pawar, S.K., Madlapure, V.R. and Pulle, J.S. (2003). Study of Zooplanktonic Community of Sirur dam Water near Mukhed in Nanded District (M.S.), India. *J. Aqua. Biol.* 18 (2):37-40.

Pearsall, W.H. (1921). A Theory of Diatoms periodicity. *J. Ecol.* 1 (2):165-183.

Peerapornpisal, Y., Sonthichai, W., Somdee, T., Mulsin, P. and Rott, E. (1999). Water Quality and Phytoplankton in the Mae Kuang Udomtara Reservoir, Chiang Mai, Thailand. *J. Sci. Fac. Cmu.* 26(1):25-43.

Pennak, R.W. (1978). Freshwater Invertebrates of the United States. 2nd edition, John Willey Sons, New York, 803 pp.

Pradhan, Arunava, Bhaumik Pranami, Das Sumana and Mishra, Madhusmita. (2008). Phytoplankton Diversity as Indicator of Water Quality for Fish Cultivation. *Am. J. Environ. Sci.* 4 (4):406-411.

Pradhan, Prasenjit, Sunirmal Giri and Susanta Kumar Chakraborty. (2006). Ecological Gradients Determining the Density and Diversity of Rotifer in a Freshwater River System of South West Bengal, India. *J. Aqua. Biol.* 21(1):19-28.

Prakash, Sadguru, Ansari, Khalid K. and Sinha, Mukul. (2002). Seasonal Dynamics of Zooplankton in A Freshwater Pond Developed from the Waste Land of Brick-Kiln. *Poll. Res.* 21(1): 81-83.

Rajashekar, M., Vijaykumar, K. and Zebra Paerveen. (2010). Seasonal Variations of Zooplankton Community in Freshwater Reservoir of Gulbarga Distrct, Karnataka, South India. *International Journal of Systems Biology*. 2 (1):6-11.

Ranjan, Goutam, Singh, N.P. and Singh, R.B. (2007). Physico-chemical Characteristics of Ghariyarwa Pond of Birganj, Nepal in Relation to Growth of Phytoplankton. *Nature Environment and Pollution Technology*. 6 (4):629-632.

Rawat, M.S. and Sharma, R.C. (2010). Analysis of Zooplankton Population in Garhwal Himalayan Lake, Deoria Tal, Uttarakhand. In: Aquatic Ecosystem and its Management (Eds. K. Vijaykumar and B. Vasanthkumar), Daya Publishing House, Delhi, pp. 102-109.

Renuga, K. and Ramnibai, R. (2006). Contribution to the Distribution of Freshwater Copepods of Kanchipuram district of Tamil Nadu. In: Ecology of Lakes and Reservoirs (Dr.V.B. Sakhare), Daya Publishing House, Delhi, pp. 143-150.

Renuga, K. and Ramnibai, R. (2010). Zooplankton Composition Present in Krishnagiri Reservoir, Tamil Nadu, India. *Current Biotica*. 3 (4):519-522.

Rawat M.S. and Sharma R.C. (2005). Phytoplankton Population of Garhwal Himalayam Lake Deoria Tal, Uttranchal. *J. Ecophysiol. Occupat. Health.* 5: 73-76.

Rawat, M.S., Sharma R.C. (2010). Analysis of Zooplankton Population in Garhwal Himalayan Lake, Deoria Tal, Uttarakhand. In: Aquatic Ecosystem and its Management (Ed. K. Vijaykumar and B. Vasanthkumar), Daya Publishing House, Delhi, pp. 102-109.

Saikia, S.K. and Das, D.N. (2003). Diversity Indices of Zooplankton and Water Quality in two Freshwater Ponds of Arunachal Pradesh, India. *Geobios*. 30 (2-3):113-116.

Sakhare, V.B. (2007). Reservoir Fisheries and Limnology, Narendra Publishing House, Delhi, pp. 187.

Sakhare, V.B. (2007). Wan Reservoir (Beed district; Maharashtra): Ecology and Fisheries. *Fishing Chimes*. 27 (6): 23-26.

Sakhare, V.B. and Joshi, P.K. (2002). Ecology of Palas-Nilegaon Reservoir in Osmanabad District, Maharashtra. *J. Aqua. Biol.* 18 (2): 17-22.

Sakhare, V.B. and P.K. Joshi. (2006). Plankton Diversity in Yeldari Reservoir, Maharashtra. *Fishing Chimes*. Vol. 25 (12):23-25.

Santhanam, R. and Krishnamurthy, K. (1985). On Planktonic Rotifers. 3rd All India Congr. Zool. (Abstracts).

Sharma, B.K. and Lyngdoh. (2003). Abundance and Ecology of Net and Phytoplankton of a Subtropical Reservoir of Meghalaya (N.E. India), Ecology, Environment and Conservation. 9 (4):497-503.

Sharma, B.K. and Lyngsker Clarobian. (2003). Plankton Communities of a Subtropical Reservoir of Meghalaya (N.E. India). *Indian Journal of Animal Sciences*. 73 (2):209-215.

Sharma, B.K. (2009). Composition, Abundance and Ecology of Phytoplankton Communities of Loktak Lake, Manipur, India. *Journal of Threatened Taxa*.1(8):401-410.

Sinha, B. and Islam, M.R. (2002). Seasonal Variation in Zooplankton Population of two Lentic Bodies and Assam State Zoo cum Botanical garden, Guwahati, Assam, *Eco. Env. and Cons*. 8: 273-278.

Sinha, K.K. and Sinha, D.K. (1993). Seasonal Trends in Physico-chemical Factors and Zooplankton in A Freshwater Pond of Munger, Bihar. *J. Ecobiol*. 5(4):299-302.

Singh, Meena and Sinha, R.K. (1995). Diel Variation of Water Quality and Zooplankton Community in A Freshwater Pond of Patna, Bihar. *Eco. Env. and Cons*. 1(1-4):57-64.

Singh, Y. (1979). Ecological Studies on River Algae with Special Reference to Bacillariophyceae. Ph.D. thesis, Lucknow University, Lucknow.

Sivakumar, K. and Karuppasamy, R. (2008). Factors Affecting Productivity of Phytoplankton in a Reservoir of Tamil Nadu, India. *American – Eurasian Journal of Botany*. 1 (3): 99-103.

Sprules, W.G. (1977). Crustacean Zooplankton Communities as Indicators of Limnological Conditions: An Approach using Principal Component Analysis. *J. Fish. Res. Board Can*. 34: 962-975.

Sugunan, V.V. and Yadava, Y.S. (1991b). Feasibility Studies for Fisheries Development of Nongamahir Reservoir, CIFRI, Barrackpore, pp. 30.

Sukumaran, P.K and Das, A.K. (2001). Distribution of Phytoplankton in some Fresh Water Reservoirs, Karnataka. *J. Inland Fish Soci. India*, 33 (2): 29-36.

Sukumaran, P.K. and Das, A.K. (2002). Plankton Abundance in Relation to Physico-chemical Features in a Peninsular man-made Lake. *J. Environ. Ecol*., 20 (4): 873-879.

Sunkad, B.N. (2005). Diversity of Zooplankton in Rakasakoppa Reservoir of Belgaum, North Karnataka. In Kumar, A. (Ed.) Ecology of Plankton. Daya Publishing House, New Delhi, 147-152.

Sunkad, B.N. and Patil, H.S. (2004). Water Quality Assessment of Fort Lake of Belgaum (Karnataka) with Special Reference to Zooplankton. *J. Environ. Biol*. 25:99-102.

Telkhade, P.M., Dahegaonkar, N.R., Zade, S.B. and Lonkar, A.N. (2008). Quantitative Analysis of Phytoplankton and Zooplankton of Masala Lake, Masala, Distt. Chandrapur, Maharashtra. *Environment Conservation Journal*, 9:37-40.

Thirumathal, K. (2006). Cladocerans of Amaravathy Reservoir, Udumalpet, Coimbatore district, Tamil Nadu, India. In: Ecology of Lakes and Reservoirs (Dr. V.B. Sakhare), Daya Publishing House, Delhi, pp. 105-110.

Tiwari, Ashesh and Chauhan, S.V.S. (2006). Seasonal Phytoplanktonic Diversity of Kitham Lake, Agra. *J. Environ. Biol*. 27 (1):35-38.

Uttangi, J.C. (2001). Conservation and Management Strategy for the Water Fowls of Minor Irrigation tank Habits and their Importance as Stopover site in Dharwad Dist. In: Hosetti, Venkatsehwarlu (Eds.). Trends in Wildlife and Management, Daya Publishing House, Delhi, pp. 179-221.

Velecha, V. and Bhatnagar, G.P. (1988). Seasonal Changes of Phytoplankton in Relation to some Physico-chemical Factors in Lower Lake Bhopal. *Geobios*, 15: 170-173.

Venu, P. and Seshavatharam, V. (1984). Phytoplankkton Production in Relation to Physic-chemical Conditions in Lake Kondakarla. *Proc. Indian Natn. Sci. Acad.* B51 No. 6, pp. 588-595.

Verma, S.R. and Shukla, G.R. (1970). The Physico-chemical Conditions of Kamla Nehru Tank, Muzzafarnagar (U.P.) in Relation to the Biological Productivity. *Environment.* 12:110-128.

Victor, R. and Fernando, C.H. (1982). The Freshwater Ostracods (Crustacea-Ostracoda) of India. Records of the Zoological Survey of India. 74:147-242.

Vyas, L.N. and Kumar, H.D. (1968). Studies on the Phytoplankton and other Algae of Indrasagar tank, Udaipur, India. *Hydrobiol.* 31 (3-4): 421-434.

Yousuf, A.R. and Parveen, M. (1990). Phytoplankton Dynamics in Dal Lake, Kashmir. In: Contributions to the Fisheries of Inland Open Water Systems in India (Ed. A.G. Jhingran, V.K. Unnithan and Amitabha Ghosh), Inland Fisheries Society of India, pp. 58-63.

Walujkar, A.G. and Hiware, C.J. (2006). Seasonal Variation in Zooplankton Population of Shirsatwadi Reservoir from Pathardi Tehasil (Maharashtra), India. (In Biodiversity and Environment, Edtd by B.N. Pandey and G.K. Kulkarni, APH Publishing Corporation, New Delhi).

Welch, P.S. (1948). Limnological Methods. Mc Graw-Hill Book Company, Inc., New York.

Whitton, B.A. and Patts, M. (2000). The Ecology of Cyanobacteria. Kluwer Academic Publishers, Netherlands.

Zafar, A.R. (1986). Seasonality in Phytoplankton in some South Indian Lakes. *Hydrobiol.*, 138: 117-187.

Page 136-141

PLANKTON AND FISHERIES
Edited by : V.B. Sakhare; H.K. Jadhav and S.S. Jadhav
Edition : 2017
ISBN : 978-93-5056-811-8
Published by : Discovery Publishing House Pvt. Ltd., New Delhi (India)

10 Reservoir Fisheries of Ahmednagar District, Maharashtra

Vishwas Balasaheb Sakhare
Post Graduate Department of Zoology
Yogeshwari Mahavidyalaya, Ambajogai - 431 517.

Indian reservoirs form an important source of fish production. In India, 19370 reservoirs are there, spread over in 15 states, covering an area of 3.15 million ha. This area is expected to grow further to 6 million ha in due course of time of 25 years. It is due to the execution of new reservoirs for irrigation and power generation. In spite of the huge water area available under reservoirs, the utilization of these water bodies from the fisheries point of view is poor. The average productivity from all categories of reservoirs is estimated to about 15 kg/ha/yr, although potential exists for manifold increase as demonstrated in some small, medium and large reservoirs in the country.

Maharashtra state has vast potential for fish production from reservoirs in most of the districts. Fishing in the reservoirs is normally carried out by the members of fishermen co-operatives. There are 2603 primary inland fishermen co-operatives in the state and the reservoirs are given on the lease for a period of five years to eligible fishermen co-operatives. Maharashtra State is endowed with 3.18 lakh ha., water spread area under 192 large and medium, 2065 minor Irrigation projects .Reservoir fisheries contributes in socio-economic developments of economically backward population. It is one of the major sources of livelihood for economically backward population.. The present study has been undertaken to have knowledge on the fish and fishery potential of Ahmednagar district.

Ahmednagar is the largest district of the state covering an area of 17,412 sq.km., constituting 5.54 per cent of the total area of the state. The district is named after its founder Ahmed Shah Nizam Shah. The district owes its own historical importance and has witnessed the historical events of Indian history of Freedom for Indpendence. It is the place where national leaders like Pandit Jawahar Lal Nehru were prisoned during the freedom movement and he wrote his famous book titled 'Discovery of India' in Ahmednagar Jail.

The entire Ahmednagar district is covered by basaltic lava flows of the Deccan Traps belonging to the Upper Cretaceous to Eocene age. The Deccan Trap basalts are overlain by alluvial deposits along the river Godavari and occupy the northern part of the district. The stratigraphical sequence of the different lithological units occurring in the district is give below.

The climate of the Ahmednagar district is hot and dry in general. The maximum temperature recorded in the month of May rises to about 40° C while the lowest temperature recorded in the month of January goes down to about 5-8°C. It receives an annual average rainfall of about 556 mm. The rainfall varies between 360 mm to 1034 mm. The cold season in the district commences from December and ends in the month of February. The period from March to the first Week of June is the hot season which is followed by southwest monsoon season which lasts till the end of September. October and November constitute the post monsoon season.

- *Reservoir fisheries:* According to District Fisheries Department, there are 40 small reservoirs in the area of 15 to 99 hectares. Fishery of these water bodies is supported by different fish species (Table 10.1). Fish production in these reservoir varies from 5 MT (Balthan reservoir) to 40 MT (Therwadi reservoir). Fish seed of economically important Indian major carps *i.e., Catla catla, Labeo rohita, Cirrhinus mrigala* along with exotic species like: *Cyprinus carpio, Hypophthlamichthys molitrix* and *Ctenopharyngodon idella* is regularly stocked. Details of reservoir wise seed stocking and fish production are depicted in Table 10.2.

Beside these reservoirs, information is also available on different reservoirs which are not included in list of District Fisheries Department.

Pandarkar *et al.* (2014) studied zooplankton diversity of Visapur reservoir and reported 31 species of zooplankton, out of them 20 species belonged to rotifers, 5 species to cladocerans, 4 species to copepods and 2 species to ostracods. Rotifers dominated followed by cladocerans, copepods and ostracods. The authors revealed that the reservoir is productive and capable of fish culture.

Table 10.1: Fish Fauna of Ahmednagar District

1.	*Catla catla*
2.	*Cirrhinus mrigala*
3.	*Labeo rohita*
4.	*Labeo boggut*
5.	*Cyprinus carpio*
6.	*Ctenopharyngodon idella*
7.	*Hypophthalmichthys molitirx*
8.	*Oreochromis mossambicus*
9.	*Punitus sarana*
10.	*Puntius chola*
11.	*Punitus sophore*
12.	*Nemacheilus botia*
13.	*Nemacheilus beavani*
14.	*Notopterus notopterus*
15.	*Notopterus chitala*
16.	*Chanda nama*
17.	*Chanda ranga*
18.	*Glossogobius giuris*
19.	*Mastacembelus armatus*
20.	*Amblypharyngodon mola*
21.	*Discognathus modestus*
22.	*Oxygaster bacaila*
23.	*Barbus pinnauratus*
24.	*Barbus chilinoides*
25.	*Clarias batrachus*
26.	*Wallago attu*

Sadatpur reservoir is located between Latitude 19°34 to 19°36N and Longitude 74°26 to 74°27 E near Sadatpur village in Sangamner tehasil. Pawar (2009) reported 24 fish species belonging to 17 genera and 2 orders. Water quality of this reservoir is within the permissible limit for fish and fisheries (Pawar, 2009). Dhembare (2005) reported 21 species of zooplankton belonging to four groups *i.e., (i)* protozoa (7 species); *(ii)* rotifera (7 species), *(iii)* cladocera (4 species) and *(iv)* copepoda (3 species).

Table 10.2: Fisheries of Small Tanks in Ahmednagar District of Maharashtra

Sr. No.	Reservoir	Taluka	Area (ha)	Seed Stocked	Fish Production (MT)
1.	Baradari	Ahmednagar	30	50,000	25
2.	Cichondi Patil	Ahmednagar	48	60,000	27
3.	Kaudgaon	Ahmednagar	49	70,000	25
4.	Kamargaon	Ahmednagar	63	70,000	28
5.	Deulgaon siddhi	Ahmednagar	67	50,000	23
6.	Musalwadi	Rahuri	52	100,000	23
7.	Taklibhan	Shrirampur	92	125000	30
8.	Mutewadgaon	Shrirampur	31	80,000	16
9.	Shiral chichondi	Pathardi	30	75000	13
10.	Mohari (P)	Pathardi	40	50000	24
11.	Pampalgaon tappa	Pathardi	43	100000	20
12.	Kuttarwadi	Pathardi	38	70000	15
13.	Pargaon sudrik	Shrigonda	45	100000	25
14.	Autewadi	Shrigonda	60	70000	18
15.	Ghodegaon	Shrigonda	62	300000	22
16.	Limgewadi	Shrigonda	23	50000	20
17.	Kolgaon	Shrigonda	33	110000	20
18.	Rakshaswadi (K)	Shrigonda	54	200000	30
19.	Rui chatrapati	Parner	37	80000	20
20.	Bhalwani	Parner	36	80000	18
21.	Tikhol	Parner	35	50000	15
22.	Jadhavwadi	Parner	22	50000	25
23.	Thergaon	Karjat	27	80000	20
24.	Therwadi	Karjat	99	100000	40
25.	Gurav pimpri	Karjat	96	110000	38
26.	Durgaon	Karjat	67	110000	30
27.	Bhairobawadi	Karjat	76	75000	25
28.	Takli (K)	Karjat	47	100000	25
29.	Rakshaswadi (B)	Karjat	43	100000	30
30.	Yesodi	Karjat	35	80000	22
31.	Naigaon	Jamkhed	57	100000	25
32.	Mohari (J)	Jamkhed	68	70000	22
33.	Bhutwada	Jamkhed	26	70000	19
34.	Pimpalgaon (A)	Jamkhed	48	100000	25
35.	Dhondpargaon	Jamkhed	37	80000	20
36.	Dhotri	Jamkhed	34	50000	18
37.	Kelewadi	Sangamner	15	50000	16
38.	Malunje	Sangamner	28	70000	18
39.	Sangwi	Akole	33	126000	10
40.	Balthan	Akole	27	50000	5

The Bhandardara reservoir (19°31′45"N and 73°45′5"E) located in the western part of Ahmednagar district in the middle of Sahyadri mountain hills. The reservoir is also known as 'wilson dam'. It is the oldest dam which was built in year 1910 on the river Pravara about 500 feet above the mean sea level. The detail morphometry of the reservoir is presented in Table 10.3.

Fig. 10.1: **Bhandardara reservoir**

Table 10.3: Morphometry of Bhandardara Reservoir in Ahmednagar District

1.	River	Pravara
2.	Year of completion	1926
3.	Length of dam (m)	2717
4.	Maximum height above foundation (m)	82.35
5.	Maximum water level (m)	746.04
6.	Full reservoir level (m)	744.725
7.	Gross storage capacity (mcm)	312.4
8.	Live storage capacity (mcm)	307.31
9.	Length of spillway (m)	214.95
10.	Number of spillway gates	2

Gears commonly used in Bhandardara reservoir are hook and line, surface gill net and cast net. Cast net is generally operated in shallow area of the reservoir. Gill net is made up of Garware nylon rope. Wooden boats are commonly used for fishing. The fishery of reservoir is mainly supported by: *Catla catla, Labeo rohita, Cyprinus carpio, Wallago attu, Discognathus modestus, Puntius* spp., and *Mastacembelus armatus.*

REFERENCES

Dhembare, A.J. (2005). Diversity of Zooplankton and Limnological Investigations from Sadatpur dam, Ahmednagar, Maharashtra. *Journal of Experimental Zoology,* 8(2): 313-320.

Pandarkar, A.K., Pawar, B.A. and Shendge, A.N. (2014). Zooplankton Diversity of Visapur Reservoir in Ahmednagar District, Maharashtra. *Journal of Experimental Zoology,* 17(1):327-329.

Pawar, B.A. (2009). Studies on Water Quality and Fish Diversity of Sadatpur Lake in Ahmednagar district, Maharashtra. *J. Indian Fish. Assoc.,* 36:93-100.

Page 142-146

PLANKTON AND FISHERIES
Edited by : V.B. Sakhare; H.K. Jadhav and S.S. Jadhav
Edition : 2017
ISBN : 978-93-5056-811-8
Published by : Discovery Publishing House Pvt. Ltd., New Delhi (India)

11 Studies on Abundance of Zooplankton in Girzani Lake of Soalpur District, Maharashtra

P.H. Agarwal and A.C. Kumbhar
Department of Zoology,
Shankarrao Mohite Mahavidyalaya, Akluj - 413 101

ABSTRACT

Zooplankton are the microscopic heterotropic animals floating in water. Since planktons play a great role in food chain for fish community, understanding of the population of zooplankton is essential. They serve as good indicators of water quality. The present work deals with the study of abundance of zooplankton in Girzani lake of Malshiras Taluka of Solapur District (M.S.) during the period of April 2014 to March 2015. Girzani Lake is situated near Akluj town 130 kms., from Solapur city. The study of the abundance of zooplankton showed that the copepods were found in more percentage during summer of 2015 and less percentage of copepods were found during monsoon season. Percentage of cladoceran was increased in summer followed by monsoon and winter season. Hence no definite pattern of variation was observed.

Keywords: Girzani Lake, Zooplankton, Copepods, Cladoceran, Fish community.

INTRODUCTION

Biodiversity is the variety of organisms present at all levels which includes different ecosystems which comprises of different communities of organisms within particular habitats and the physical conditions under which they live. Aquatic ecosystems are known to support work to range of organisms. Zooplankton are the microscopic heterotrophic animals found floating in water. They play an important role in balancing of food chain of water ecosystem. They act as primary consumers and constitute an important link between primary produces *i.e.,* phytoplanktons and higher consumers like fish. They play a key role in energy transfer. Adequate knowledge of zooplankton communities and their population dynamics is a major requirement for better understanding of life processes in a fresh water body since eutrophication influences both the composition and productivity of zooplanktons. (Shinde *et al.* 2011)

The zooplankton respond quickly to changes of aquatic environment. Therefore they are used as indicator for monitoring the water quality, tropic status and pollution level. The zooplanktons consist of Protozoans, Cladocera, Copepod and Rotifer etc. The present study deals with the study of diversity of zooplanktons from Girazani lake, Malshiras Taluka of Solapur District (M.S.).

Materials and Methods

Water sample for zooplankton analysis was collected from Girzani lake for a period of 12 months from April 2014 to March 2015. Three sampling sites were selected. The zooplanktons were collected by using plankton net. Immediately after collection the zooplanktons were preserved in 4 per cent formalin solution. Stereoscopic microscope was used for the identification of zooplankton. Counting was done by using a device called as Sedgwick Rafter cell. Identification was done by using identification keys described in Edmonson (1959) and Trivedi and Goel (1988).

Results

The results of zooplankton diversity from Girzani lake of Malshiras Taluka of district Solapur is given in the Plate I.

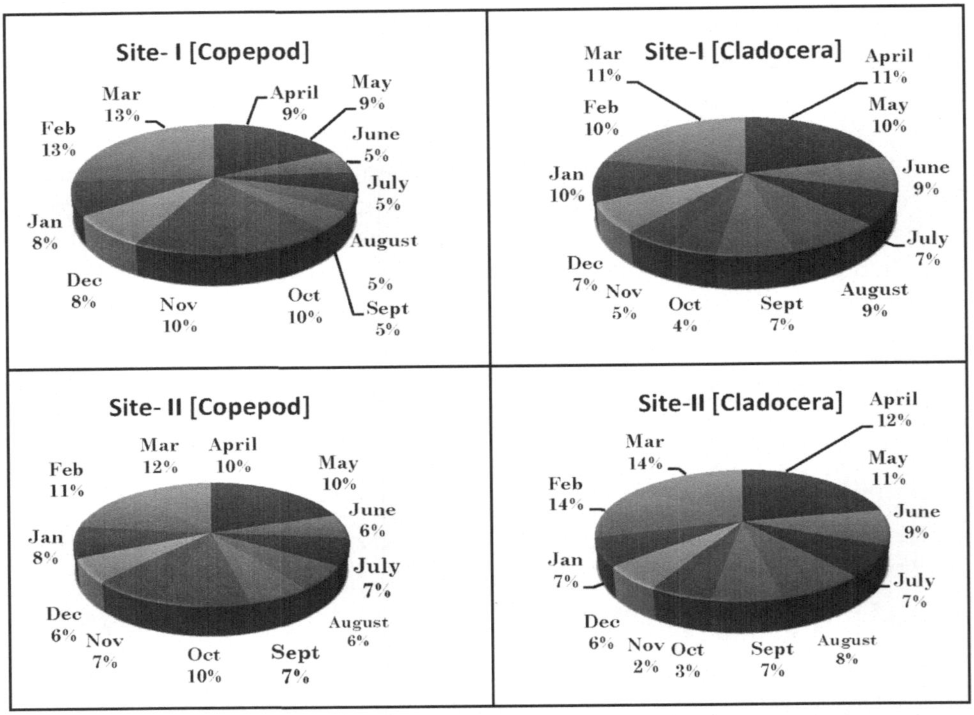

Plate I: Representation of abundance of zooplankton at all sites

The present study reports the zooplankton diversity from Girzani lake of Malshiras Taluka of Solapur district (M.S.). The study reports the abundance of Cladocera and Copepods from the Girzani lake. At site I, the Copepods were very less *i.e.* 5 per cent from June to September and the more percentage of Copepods was 13 per cent in month of February and March. December and January showed 8 per cent Copepods and April and May showed 9 per cent while very less percentage of Cladocerans were present in month of October *i.e.* 4 per cent and in the month of March and April the percentage of Cladocerans were more *i.e.* 11 per cent. In January, February and May the Cladocerans were 10 per cent while in June and August they were 9 per cent and in July, September and December it was 7 per cent while in November they were 5 per cent.

At Site II, the maximum percentage of Copepod was 12 per cent in month of March and minimum percentage was 6 per cent in month of June, August and December. April, May and October showed 10 per cent of

Copepods while July, September and November showed 7 per cent of copepods. In January it showed 8 per cent while in February it showed 11 per cent of Copepods. Whereas, maximum percentage of Cladocerans at site II was 14 per cent in month of February and March and minimum percentage was 2 per cent in month of November. April showed 12 per cent, May showed 11 per cent, June showed 9 per cent while July, September and January showed 7 per cent of Cladocerans. In month of August the percentage of Cladoceran was 8 per cent, in October it was 3 per cent and in December it was 6 per cent.

At Site III, the more percentage of Copepod was 12 per cent in month of November and February while less percentage of Copepod was 4 per cent in month of August and September. April, May and January showed 9 per cent of Copepods while June and July showed 6 per cent of Copepods. In month of October the percentage of Copepods was 10 per cent, in December it was 8 per cent and in March it was 11 per cent. More percentage of Cladocerans at Site III was 12 per cent in month of April while less percentage of Cladoceran was 5 per cent in month of September to November. May and June showed 10 per cent of Cladocerans while July and December showed 7 per cent of Cladocerans. In August the percentage of Cladocerans was 6 per cent while January, February and March showed 11 per cent of Cladocerans.

Discussion

During February to May and also in October and November months there is an increase in temperature which results in enhancement of the water evaporation and production of more number of phytoplanktons which ultimately lead to growth of Copepods. Similar results were noticed at Site II and Site III. Similar results were observed by Dede and Deshmukh (2015) by their study from Bhima river of Solapur district. In the month of December and January appreciable decrease in percentage of Copepods was observed during monsoon season. Opposite findings was observed by Pradhan V.P. (2014) from the study of Wunna lake.

During summer season percentage of Cladocerans were increased followed by monsoon and winter season from all sites. This may be due to favourable environmental condition. Similar observation was done by Thirupathaiah *et al.* (2011) and Patel *et al.* (2013). Copepods were dominant may be due to their feeding on diatoms and Cladocerans and high reproductive capacity (Manickam *et al.* 2014). In the present study similar results were observed at Site II and III.

Conclusion

Our result indicates that as the environmental variation has occurred in the whole year it directly and indirectly affected the total percentage of Cladocerans and Copepods. This finding indicates that the resources available would also help in increasing abundance of zooplanktons. As the site no. II is nearer to the agricultural land, there is an impact of pollution load on this water body. This is because of run off of water used in farming that may cause an effect on abundance of zooplankton, which indicates the lake may undergo the state of eutrophication. Further detailed investigation through regular monthly sampling of zooplankton showed no definite pattern of their variation. To confirm the exact status of water body further investigations are required which would help in conservation of zooplankton diversity and its abundance and also water quality of the Girzani lake.

REFERENCES

Dede, A.N. and Deshmukh, A.L. (2015). Study on Zooplankton Composition and Seasonal Variation in Bhima River near Ramwadi Village, Solapur District (Maharashtra), India, 4 (3) : 297-306.

Javaid, A.S., Ashok, K.P. and Mustafa, G.S. (2013). Distribution, Diversity and Abundance of Copepod Zooplankton of Wular lake, Kashmir Himalaya, 24-29.

Madhusudhana Rao, K., Krishna, P.V., Jyothirmayi, V and Hemanth Kumar, V. (2014). Biodiversity of Zooplankton Communities in a Perennial Pond at Lake Kolleru Region of Andhra Pradesh, India, 7 : (33-41).

Manickam, N., Saravana, B.P., Santhanam, P., Muralisankar, T., Srinivasan, V., Radhakrishnan, S., Vijayadevan, K., Chitrarasu, P. and Jawahar, A.A. (2014). Seasonal Variations of Zooplankton Diversity in a Perennial Reservoir at Thoppaiyar, Dharmapuri District, South India, 1(1) : 7.

Manickam, N., Saravana, B.P., Santhanam, P., Muralisankar, T., Srinivasan, V., Vijayadevan, K., Bhuvaneshwari, R. (2015). Biodiversity of Freshwater Zooplankton and Physic-chemical Parameters of Barur Lake, Krishnagiri District, Tamil Nadu, India, 2(1) : 1-12.

Patel, V., Shukla, S.N. and Patel, V.K. (2013). Studies on the Diversity of Zooplankton and their Seasonal Variation in Govindgarh Lake at Rewa (M.P.), India, 3 (11) : 544-546.

Pradhan, V.P. (2014). Zooplankton Diversity in Fresh Water Wunna lake, 2(3) : 268-272.

Rajashekhar, M., Vijaykumar, K. and Zeba Parveen (2009). Zooplankton Diversity of Three Freshwater Lakes with Relation to Trophic Status, Gulbarga district, North – East Karnataka, South India, 32-37.

Shinde, S.E., Pathan, T.S. and Sonawane, D.L. (2012). Seasonal Variations and Biodiversity of Zooplankton in Harsool-Savangi dam, Aurangabad, India, 741-744.

Sivakami, R., Anumugam, V. and Premkishore, G. (2015). An Analysis of Zooplankton in a Lake, Pudukkottai District, Tamil Nadu, India, 377-389.

Tapas, K.D. and Bidhan, C.P. (2013). Biodiversity and Seasonal Abundance of Zooplankton and its Relation to Physico-chemical Parameters of Jamunabundh, Bishnupur, India.

Thirupathiah, M., Sammatha, C.H. and Sammaiah, C.H. (2011). Diversity of Zooplankton in Freshwater Lake of Kamalapur, Karimnagar District (A.P.) India, 5 (1-2) : 35-40.

Page 147-186

PLANKTON AND FISHERIES

Edited by : **V.B. Sakhare; H.K. Jadhav** and **S.S. Jadhav**

Edition : **2017**

ISBN : 978-93-5056-811-8

Published by : **Discovery Publishing House Pvt. Ltd., New Delhi (India)**

12 Plankton Diversity of Two Reservoirs in Beed District, Maharashtra

P.P. Buktar

Department of Zoology

Yogeshwari Mahavidyalaya, Ambajogai - 431 517.

INTRODUCTION

The word 'plankton' is originated from the Greek term 'planktos' which means 'drifting'. Reservoirs, like: the oceans and streams, have a rich biodiversity within their waters. Two types of plankton are recognized *i.e.,* phytoplankton, which is plants and plant-like forms and zooplankton, which are tiny animals. Knowledge of the plankton in any aquatic ecosystem is crucial for understanding of the entire community of forms living there.

Diurnal variation in light penetration causes some plankton to migrate up and down the water column on a 24-hour cycle. Since algae are plants on which the zooplankton graze and since zooplankton, in turn, provide food for some fish, zooplankton production in a lake is dependent on the algae and in turn, influences fish production and water quality (Mills and Schiavone, 1982). Because of their vast numbers, small size, fragility, and variability, the study of plankton is an involved and demanding process.

The first use of the term 'plankton' is attributed to the German marine biologist, Victor Hensen. According to Hensen's terminology 'plankton' included all organic particles 'which float and involuntarily in the open water, independent of shores and bottom'. The dependence of plankton upon water movements for maintenance and transport is accurately implied in this definition (Greek planktos meaning wandering).

Plankton is used as an indicator to observe and understand changes in the ecosystem because it seems to be strongly influenced by climatic features. (Beaugrand *et al.* 2000; Li *et al.* 2000).

Plankton productivity of water differs considerably from very high to scanty plankton production. The quantitative measure of the production can be expressed by the standing crop, annual crop and average individual weight of each kind of plankton in different environmental conditions.

The larval forms of nearly all species are plankton feeder and growth of a particular fish can be successfully carried out in ponds with good growth of planktons. The presence of a specific type of plankton on which a particular fish lives is absolutely necessary. Thus, the knowledge of about specific plankton is essential for the development of the fishes as it forms the essential diet of particular fish which feeds on the water surface.

Phytoplankton forms the very basis of aquatic food chain. The water quality especially the nutrients influence its population. Phytoplankton survey thus indicates the trophic status and the presence of organic population in the ecosystem. Nutrients enrichment in water bodies is known as 'eutrophication', which is a common phenomenon with algal blooms. Phytoplankton are ecologically significant as they trap radiant energy of sunlight and convert into chemical energy. Many herbivores, mostly zooplankton, graze upon the phytoplankton thus, passing the stored energy to its subsequent trophic levels. The role of phytoplankton in energy budgets of aquatic systems and their importance in establishing their states is well known. The phytoplankton float passively and spread uniformly and extend down to various depths, where light is available for photosynthesis. Excessive nutrient and organic inputs from human activities in lakes and their watersheds lead to eutrophication, characterized by increases in phytoplankton biomass, nuisance algal blooms, loss of water clarity from increased primary production and loss of oxygen in bottom waters. Phytoplankton also are biological indicators of water quality in pollution studies. To summarize, due to their involvement in cycling of energy and matter in an ecosystem, evaluation of phytoplankton population terms of their diversity, density, biomass, spatial and temporal distribution, periodicity and productivity and population turnover, is vital in management of an ecosystem.

Cyanophyceae comprises of prokaryotic organisms popularly known as 'blue-green algae'. They are like gram-negative bacteria and due to the nature of the cell wall, cell structure and capacity to fix atmospheric nitrogen these are considered as bacteria and named cyanobacteria. However, they possess the oxygen evolving photosynthetic system, chlorophyll a accessory pigments and thallus organizations resembling other algae. They occur abundantly in freshwater habitats along with other groups of algae. Cyanophyceae members are broadly classified into coccoid and filamentous forms. The coccoid forms range from single individual cell to aggregates of unicells into groups or in regular or irregular colonies and pseudoparenchymatous conditions. The filament forms range from simple uniseriate filaments to heterotrichous filaments, which may be differentiated into heterocysts and akinetes (spores). These are truly cosmopolitan organisms occurring in habitats of extreme conditions of light, pH and nutritional resources. They abound various types of natural and artificial aquatic ecosystems.

Chlorophyceae (green algae) constitutes one of the major groups of algae occurring in freshwater habitats. The cells are typically green in colour due to the presence of chlorophyll a and b. The cells contain chloroplast of various shapes, which are dispersed differently in each group of organisms. The chloroplast also contains pyrenoids. In majority of the organisms there is a single nucleus but some genera are multinucleate. Flagellated cells are common either in the vegetative phase or reproductive units. Chlorophyceae is generally divided into several orders based on the diversity of the thallus.

The members of Euglenophyceae are single cells, motile found swimming with the help of usually one prominent flagellum and in some cases with two flagella. In the anterior portion a gullet is visible and there are many chloroplasts in the autotrophic forms and the chloroplasts vary in shape. Euglenoid cells are covered by a proteinaceous pellicle and at times help the organisms attain various shapes. These are widely distributed in all types of water bodies specifically in organically rich aquatic ecosystems.

The members belonging to bacillariophyceae are popularly known as 'diatoms'. All are basically unicellular, in some cases become pseudofilamentous or aggregated into colonies. The cell wall of diatoms is impregnated with silica and several diatoms have been well preserved as microfossils. The diatom cell is also called as 'frustule' and the classification of diatoms is based on the pattern of ornamentation on the wall of the 'frustule'. The cells have either bilateral or radial symmetry. The frustules are composed of two halves, epitheca and hypotheca and connecting girdle bands. The valve surfaces have several types of markings. Radial symmetry forms are grouped as Centrales and bilaterally symmetric ones are pennales.

Phytoplankton constitutes the base of the ecological pyramid providing food energy for the higher trophic levels of the aquatic ecosystems. In view of this relationship, attempts have been made to correlate primary productivity and fish yields (*e.g.,* Sreenivasan 1964, 1968; Melack 1979). In addition, phytoplankton is also important as an index of the trophic status of a water body. Relationship between algal associations and lake fertility is also discussed in detail by Hutchinson (1957). Various ecological aspects of phytoplankton have been a subject of study in India by several workers (Singh 1979, Hosmani and Bharathi 1980, Nandan and Patel 1985, 1986, Nandan and Ansari 1999, Khare 1999, Nandan and Jain 2005, Ranjan *et al.* 2007, Sivakumar and Karuppasamy 2008, Dhavale *et al.* 2009, Mohite and Joshi 2009, Nasare *et al.* 2009).

Zooplankton by their heterotrophic activity plays a key role in the cycling of organic materials in aquatic ecosystems and used as bioindicators. The biondicators are evaluated through presence/absence, condition, relative abundance, reproductive success, community structure (*i.e.*, composition and diversity), community function (*i.e.*, trophic structure), or any combination thereof (Hellawell, 1986).

Zooplankton support the economically important fish population. They are the major mode of energy transfer between phytoplankton compositions, abundance and seasonal variations is helpful in planning and successful fishery management (Jhingran, 1974).

Potentiality of zooplankton as bioindicator is very high because their growth and distribution are dependent on some abiotic (*e.g.*, temperature, salinity, stratification, pollutants) and biotic parameters (*e.g.*, food limitation, predation, competition).

Zooplanktons are the central trophic link between primary producers and higher trophic levels. The freshwater zooplankton comprise of Protozoa, Rotifers, Cladocerans, Copepods and Ostracods. Most of them depend to a large extent, on various bacterioplankton and phytoplankton for food. Many of the larger forms feed on smaller zooplankton, forming secondary consumers. Some of them are detritivore feeders, browsing and feeding on the substrate attached organic matter, phytoplankton or concentrating on the freely suspended organic matter particles or those lying on the bottom sediment. Many of these organisms are also fish food organisms and are consumed by the other aquatic macrofauna. The freshwater zooplankton is mainly constituted of five groups:

1. Rotifers, typically an order of magnitude less abundant the protozoans, are the most important soft-bodied metazoans (invertebrates) among the plankton. Their name comes from the apparently rotating wheels of cilia, known as corona, used for locomotion and sweeping food particles towards the mouth. The mouth is generally anterior and the digestive tract contains a set of jaws (trophi) to grasp the food particles and crush them. Relatively few (about 100) ubiquitous rotifer species are planktonic and a much larger number (about 300) are sessile and are associated with sediments and the vegetation of the littoral zones. Planktonic rotifers have a very short-life cycle under favourable conditions of temperature, food and photoperiod. Since the rotifers have short reproductive stages they increase in abundance rapidly under favourable environmental conditions (Dhanapathi, 2000).
2. Crustacea comprises of members all belonging to the well-known phylum arthropoda. This is the largest phylum in terms of number of species and among zooplankton holds the highest position both in terms

of systematics and as secondary consumers in the food chain. In healthy habitats wherein external influences of pollution are absent or at least low, members of this group constitute a sizeable population.

3. Cladocerans are a crucial group among zooplankton and form the most useful and nutritive group of crustaceans for higher members of fishes in the food chain. Cladocerans are normally covered by the chitinous covering termed as the carapace. The two large second antennae are responsible for giving the cladocerans their common name, water fleas and are used for rowing through the water. Cladocerans are filter feeders as they filter the water to trap the organisms in it. Cladocerans are highly sensitive against even low concentrations of pollutants. The food source of this group is smaller zooplankton, bacterioplankton and algae (Murugan *et al.* 1998). Cladocerand have been described from all over the world including the Indian subcontinent (Birge 1918, Daday 1911 and Pennak 1978). Out of the eleven families of cladocera, 8 families have been reported from Indian waters which represents about one-fourth of the world cladoceran fauna Rao and Chaubey (1993).
4. The Copepods comprise of calanoids, cyclopoids and harpacticoids. The copepods also form important organisms for fish and are influenced by negative environmental factors as caused by excessive human interference in water bodies but to a lesser extent than the Cladocerans. Copepods are much hardier and strongly motile than all other zooplankton with their tougher exoskeleton and longer and stronger appendages. They have long developmental time and a complex life history with early larval stages difficult to distinguish. They are almost wholly carnivorous on the smaller zooplankton for their food needs. Among the three orders of copepods, cyclopoid copepods are generally predatory on (carnivorous) on other zooplankton, and fish larvae. The cyclopoid copepods also feed on algae, bacteria and detritus. The second group of copepods, calanoid copepods change their diet with age, sex, season, and food availability. The calanoid copepods are omnivorous feeding on ciliates, rotifers, algae, bacteria and detritus. The third group harpacticoid copepods are primarily benthic. Copepods, in general can withstand harsher environmental conditions as compared to cladocera (Kalff, 2002).
5. The Ostracods are bivalved organisms and belong to phylum Arthropoda. They mainly inhabit the lake bottom and among macrophytes and feed on detritus and dead plankton. Ostracods are in turn consumed by fishes and benthic macro-invertebrates (Chakrapani *et al.* 1996). There are over 1700 species of known ostracods of which about one-third are freshwater forms. They inhibit a wide variety of freshwaters likes: lakes, pools, swamps, streams and heavily polluted areas (Edmondson, 1959).

Zooplankton constitutes an important link in food chain as grazers (primary and secondary consumers) and serves as food for fishes directly or indirectly. Therefore any adverse effect to them will be indicated in the wealth of the fish populations. Thus, monitoring them as biological indicators of pollution could act as a forewarning for the fisheries particularly when the pollution affects the food chain (Mahajan, 1981). Thus, the use of zooplankton for ecological biomonitoring of the water bodies helps in the analysis of water quality trends, development of cause-effect relationships between water quality and environmental data and judgment of the adequacy of water quality for various uses.

Zooplankton communities of freshwaters constitute an extremely diverse assemblage of organisms represented by nearly all the phyla of invertebrates. The most significant feature of zooplankton is its immense diversity over space and time. In an ecosystem 90 per cent of zooplankton species are herbivorous, remaining 10 per cent being carnivore. Studies on the aquatic systems reveal that the structure of the zooplankton community is quite characteristic and is the product of the environmental conditions prevailing there. Several zooplankton species have been classified as indicative of polluted conditions like: *Keratella, Brachionus, Cephalopoda, Monostyla, Lecane, Bosminia, Adona, Alonella, Cyclops* and several members of the group protozoa (Rawson 1956 and Pennak 1978).

The variability observed in the distribution of zooplankton is due to abiotic parameters (*e.g.*, climatic or hydrological parameters: temperature, salinity, stratification, advection), to biotic parameters (*e.g.*, food limitation, predation, competition) or to a combination of both (Beyst *et al.* 2001, Christou, 1998, Escribano and Hidalgo, 2000 and Roff *et al.* 1988). Although zooplankton exists under a wide range of environmental conditions, yet many species are limited by temperature, dissolved oxygen, salinity and other physicochemical factors. The use of zooplankton for environmental characterization of lakes is potentially advantageous. Zooplankton species tend to have wide geographic distributions (Carter *et al.* 1980 and Shurin *et al.* 2000), so local differences in community occurrence do not generally result from dispersal limitation. Tropic roles (predators, herbivores, omnivores) are well represented in the zooplankton, and individual generation times are short enough that they quickly respond to acute stress but long enough for them to integrate the effects of chronic problems, making them favourable candidates for a community indicator of ecosystem health (Cairns *et al.* 1993). Finally, zooplankton are relatively easy to identify, so they are particularly useful when community sensitivity can be detected based on zooplankton body sizes or gross taxonomic classifications.

Multi-lake studies have been used to explore variations in the zooplankton community along a number of limnological gradients. For example, zooplankton community size structure has been used as an indicator of lake trophic status (Bays and Crisman, 1983, Beaver and Crisman, 1990, Canfield and Jones, 1996 and Pace, 1986). Studies have compared the abundance and biomass of micro - and macro-zooplankton (Bays and Crisman, 1983, Pace, 1986 and Sprules *et al.* 1988) to algal chlorophylls (Canfield and Jones, 1996), Carlson's Trophic State Index (Bays and Crisman, 1983), and nutrients (Pace, 1986 and Sprules, 1977). Zooplankton indicator species have been used to determine shifts in trophic state (*e.g.*, Fuller *et al.* 1977 and Sprules, 1977). Several studies have examined differences in rotifer communities in lakes of various trophic states (Beaver and Crisman, 1990, Fuller *et al.* 1977 and Gannon and Stemberger, 1978). Abundance of selected major zooplankton groups (*e.g.*, Rotifera, Copepoda) has also been used to show changes in trophic state (Gannon and Stemberger, 1978 and Pace, 1986).

The density of plankton in a water body determines the stocking rate of fishes because they are the chief source of food of many economically important fishes. Plankton, due to its key role in the ecosystem of the environment, is directly related to the fish catch potential of a reservoir. An insight into the distribution, composition and succession of plankton gives valuable clue for determining the fishing grounds, selection of suitable species for stocking and determining the level of utilization of the available food by the existing fish stock.

The zooplankton study has been a fascinating subject for a long time. Enough literature exists on the plankton of various water bodies (Saha and Pandit, 1990, Singh and Ahmed 1990, Sugunan 1980, Singh 1960, More and Nandan 2000, Yazdandoost and Katdare 2000, Pendse *et al.* 2000, Bahura 2001 and Shukla *et al.* 1989). Such studies from state of Maharashtra have been very recently initiated and the only contributions on this aspect are those of Deshmukh (2001), Meshram and Dhande (2000), Pulle and Khan (2003), Sakhare (2007), Sakhare and Joshi (2002, 2006) and Goel and Autade (1995).

Morphometry of Reservoirs

Wan reservoir was constructed in 1963 at village Nagapur of Parli Vaijanath tahsil in Beed district of Marathwada region, Maharashtra. Reservoir site is about 14 kms., away to west side of Parli vaijanath town. Reservoir lies in between 180-53′-0" N. latitude and 760-27′-0" E. longitude. It is an earthen dam with 19.81 meters height and 2188.40 meters length. It was constructed across river Wan. Reservoir have 379.92 sq.kms., catchment area with gross capacity of 25.181 MCM (Table 12.1).

Reservoir was mainly constructed for irrigation, drinking water and water supply for thermal power station at Parli-Vaijanath. Reservoir has two canals *viz;* left canal and right canal. The length of left canal is 12.87 kms., head discharge capacity is 1.77 m^3/s, and area under irrigation is 3965 hectare. Near about 13 villages are benefited by this canal *viz;* Safdarabad, Mandekhel, Tadoli, Parchondi, Malhiwra, Gopalpur, Bhilegaon, Malnithpur, Selu, Revali, Pimpalgaon, Sirsala, Kanadi etc.

The length of right canal is 9.65 kms., head discharge capacity 1.75 m^3/s, irrigational area is 3602 hectare. Near about 10 villages are benefited by right canal *viz;* Nagapur, Limbota, Pangari, Deshmukh Takli, Talegaon, Kowthali, Belamba, Tokwadi, Sangam, Wagbet.

Table 12.1: Morphometry of Wan Reservoir

1.	Location	Latitude 180-53'-0" N. and Longitude.760-27'-0" E.
2.	Catchment Area	379.92 sq. kms.
3.	Average rainfall	525.00 mm.
4.	Annual yield	40.662 McM.
5.	Submergence area	347.00 ha.
6.	Gross storage	25.181 McM.
7.	Net storage	21.912 McM.
8.	Silt pocket	3.270 McM.
9.	Lowest sill level	446.34 m.
10.	Full tank level	454.87 m.
11.	High flood level	456.40 m.
12.	Top bund level	457.92 m.
13.	Length of west-weir	617.50 m.
14.	Designed flood discharge	2348 Cumes
15.	Irrigation area	7567 ha
16.	Length of canal	12.3 kms. (Right canal) 9.65 kms. (Left canal)
17.	Head discharge of canal	1.77 m^3/s (left) 75 m^3/s (right)
18.	Area under irrigation	3602 ha (right canal) 3965 ha(left canal)
19.	Total cost of the project	154.49 lac.
20.	Year of filling	1966

Borna reservoir is located at village Nandnaj in Parli Vaijanath tahsil of Beed district. Reservoir is about 12 kms., away from east side of Parli vaijanath town. Construction of reservoir was started across river Borna in 1976 and completed in 1981. Reservoir lies in between 180-51'-30" N. latitude and 760-36'-30" E. longitude. It is an earthen dam of 21.65 meters height and 856 meters in length. Catchment area and gross capacity of reservoir is 110.59 sq.kms., and 10.81 McM respectively (Table 12.2).

Reservoir has two canals *viz;* left canal and right canal. The length of left canal is 10.18 kms., head discharge capacity is 0.621 m^3/s. The length of right canal is 14.80 kms., head discharge capacity 0.81 m^3/s. The collective irrigational area of both canals is 2405 hectare. Near about 8 villages are benefited by both canals *viz;* Kasarwadi, Ukhali, Mankadevi, Kuram, Dadahari vadgaon, Mandva, Saradgaon, Nandnaj.

Table 12.2: Morphometry of Borna Reservoir

1.	Location	Latitude 180-51'-30" N. and Longitude.760-36'-30" E.
2.	Catchment Area	110.59 sq. kms.
3.	Submergence area	219 ha.
4.	Gross storage	10.81 McM.
5.	Net storage	8.97 McM.
6.	Silt pocket	1.84 McM.
7.	Lowest sill level	429.50 m.
8.	Full tank level	439.45 m.
9.	High flood level	439.45 m.
10	Top bund level	441.45 m.
11.	Designed flood discharge	1246 Cumes.
12.	Irrigation area	2405 ha.
13.	Length of canal	14.80 kms. (Right canal), 10.18 kms. (Left canal)
14.	Head discharge of canal	0.621 m^3/s (left) 0.81 m^3/s (right)
15.	Area under irrigation	1376 ha.
16.	Year of filling	1981

Materials and Methods

Standard methodology after Welch (1952) with suitable modifications to suit local availability was used. Procedure adopted is briefly described below:

(a) Collection.

(b) Preservation and transportation.

(c) Washing.

(d) Qualitative analysis.

(e) Quantitative analysis.

(a) *Collection:* Collection of planktons was done by using a plankton net with 38 cm diameter of the mouth and a bolting silk No. 20 (173 meshes/ inch). An iron tube was firmly tied to the tapering end of the net and the open end of the plankton collecting tube was covered by a piece of bolting silk, securely tied with cotton thread so that plankton collected through the net could be easily transferred into separate plastic bottles.

(b) *Preservation and transportation:* Initial study for taxonomic identification and general behaviour was carried out on live plankton. Subsequently, quantitative estimations were made on plankton preserved in 5 per cent formalin. An ice container was used for live transportation to the laboratory.

Satellite Image of Wan Reservoir

Satellite Image of Bora Reservoir

(c) *Washing:* Samples collected from Wan and Borna reservoir were easily washed with formalin water. For this purpose a glass funnel and a piece of bolting silk were used. By using a wash bottle containing formalin water, washing was carried out in the following manner:

The whole plankton sample was measured (used for quantitative estimation) and diluted to a desirable concentration depending upon the density of plaktonic population in such a way that they could be easily counted individually under light binocular microscope. For dilution a polson plankton splitter was used. Generally one fourth of the total biomass in a sample was used for washing to minimize error. This small fraction of collected plankton material was transferred on a set of different mesh size sieves and shaken gently. By this procedure, it was possible to remove easily the fine debris and soil particles. After that, the whole plankton material was collected in Petri-plate containing formalin water. At this stage, the sample containing some plant material and some other foreign particles were easily removed with the help of different size brushes. Finally, the remaining plankton material was transferred to fresh formalin solution and the whole plankton concentration was measured and multiplied with the dilution factor, already made by splitter.

(d) *Qualitative analysis:* For qualitative analysis, a light binocular and an inverted plankton microscope are used. As far as possible, the animals were identified up to species level.

Preliminary identification was made by using Pennak (1978), Battish (1992), Michael (1973) and Dhanapathi (2000) as basic references.

The rotifers were ordinarily distinguished at species level by trophic characteristics in whole animal. Although in some difficult cases animals were crushed with the help of 2 micro-needles to force animal out.

Generally, the cladocerans were identified by carapace characteristics, although in a number of cases a minor dissection of post abdominal segment with the help of 2 mico-needles was carried out. After dissection, these abdominal segments were observed under high power in a glycerine mount.

Copepods were generally identified with the help of body appendages and for species identification a minor dissection on the 5th leg was carried out in a glycerine mount. Animal or dissected part as observed under high power.

For identification of ostracods, body shell was removed to study detailed structure. These animals also required a minor dissection of furca. After dissection, furca was observed under high power in glycerine.

(e) *Quantitative estimation:* For quantitative estimation of plankton, a Sedgwick-Rafter counting cell of mm2 and micropipette of glass van grade I of 1, 2 and 5 ml capacity were used. For this purpose, 1 ml of plankton sample was drawn and transferred to the Sedgwick-Rafter counting cell. Observations were made under the binoculars and counting was done up to genetic level. For the sake of convenience, blood cell counter make was used for accurate and quick counting. The procedure was repeated 5 times to get an average. The total population of individual plankton genera in a reservoir was calculated by the following formula:

N = n x1/w

Where,

N = Number of individuals of a species per cubic meter

n = Number of individuals of a species in 1 ml.

1 = Dilution factor

w = Amount of water hauled

When the plankton were collected by filtration the pollution of a species was calculated as follows:

N = nxdx10/w

Where,

N = Number of individuals of a species in cubic meter

n = Average number of individual of a species in one ml

d = Dilution factor

w = Amount of water filtered.

Results

Zooplankton Diversity in Wan Reservoir

Zooplanktons were represented by protozoa, rotifera, cladocera, copepoda and ostracoda. The seasonal variation in zooplankton of Wan reservoir during year 2009-10 and 2010-11 are presented in Table 12.3 and 4 respectively.

Rotifers were dominant with eight species *i.e., Branchionus flacatus, Brachionus calyciflorus, Brachionus diversicornis, Filina longiseta, Keratella tropica, Keratella quadrata, Lecane bulla,* and *Trichocera porecellus* in Wan reservoir throughout the study period.

During 2009-10 Rotifers accounted for 38.2 per cent of the total zooplankton showing maximum (265 org./liter) in April during summer and minimum (51 org./liter) in September during monsoon. While during 2010-11 Rotifers accounted for 37.33 per cent of the total zooplankton with maxima (245 org./liter) in April during summer and minimum (41 org./liter) in June during monsoon.

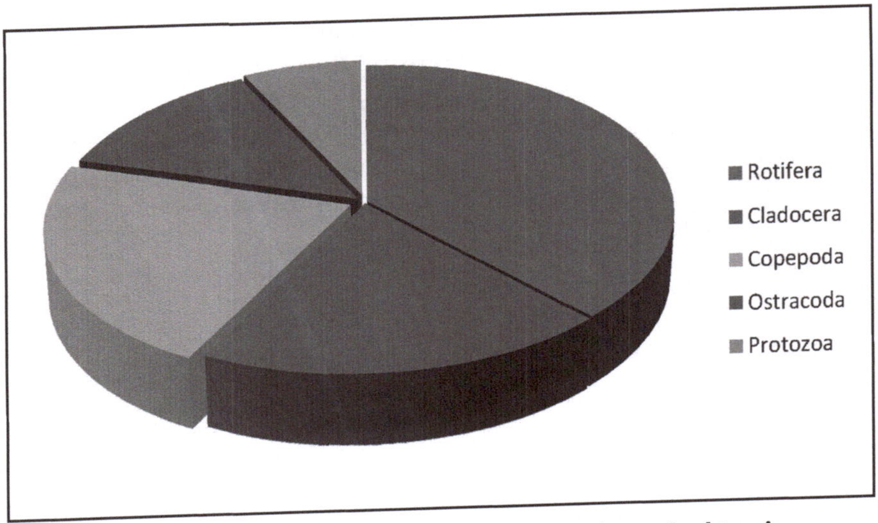

Fig. 12.1: **The percentage of composition of zooplankton in Wan reservoir (Year 2009-2010)**

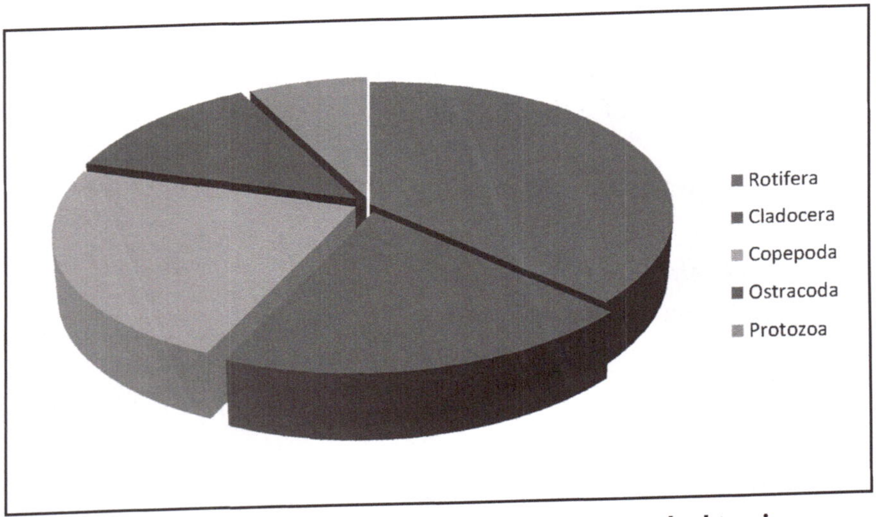

Fig. 12.2: **The percentage of composition of zooplankton in Wan reservoir (Year 2010-11)**

During 2009-10 Cladocera accounted for 19.6 per cent of the total zooplankton with six species *i.e., Indialona ganapati, Moina micrura, Diaphanosma sarsi, Alona rectangular, Ceriodaphnia cornuta,* and *Diaphanosoma excisum.* The maximum (164 org./liter) in April during summer and minimum (14 org./liter) in June during monsoon. While during 2010-11 Cladocera accounted for 19.6 per cent of the total zooplankton with maxima (155 org./liter) in April during summer and minimum (17 org./liter) in August during monsoon.

Copepods were with five species *i.e., Diaptomus marshianus, Phylladiaptomus linddbergi, Mesocyclops leukarti, Mesocyclops hyalinus,* and *Cyclops viridis* in Wan reservoir throughout the study period.

During 2009-10 Copepoda accounted for 22.2 per cent of the total zooplankton showing maximum (155 org./liter) in April during summer and minimum (28 org./liter) in June during monsoon. While during 2010-11 Copepoda accounted for 23.2 per cent of the total zooplankton with maxima (149 org./liter) in April during summer and minimum (29 org./liter) in June during monsoon.

During 2009-10 Ostracoda accounted for 12.8 per cent of the total zooplankton showing maximum (85 org./liter) in month of may during summer and minimum (05 org./liter) in June and July during monsoon. While during 2010-11 Ostracoda accounted for 12.4 per cent of the total zooplankton with maxima (79 org./liter) in month of May during summer and minimum (07 org./liter) in July during monsoon.

Table 12.3: Monthly Analysis of Zooplanktons Diversity in Wan Reservoir (2009-10)

Species/Month	Feb.	Mar.	Apr.	May	June	July	Aug.	Sept.	Oct.	Nov.	Dec.	Jan.
1	2	3	4	5	6	7	8	9	10	11	12	13
Rotifera												
Brachionus calyciflorus	18	29	35	25	05	10	10	16	17	20	23	22
Brachionus falcatus	17	23	39	24	00	05	05	08	17	16	23	24
Brachionus diversicornis	23	19	35	22	10	10	10	12	14	23	17	19
Keratella tropica	20	35	34	25	15	10	05	05	05	16	18	21
Keratella quadrata	17	21	35	20	05	05	05	00	08	14	21	18
Lecane (monostyla) bulla	16	23	34	25	10	05	10	05	13	15	16	21
Trichocera porcellus	26	31	35	26	05	04	10	05	14	17	21	23
Filina longiseta	15	10	18	22	10	05	00	00	12	14	11	15
Total	152	191	265	189	60	54	55	51	100	135	150	163
Cladocera												
Indialona ganapati	21	22	28	22	02	05	00	00	04	04	15	20
Moina micrura	18	27	30	20	04	04	00	04	02	05	04	10
Diaphanosoma sarsi	16	25	28	21	02	05	02	00	02	05	04	20
Diaphanosoma excisum	18	23	28	21	02	00	05	05	05	05	10	12
Alona rectangular	17	22	28	20	02	02	02	00	05	05	15	15
Ceriodaphnia cornuta	10	14	22	12	12	14	15	18	11	08	05	00
Total	100	133	164	116	14	30	24	27	29	32	53	77

Contd...

1	2	3	4	5	6	7	8	9	10	11	12	13
Copepoda												
Diaptomus marshianus	19	24	28	21	05	05	04	05	10	12	15	15
Phylladiaptomus lindbergi	24	26	29	22	10	10	04	05	10	10	16	20
Mescyclops leukarti	23	28	34	21	05	04	04	10	15	15	10	18
Mesocyclops hyalinus	22	26	35	19	04	04	04	10	15	18	15	18
Cyclops viridis	18	22	29	10	05	06	12	15	18	10	20	18
Total	106	126	155	93	29	29	28	45	68	65	76	89
Ostracoda												
Cypris obensa	24	27	24	28	00	00	05	05	14	16	17	19
Cyclocypris globosa	19	25	25	33	00	00	10	10	08	12	18	20
Candocypria osborni	18	23	28	24	05	05	15	20	15	05	00	08
Total	61	75	77	85	05	05	30	35	37	33	35	47

Table 12.4: Monthly Analysis of Zooplanktons Diversity in Wan Reservoir (2010-11)

Species/Month	Feb.	Mar.	Apr.	May	June	July	Aug.	Sept.	Oct.	Nov.	Dec.	Jan.
1	2	3	4	5	6	7	8	9	10	11	12	13
Rotifera												
Brachionus calyciflorus	16	25	32	22	05	05	05	10	15	18	21	19
Brachionus falcatus	15	26	36	21	00	05	05	08	17	16	23	18
Brachionus diversicornis	20	22	33	20	05	10	10	12	14	23	17	21
Keratella tropica	18	31	35	23	11	10	05	05	05	15	16	21
Keratella quadrata	15	26	30	20	05	05	05	00	08	14	20	16
Lecane (monostyla) bulla	14	24	31	21	10	05	10	05	13	15	16	24
Trichocera porcellus	22	30	32	22	05	04	10	05	14	17	21	21
Filina longiseta	13	15	16	20	00	05	00	00	12	13	11	10
Total	133	199	245	169	41	49	50	45	98	131	145	150
Cladocera												
Indialona ganapati	18	24	26	20	05	10	00	00	04	04	16	21
Moina micrura	16	25	31	22	04	04	00	04	02	05	04	10
Diaphanosoma sarsi	14	23	24	24	02	05	02	00	02	05	04	22
Diaphanosoma excisum	15	21	25	20	02	00	05	05	05	05	10	12
Alona rectangular	16	20	26	18	02	02	02	00	05	05	14	12
Ceriodaphnia cornuta	06	12	23	10	10	05	08	18	11	08	05	00
Total	85	125	155	114	25	26	17	27	29	32	53	77

Contd...

1	2	3	4	5	6	7	8	9	10	11	12	13
Copepoda												
Diaptomus marshianus	17	26	26	25	05	05	04	05	10	12	16	17
Phylladiaptomus lindbergi	25	26	29	23	10	10	05	05	10	13	16	22
Mescyclops leukarti	21	25	34	22	05	06	06	10	15	16	18	21
Mesocyclops hyalinus	22	26	35	15	04	04	04	10	15	18	15	14
Cyclops viridis	16	20	25	11	05	06	12	15	18	10	14	13
Total	101	123	149	96	29	31	31	45	68	69	79	87
Ostracoda												
Cypris obensa	23	21	20	25	04	00	05	05	12	15	16	18
Cyclocypris globosa	17	22	21	31	00	02	12	10	08	12	18	21
Candocypria osborni	16	21	24	23	05	05	15	12	15	05	00	07
Total	56	64	65	79	09	07	32	27	35	32	34	46

Zooplankton Diversity in Borna Reservoir

Zooplanktons were represented by protozoa, rotifera, cladocera, copepoda and ostracoda. The seasonal variation in zooplankton of Borna reservoir during year 2009-10 and 2010-11 are presented in Table 12.5 and 12.6 respectively.

Rotifers were dominant with eight species *i.e., Branchionus flacatus, Brachionus calyciflorus, Brachionus diversicornis, Filina longiseta, Keratella tropica, Keratella quadrata, Lecane bulla,* and *Trichocera porecellus* in Borna reservoir throughout the study period.

Cladocera was with six species *i.e., Indialona ganapati, Moina micrura, Diaphanosma sarsi, Alona rectangular, Ceriodaphnia cornuta,* and *Diaphanosoma excisum.* Copepods were with five species *i.e. Diaptomus marshianus, Phylladiaptomus linddbergi, Mesocyclops leukarti, Mesocyclops hyalinus,* and *Cyclops viridis.*

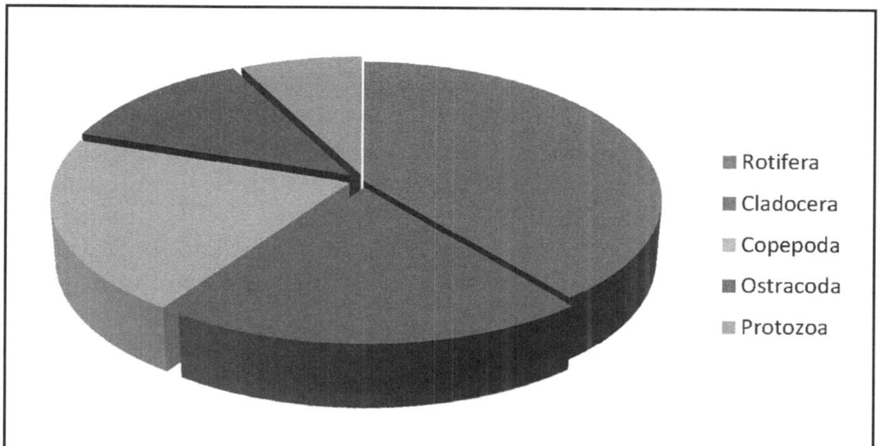

Fig. 12.3: **The percentage of composition of zooplankton in Borna reservoir (Year 2009-10)**

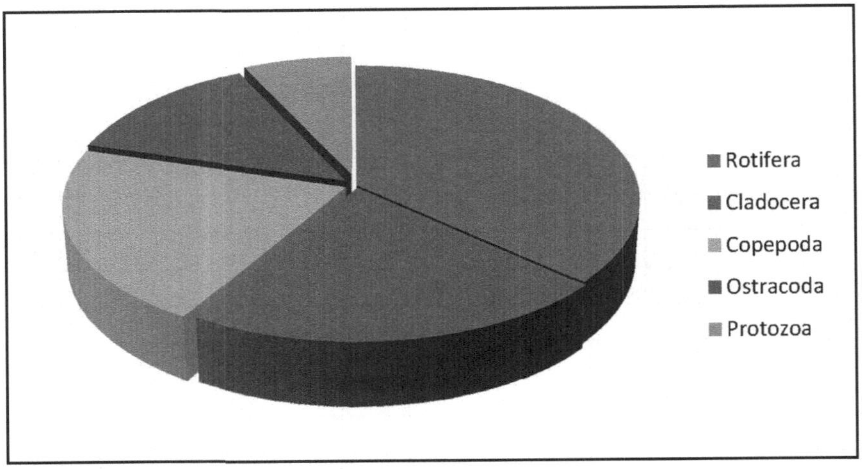

Fig. 12.4: **Thepercentage of composition of zooplankton in Borna reservoir (Year 2010-11)**

Ostracoda included just three species *Cypris obensa, Cyclocypris globosa,* and *Candocypria osborni* in Borna reservoir during study period.

During 2009-10 Rotifers accounted for 39.10 per cent of the total zooplankton showing maximum (224 org./liter) in April during summer and minimum (53 org./liter) in September during monsoon. While during 2010-11 Rotifers accounted for 36.7 per cent of the total zooplankton with maxima (218 org./liter) in April during summer and minimum (21 org./liter) in June during monsoon.

During 2009-10 Cladocera accounted for 20.25 per cent of the total zooplankton showing maximum (160 org./liter) in month of May during summer and minimum (20 org./liter) in August during monsoon. While during 2010-11 Cladocera accounted for 21.8 per cent of the total zooplankton with maxima (181 org./liter) in month of May during summer and minimum (19 org./liter) in July, August and September during monsoon.

During 2009-10 Copepoda accounted for 20.7 per cent of the total zooplankton showing maximum (138 org./liter) in April during summer and minimum (15 org./liter) in July during monsoon. While during 2010-11 Copepoda accounted for 21.13 per cent of the total zooplankton with maxima (149 org./liter) in month of May during summer and minimum (12 org./liter) in June during monsoon.

During 2009-10 Ostracoda accounted for 12.4 per cent of the total zooplankton showing maximum (78 org./liter) in month of may during summer and minimum (10 org./liter) in June and July during monsoon. While during 2010-11 Ostracoda accounted for 13.23 per cent of the total zooplankton with maxima (75 org./liter) in April during summer and minimum (02 org./liter) in July during monsoon.

Table 12.5: Monthly Analysis of Zooplanktons Diversity in Borna Reservoir (2009-10)

Species/Month	Feb.	Mar.	Apr.	May	June	July	Aug.	Sept.	Oct.	Nov.	Dec.	Jan.
1	2	3	4	5	6	7	8	9	10	11	12	13
Rotifera												
Brachionus calyciflorus	24	30	26	28	10	15	18	19	19	22	24	26
Brachionus falcatus	23	25	29	35	15	05	05	08	15	10	20	26
Brachionus diversicornis	20	22	27	23	12	11	10	14	14	20	19	20
Keratella tropica	23	30	34	35	15	10	05	05	05	12	11	18
Keratella quadrata	22	23	27	23	08	06	05	00	05	11	20	16
Lecane (monostyla) bulla	21	18	21	23	04	03	10	02	13	10	15	20
Trichocera porcellus	25	27	32	26	05	04	08	05	14	16	21	19
Filina longiseta	17	20	28	21	04	05	00	00	10	11	13	15
Total	175	195	224	214	73	59	61	53	95	112	143	160
Cladocera												
Indialona ganapati	16	18	15	27	02	06	00	00	03	06	12	19
Moina micrura	15	21	32	21	04	05	00	03	02	06	04	16
Diaphanosoma sarsi	17	18	23	27	05	05	04	00	03	04	05	21
Diaphanosoma excisum	14	22	26	29	03	00	05	05	06	05	10	16
Alona rectangular	18	23	27	33	02	04	06	00	05	04	16	17
Ceriodaphnia cornuta	06	15	18	23	18	10	05	00	10	08	05	11
Total	86	117	141	160	34	30	20	08	29	33	52	100
Copepoda												
Diaptomus marshianus	16	23	29	21	05	06	04	00	10	12	15	19
Phylladiaptomus lindbergi	20	23	27	21	10	00	03	02	10	11	15	15
Mescyclops leukarti	17	25	28	26	05	04	02	10	13	14	11	16
Mesocyclops hyalinus	15	23	28	18	00	00	04	11	12	18	16	14
Cyclops viridis	12	20	24	06	10	05	10	05	16	21	24	26
Total	80	114	138	92	30	15	23	28	61	76	81	90
Ostracoda												
Cypris obensa	15	27	25	26	00	05	08	05	12	12	13	16
Cyclocypris globosa	16	21	23	32	05	00	10	12	08	10	15	18
Candocypria osborni	15	16	15	20	05	05	15	20	14	05	00	05
Total	46	64	63	78	10	10	33	37	34	27	28	39

Table 12.6: Monthly Analysis of Zooplanktons Diversity in Borna Reservoir (2010-11)

Species/Month	Feb.	Mar.	Apr.	May	June	July	Aug.	Sept.	Oct.	Nov.	Dec.	Jan.
1	2	3	4	5	6	7	8	9	10	11	12	13
Rotifera												
Brachionus calyciflorus	23	29	33	27	02	07	11	12	12	18	24	23
Brachionus falcatus	17	21	28	32	02	03	03	04	15	15	20	21
Brachionus diversicornis	20	22	23	21	03	04	10	14	15	20	15	17
Keratella tropica	23	31	34	28	10	02	00	05	06	14	11	19
Keratella quadrata	17	21	26	30	00	02	03	00	05	11	21	18
Lecane (monostyla) bulla	20	22	21	16	00	06	10	05	11	13	16	23
Trichocera porcellus	23	31	34	28	00	04	11	04	16	14	21	23
Filina longiseta	14	11	19	28	04	02	00	00	04	13	13	17
Total	157	188	218	210	21	30	48	44	84	118	141	161
Cladocera												
Indialona ganapati	17	18	16	28	00	06	00	00	05	06	16	21
Moina micrura	19	21	31	23	02	05	00	04	02	06	03	12
Diaphanosoma sarsi	16	18	28	29	00	04	02	00	03	05	04	10
Diaphanosoma excisum	13	21	28	35	05	00	05	04	05	06	11	15
Alona rectangular	16	21	31	34	08	00	02	00	05	02	14	11
Ceriodaphnia cornuta	18	21	24	32	10	04	10	11	12	05	06	12
Total	99	120	158	181	25	19	19	19	32	30	54	81
Copepoda												
Diaptomus marshianus	15	21	17	30	02	04	02	06	11	14	16	10
Phylladiaptomus lindbergi	20	24	28	32	05	04	04	05	10	12	15	14
Mescyclops leukarti	18	21	20	29	00	03	03	10	12	12	10	15
Mesocyclops hyalinus	15	21	25	30	00	02	04	11	14	15	14	15
Cyclops viridis	14	11	14	28	05	00	10	15	18	20	21	15
Total	82	98	104	149	12	13	23	47	65	73	76	69
Ostracoda												
Cypris obensa	19	27	24	26	00	00	04	03	14	14	16	18
Cyclocypris globosa	20	26	32	30	05	00	11	12	06	11	19	21
Candocypria osborni	18	16	19	12	00	02	10	14	17	08	15	19
Total	57	69	75	68	05	02	25	29	37	33	50	58

Table 12.7: List of Zooplanktons in Wan and Borna Resevoirs

Rotifera:	*Branchionus flacatus, Brachionus calyciflorus, Brachionus diversicornis, Filina longiseta, Keratella tropica, Keratella quadrata, Lecane bulla, Trichocera porecellus*
Cladocera:	*Indialona ganapati, Moina micrura, Diaphanosma sarsi, Alona rectangular, Ceriodaphnia cornuta, Diaphanosoma excisum*
Copepoda:	*Diaptomus marshianus, Phylladiaptomus linddbergi, Mesocyclops leukarti, Mesocyclops hyalinus, Cyclops viridis*
Ostracoda:	*Cypris obensa, Cyclocypris globosa, Candocypria osborni*

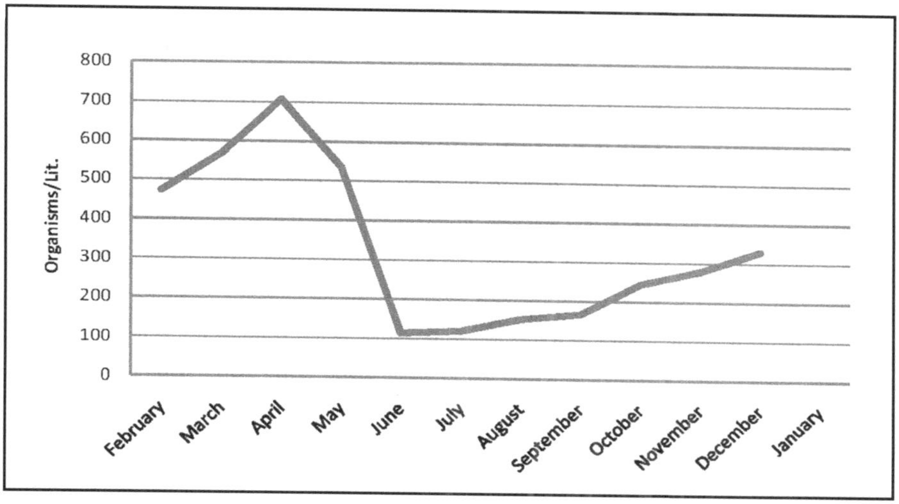

Fig. 12.5: **Monthly fluctuations in zooplanktons in wan reservoir during year 2009-10**

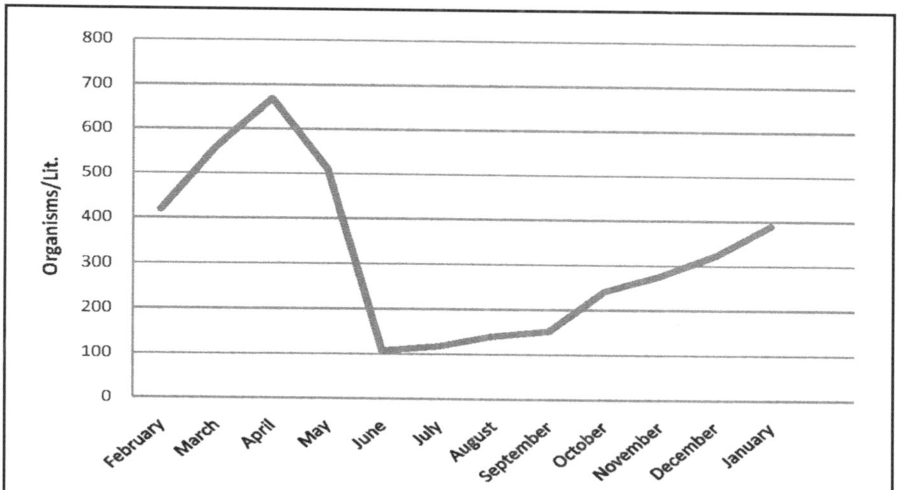

Fig. 12.6: **Monthly fluctuations in zooplanktons in wan reservoir during year 2010-11**

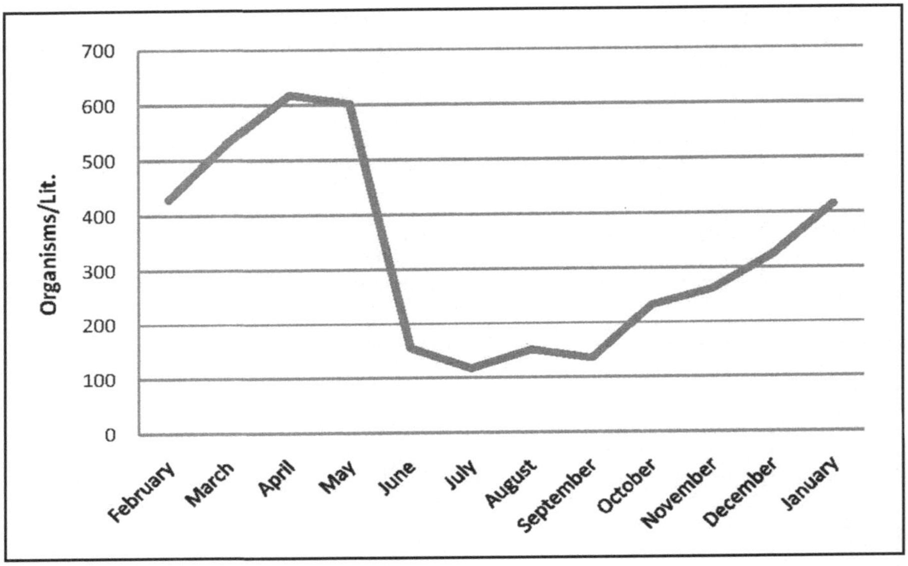

Fig. 12.7: **Monthly fluctuations in zooplanktons in Borna reservoir during year 2009-10**

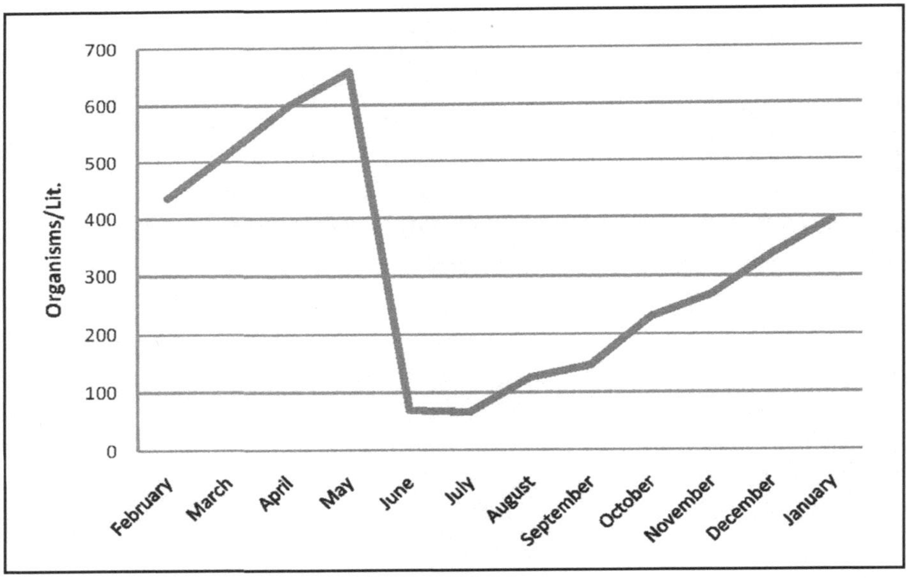

Fig 12.8: **Monthly fluctuations in zooplanktons in Borna reservoir during year 2010-11**

Phytoplankton Diversity

Altogther, 10 species of chlorophyceae, 5 species of cyanophyceae, 6 species of bacillariophyceae and 3 species of euglenophyceae were recorded from both the reservoirs (Table 12.8).

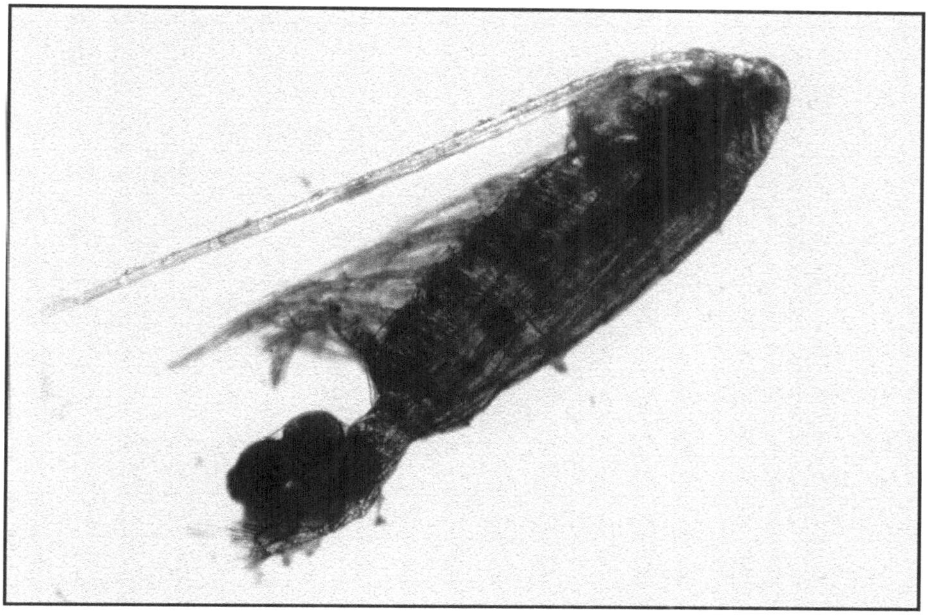

Cyclops Sp.

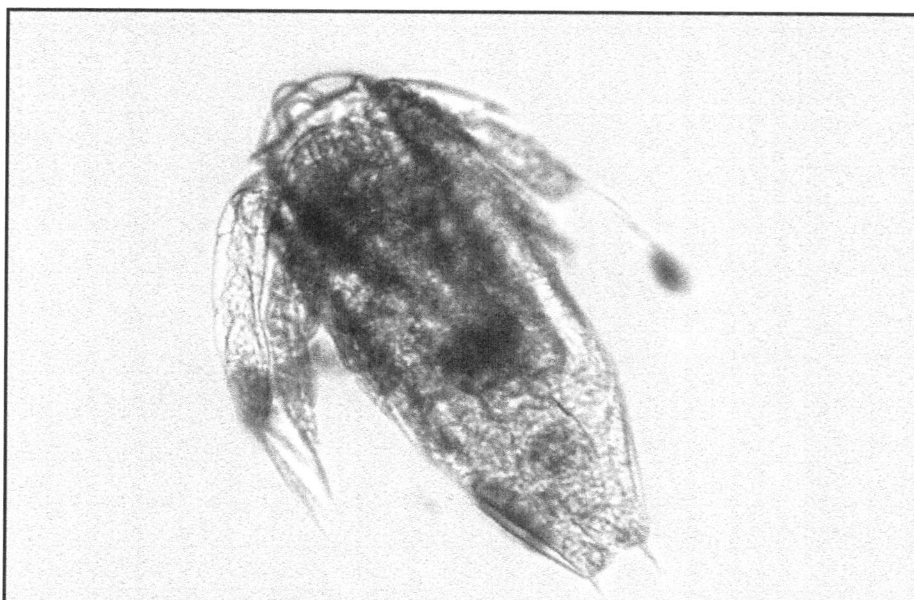

Mesocyclops Sp.

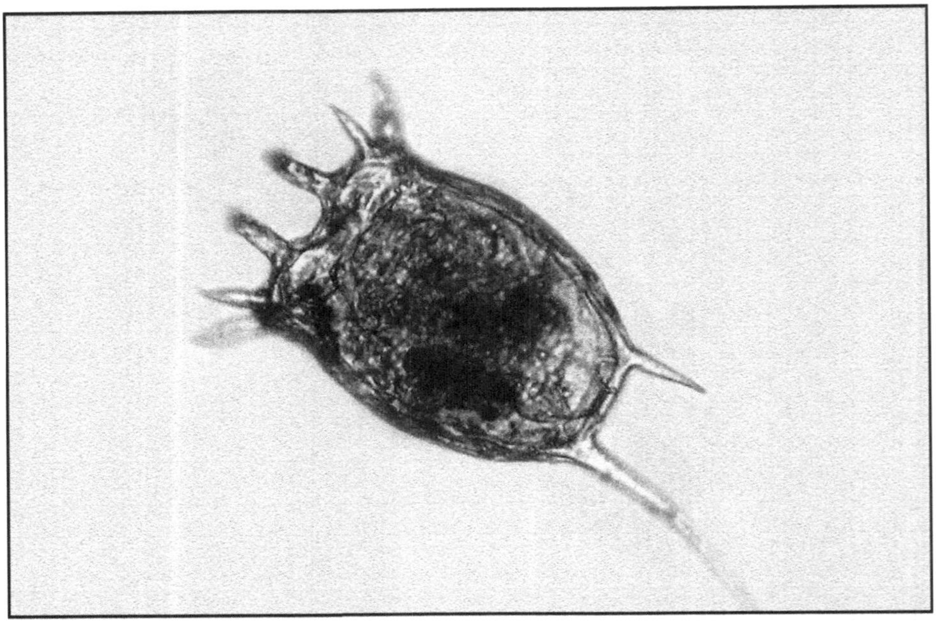

Keratella tropica

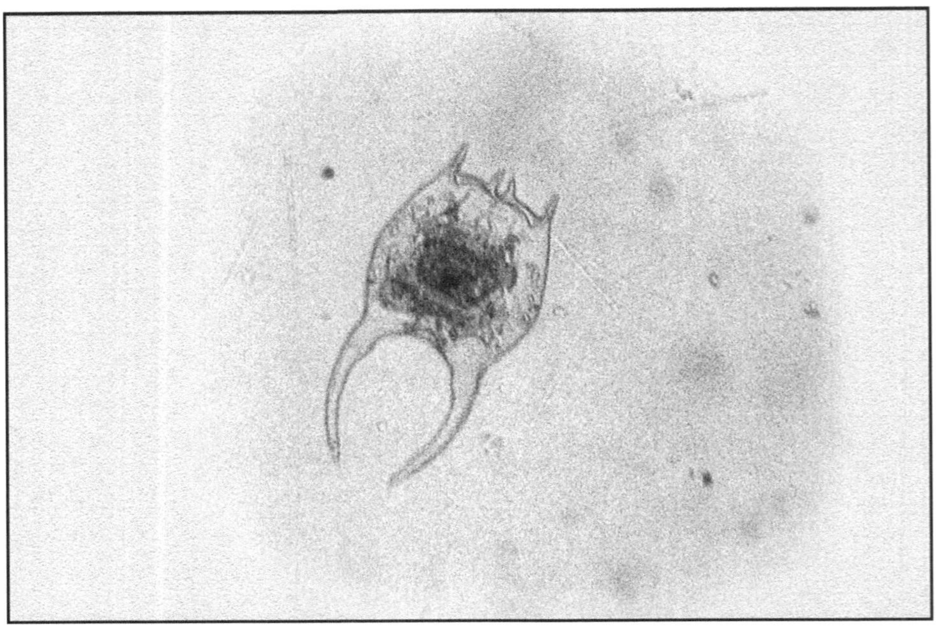

Brachionus caudatus

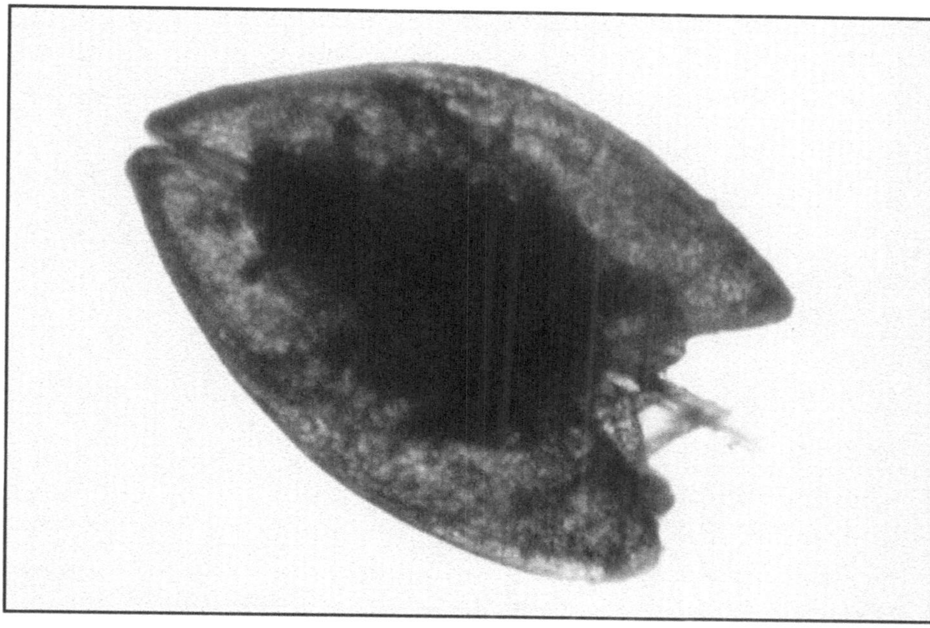

Eucypris Sp.

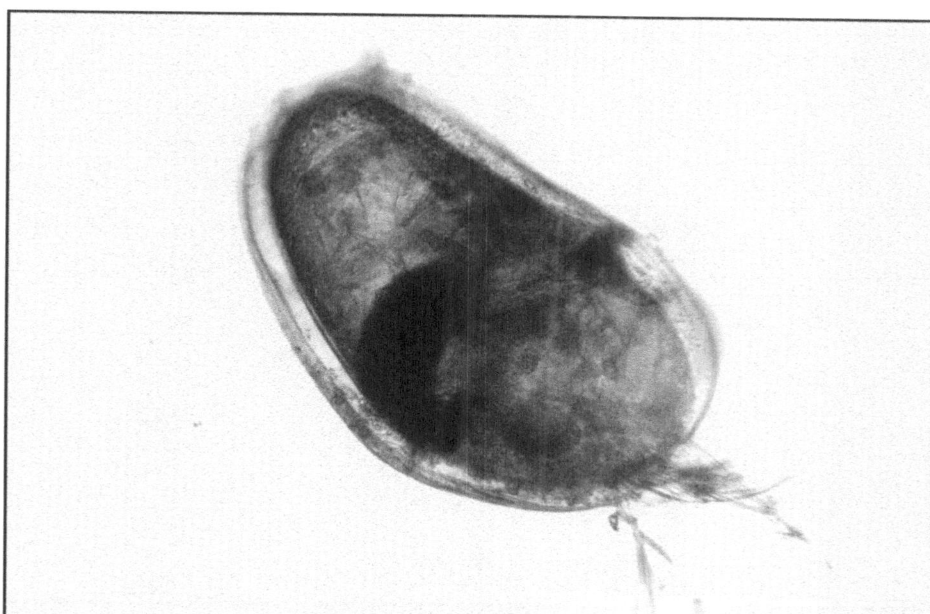

Stenocypris major

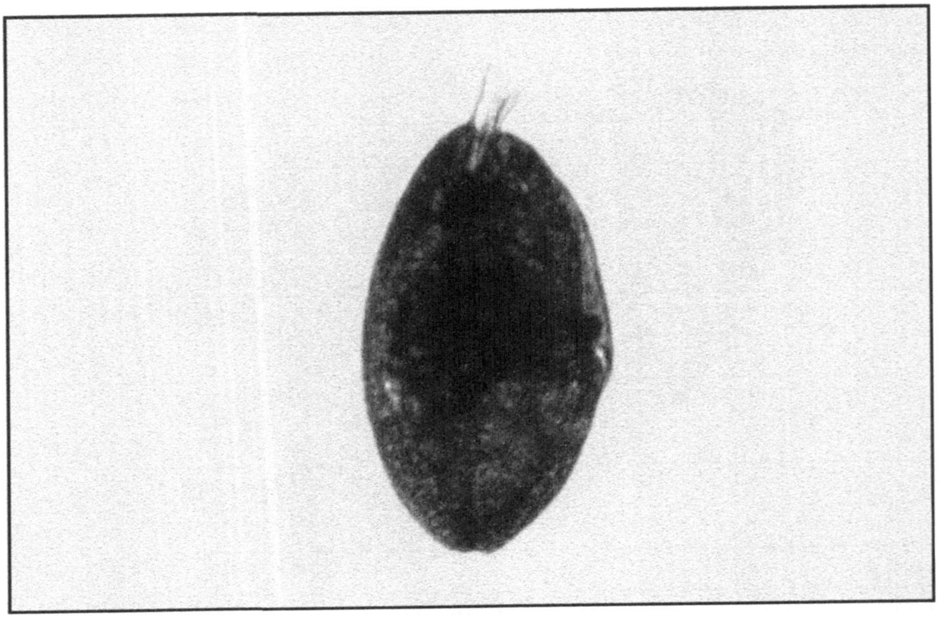

Eucypris pigra

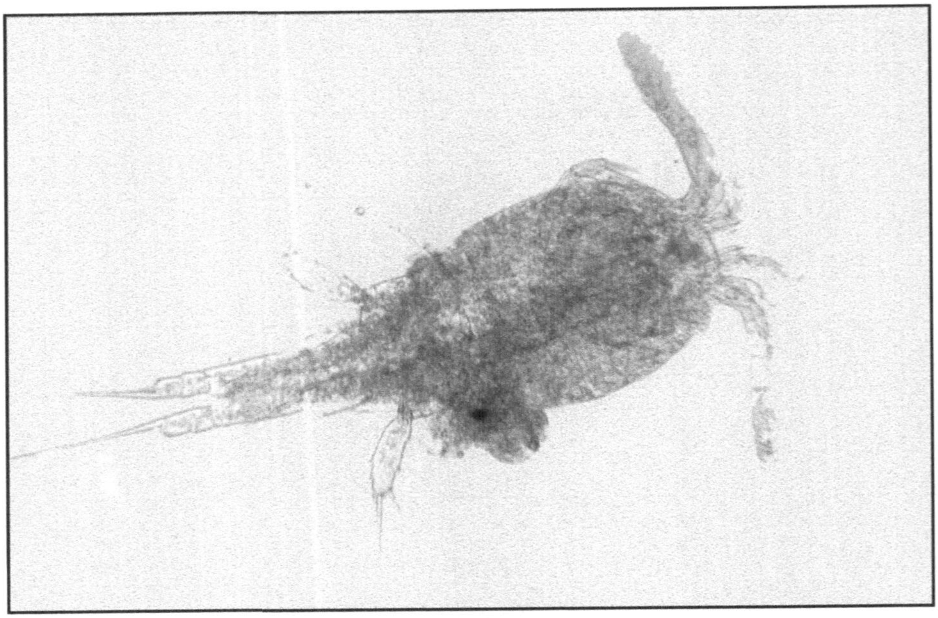

Tropocyclops pransinus

In wan reservoir during 2009-11, chlorophyceae included *Chlorella vulgaris, Pediastrum* spp., and *Scendesmus armatus* dominated the reservoir. The maximum population of chlorophyceae was recorded in April (9855 l^{-1}). From cyanophyceae *Oscillatoria* spp., and *Microcystis aeurogenose* dominated the reservoir. This group attained a highest peak in summer, with maxima in May (6545 l^{-1}). Among bacillariophyceae *Navicula* spp., *Synedra affinis* and *Bacillaria paradoxa* dominated the reservoir. Their population was maximum (4820 l^{-1}) in July. The maximum population of bacillariophyceae in rainy season may be due to the inflow of water inside the reservoir. Euglenophyceae was represented by 3 species. *Euglena* spp., increased in number in summer season. The maximum population of euglenophyceae was recorded in May (2110 l^{-1}).

In Borna reservoir during 2009-11, chlorophyceae included *Chlorella vulgaris, Pediastrum spp.,* and *Scendesmus armatus.* The maximum population of chlorophyceae was recorded in April (8287 l^{-1}). Among cyanophyceae *Oscillatoria* spp., and *Microcystis aeurogenose* dominated the reservoir. This group attained a highest peak in summer, with maxima in May (7942 l^{-1}). Among bacillariophyceae *Navicula spp., Synedra affinis* and *Bacillaria paradoxa* dominated the reservoir. Their population was maximum in July. The maximum population of bacillariophyceae in rainy season may be due to the inflow of water inside the reservoir. Euglenophyceae was represented by 3 species. *Eugela* spp increased in number in summer season. The maximum population of euglenophyceae was recorded in May (2242 l^{-1}).

Table 12.8: List of Phytoplanktons in Wan and Borna Reservoirs

Chlorophyceae:	*Ulothrix zonata, Zygnema sp., Pediastrum duplex, Pediastrum simplex, Scendesmus armatus, Oedogonium patulum, Ankistrodesmus falcatus, Chlorella valgoris, Cosmarium contractum, Closterium limneticum*
Cyanophyceae:	*Oscillatoria chlorine, Oscillatoria limnosa, Anabaena constricta, Merismopedia punctata, Microcystis aerugenose*
Bacillariophyceae:	*Navicula gracilis, Navicula viridula, Nitzschia subtilis, Bacillaria paradoxa, Diatoms vuloare, Synedra affinis*
Euglenophyceae:	*Eugelna stellata, Euglena viridis, Euglena pisciformis*

Discussion

Zooplankton Diversity

In present study, the zooplankton community was represented by four groups namely: *Rotifera, Cladocera, Copepoda,* and *Ostracoda.*

Present study has revealed 8 species of rotifers, 6 species of cladocera, 5 species of copepods and 3 species of ostracoda from each reservoir.

Rotifers are fresh water zooplanktons. Approximately, 1700 species of rotifers have been recorded from all over the world. Nearly 250 species are known from India. Notable Contribution to our knowledge of rotiferan fauna has been made by Pennak (1953).

Table 12.9: Plankton Groups and their Composition in Wan Reservoir (year 2009-11)

Groups	Range (Units l^{-1})	Average (%)
Chlorophyceae	6870-9855	8054 (34.02)
Cyanophyceae	4250-6545	5340 (32.03)
Bacillariophyceae	1965-4820	3137 (10.00)
Euglenophyceae	1230-2110	1603 (7.00)
Phytoplankton		18134 (83.05)
Rotifers	41-265	125.83 (7.12)
Cladocerans	14-164	65.16 (3.20)
Copepods	28-155	75.70 (4.06)
Ostracods	05-79	42.12 (2.56)
Zooplankton		3701 (16.94)
Total Plankton		21835

Table 12.10: Plankton Groups and their Composition in Borna Reservoir (Year 2009-11)

Groups	Range (Units l^{-1})	Average (%)
Chlorophyceae	6052-8287	7107 (35.05)
Cyanophyceae	4550-7942	6204 (31.07)
Bacillariophyceae	1984-3890	2953 (8.02)
Euglenophyceae	1270-2242	1853 (7.93)
Phytoplankton		18117 (83.33)
Rotifers	21-224	124.33 (6.90)
Cladocerans	08-181	68.62 (3.88)
Copepods	12-149	68.29 (3.80)
Ostracods	02-78	40.70 (2.8)
Zooplankton		3623 (16.66)
Total Plankton		21740

In the present study, eight species of Rotifers were recorded from Wan and Borna reservoirs. Genus *Brachionus* was reported by 3 species, followed by: *keratella* (two species), and *Trichocera, Filina* and *Lecane* comprises one species of each. Dominance of Rotifers was also reported by Norgeira (2001), Cavalli *et at.* (2001), Sampaio *et al.* (2002), Neves *et al.* (2003).

The numerical variation in peak periods of different group of zooplankton might be due to different biological parameters. In Wan reservoir rotifers were found dominant over the other groups. More density of rotifers is due to their special characters such as: less specialized feeding high fecundity and frequent parthenogenic reproduction.

Sakhare (2007) recorded 8 species of rotifers, 6 species of cladoerans, 7 species of copepods and 4 species of ostracods from Yeldari reservoir in Maharashtra. Deshmukh (2001) and Sakhare (2007) reported maximum rotifers in summer season, which corroborate with the present investigation.

Rajashekhar *et al.* (2010) studied seasonal variation of zooplankton from Khaji kotnar reservoir in Gulbarga district of Karnataka and reported 24 species of zooplankton, they also observed rotifers as dominant group throughout the study period and highest count was recorded in the summer season while low incidence was observed in southwest monsoon season.

Renuga and Ramanibai (2010) studied the zooplanktonic community of Krishnagiri reservoir in Tamil Nadu and recorded 23 species of zooplankton belonging to 4 groups *i.e.*, rotifer, cladocera, copepod and ostracoda. Rotifera represented by 8 species, cladocera represented by 5 species, copepod by 6 species and ostracoda by 4 species.

Pathak and Mudgal (2004) observed five genera of rotifers, three genera of cladocerans and ostracodans and two genera each in respect of protozoans and Copepods from Visla reservoir of Madhya Pradesh.

Cladocera are the freshwater zooplanktonic forms inhabiting almost all the niches of the fresh water bodies. They are found more in the lentic environment than in the lotic waters such as: dams, lakes, tanks and ponds. The greater significance of cladocera in the aquatic food chain as food for both young and adult fish was emphasized much earlier (Pennak, 1978). The stomach content of young fish has 1 to 95 per cent cladocera by volume (Sharma, 1991).

About 6000 species of freshwater cladocerans occur through the world (Korovchinsky, 1996) of which 110 species have been recorded from India (Patil and Goudar, 1989). Pandit *et al.* (2007) observed *Ceriodaphina cornuta, Bosminopsis dietersi, Biapertura karua* and *Alona pulchella* in Pravara river near Sangamner, Maharashtra. Population density of cladocerans in different water bodies have been reported by Rao and Muley (1981), Kaushik and Sharma (1994), Murugan *et al.* (1998), Mathew (1985) and Battish and Kumari (1986).

During present investigation cladocera was represented by: *Ceriodaphnia sp, Diaphanosoma* sp, *Moina* sp., *Alona* sp., and *Indialona* sp. The maximum population of cladocera was recorded in April 2008. Devi (1997) reported the maximum cladocerans population during postmonsoon and premonsoon in Ibrahimbagh and premonsoon and post monsoon in Shathamraj reservoir of Hyderabad.

Presence of lower water level in summer, remains of dead and decaying vegetation as well as burnt and half burnt dead bodies which result into the increase of organic matter and growth of bacteria population. It increased the zooplankton population (Bohra and Kumar, 2004).

Sakhare (2007) accounted plankton diversity in Yeldari reservoir in which cladocera was represented by seven species. The similar species were also recorded during present investigation.

Copepoda constitute one of the major zooplankton communities occurring in all types of water bodies and ranging from free living to parasitic forms. They serve as food to several fishes and play a major role in ecological pyramids. Free living copepods are an essential link in food chain occupying the intermediate trophic level between bacteria, algae and protozoa on one hand and small and large plankton predators on the other.

About 120 species of the free living freshwater copepods are known from India (Uttangi, 2001). Our present knowledge of the copepod fauna of India, is based on the studies from West Bengal (Gurney, 1934, Sewell, 1919, 1934); Lahore (Arora, 1931); Kashmir, Ladakh and Nilgiri hills (Kiefer, 1939, Uttangi, 2001, Sunkad and Patil, 2002, Kudari and Kanamadi, 2005).

In the present study, five species of Copepods documented in Wan and Borna reservoirs namely, *Cyclops sp.*, *Mesocyclops* sp., *Diaptomus* sp., and *Phylladiaptomus* sp. Patil and Goudar (1982, 1989) also reported seven species form Dharwad district; Kudari *et al.* (2005) also reported six species of Copepods from Shiggaon and Hanagal taluk of Haveri district.

Ostracoda are small crustaceans having the bivalve carapace enclosing the laterally compressed body. They inhabit all kinds of freshwater and marine water environments. The freshwater ostracods occur in lakes, ponds, pools, swamps, streams and even polluted waters. Majority of them are free living and few are commensals on the gills of cray fishes and in the intestine of fishes and amphibians. About 1700 species of ostracods of which about 550 species inhabit freshwater, have been recorded from various parts of the world. Approximately, 100 species are known from the inland water bodies of the Indian subcontinent.

In the present study among ostracods *Cypris obensa, Cyclocypris globosa* and *Candocypria osborni* species were recorded. In present study higher population of ostracods was recorded during pre monsoon. This is in confirmation with the findings of Chandrasekhar (1996).

According to Harshey *et al.* (1987) ostracods grow well in hard water. Hujare (2005) has reported absence of any seasonal trend in ostracods.

In the present study, the rotifera was the dominant group of zooplankton in both the reservoirs (8 Species). Maximum number of Rotifers occurred during summer indicating the influence of temperature. Similar observations were also made by Singh (2000). Rotifers respond more quickly to environmental changes than crustacean plankton and appear to be more sensitive indicators of change in water.

It is remarkable that the rotifera population was the most abundant group in both reservoirs followed by: cladocera, copepoda and ostracoda. Quantitatively also rotifera dominated over other groups and contributed as much as (38%) of the total zooplankton population. In both reservoirs, rotifera population was most abundant during summer months. Devika *et al.* (2006) also recorded high population during summer and suggested that this might be due to physical rather than chemical conditions in which the water temperature and transparency had a direct relationship with phytoplankton and zooplankton population.

The phytoplankton in a reservoir is an important biological indicator of the water quality. While phytoplankton are important primary producers and the basis of the food chain in open water, some species on the other hand can be harmful to human and other vertebrates by releasing toxic substances (hepatotoxins or neurotoxins etc.,) into the water. Proliferation of harmful organisms, particularly species should be monitored. Phytoplankton studies and monitoring are useful for control of the physico-chemical and biological conditions of the water in any irrigation project. Therefore certain groups of phytoplankton, especially blue green algae, can degrade recreational value of surface water, particularly thick surface scum, which reduces the use of amenities for contact sports, or large concentrations, which cause deoxygenation of the water leading to fish death (Whitton and Patts, 2000). Over the last few decades, there has been much interest in the processes influencing the development of phytoplankton communities, primarily in relation to physico-chemical factors (Akbay *et al.* 1999; Peerapornpisal *et al.* 1999; Elliott *et al.* 2002).

In India, many hydrobiologists have carried out a considerable amount of research on seasonal succession, production, phytoplankton abundance and the variations in the different freshwater ecosystems.

Sharma (2009) recorded 75 species of phytoplankton belonging to six groups from Loktak Lake in Manipur.

Sharma and Lyngdoh (2003) studied abundance and ecology of net and phytoplankton of a subtropical reservoir of Meghalaya (N.E. India).

Harilal (2005) recorded 23 genera of phytoplankton from Neyyar and 20 from Karamana river of Kerala. Members of chlorophyceae were found to predominate in two rivers.

Ayoade *et al.* (2009) recorded 32 genera of phytoplankton from Tehri dam.

In present investigation the phytoplanktons in Wan reservoir constituted 83.05 per cent of the total planktons and the zooplanktons was recorded at 16.94 per cent of the total planktons, while the phytoplanktons in Borna reservoir constituted 83.33 per cent and the zooplanktons was recorded at 16.66 per cent of the total planktons. Sugunan and Yadava (1991b) reported 96.41 per cent of phytoplankton and 3.59 per cent of zooplankton in the Nongmahir reservoir of Meghalaya. In Yeldari reservoir Sakhare (2007) recorded 84.03 per cent phytoplankton and 15.97 per cent zooplankton.

Tiwari and Chauhan (2006) observed maximum population of chlorophyceae in winter season. As compared to other classes of phytoplankton, the members of euglenoid were recorded least in number. The maximum population of euglenoids was recorded in winter.

The present study revealed that both the reservoirs support a rich diversity of planktons and are suitable for fish and fisheries.

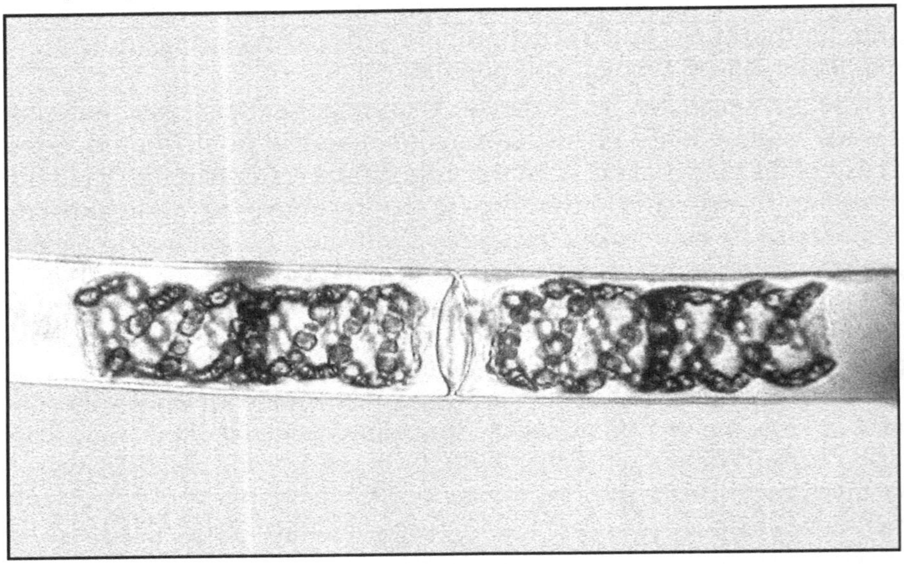

Spirogyra Sp.

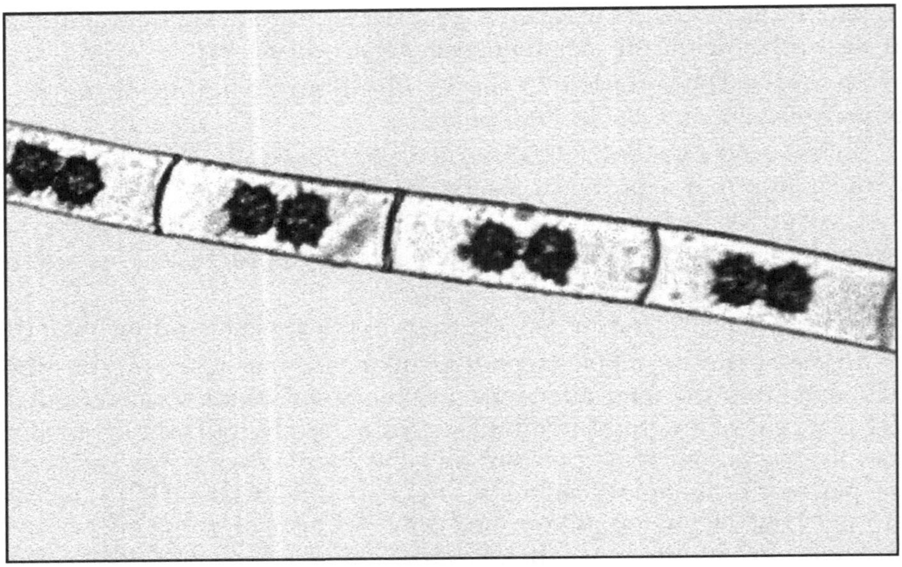

Zygnema excompressum

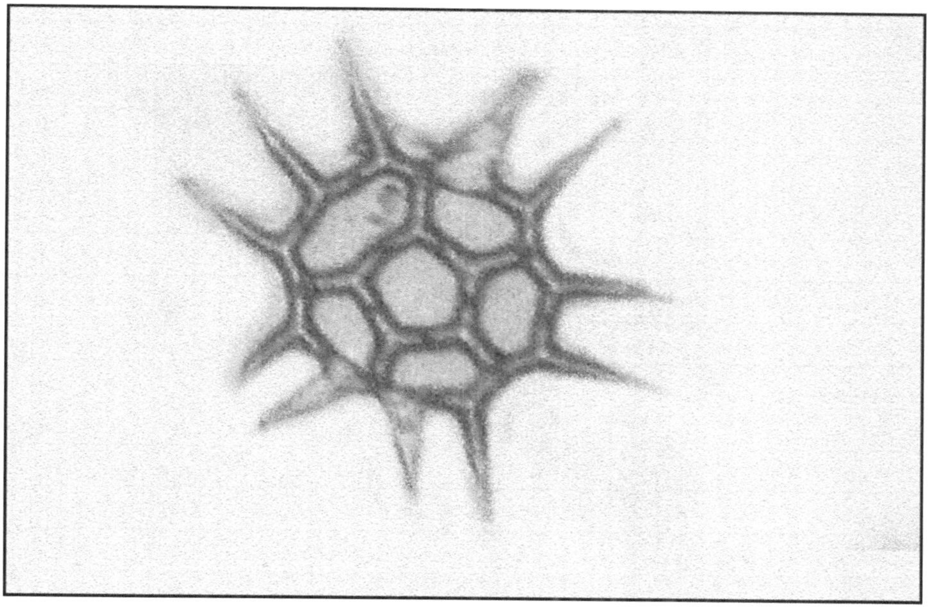

Pediastrum Simplex

Pediastrum Sp.

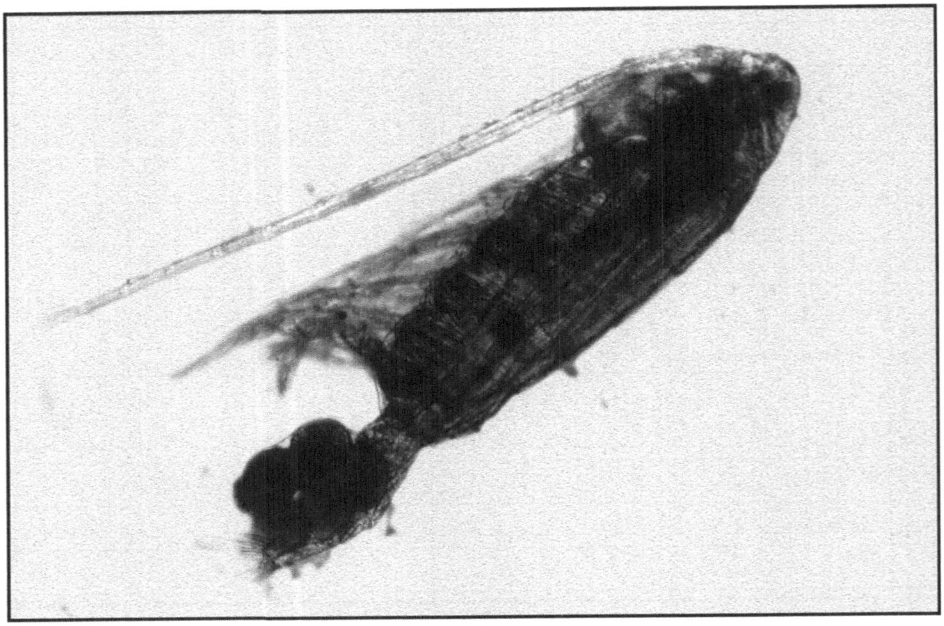

Cyclops Sp.

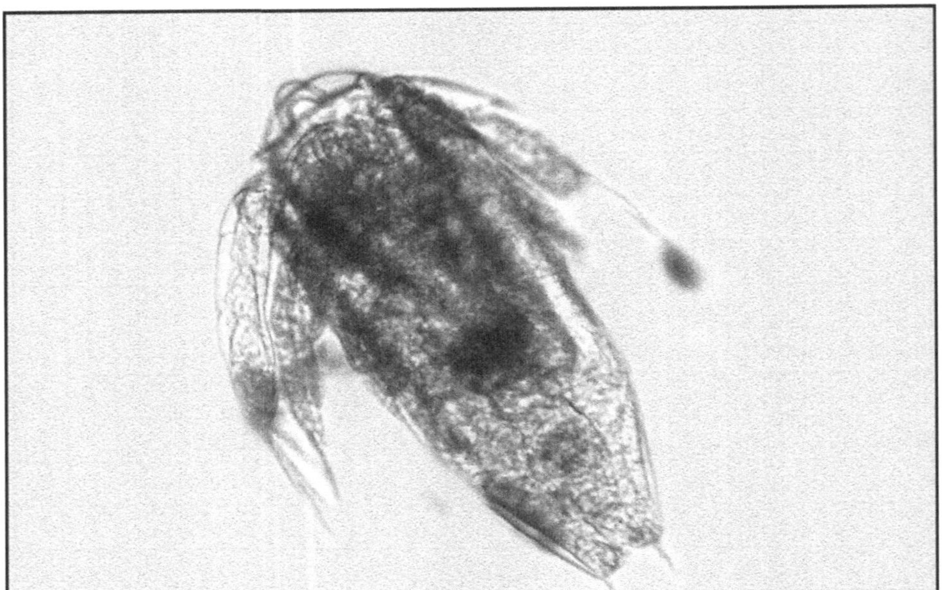

Mesocyclops Sp.

REFERENCES

Akbay, N., Anul, N., Yerti, S., Soyupak, S. and Yurteri, C. (1999). Seasonal Distribution of Large Phytoplankton in Keban dam Reservoir. *Plank. Res.*, 21(4): 771-787.

Arora, G. L., (1931). Entomostraces (water fleas) of Lahore. *Bull. Dept. Zool. Pb. Univ.*, Lahore 1: 61-100.

Ayoade, A.A., Agarwal, N.K. and Chandda Saklani, A. (2009). Changes in Physico-chemical Features and Plankton of two Regulated High Altitude Rivers Garhwal Himalaya, India. *European Journal of Scientific Research.* 27(1):77-92.

Bahura, C.K. (2001). Phytoplanktonic Community of a Highly Eutrophicated Temple Tank, Bikaner, Rajasthan. *J. Aqua. Biol.* 16 (1&2): 1-4.

Battish S.K. (1992). Freshwater Zooplankton of India. Oxford and IBH Publishing Co. Pvt. Ltd. New Delhi.

Battish, S.K. and Parminder Kumari. (1986). Effect of Physic-chemical Factors on the Seasonal Abundance of Cladocera in Typical Pond at Village of Raqba, Ludhiana. *Indian Ecol.* 13(1):146-151.

Bays J. S. and T.L. Crisman. (1983). Zooplankton and Trophic State Relationships in Florida lakes. *Can. J. Fish. Aquat. Sci.* 40:1813-1819.

Beaugrand G, F. Ibanez and P.C. Reid. (2000). Spatial, Seasonal and Long-term Fluctuations of Plankton in Relation to Hydroclimatic Features in the English channel, Celtic Sea and Bay of Biscay, Marine Ecology Progress Series 200, pp. 93-102.

Beaver, J. R. and Crisman T.L. (1990). Use of Micro-zooplankton As An Early Indicator of Advancing Cultural Eutrophication. *Verh. Internat. Verein. Limnol.* 24: 532-537.

Beyst B, D. Buysse, A. Dewicke and J. Mees. (2001). Surf zone Hyperbenthos of Belgian Sandy Beaches: Seasonal Patterns. *Estuarine, Coastal and Shelf Science.* 53: 877-895.

Birge, E.A. (1918). The Water Fleas (Cladocera). H.B. Ward and G.C. Whipple, Eds. Freshwater Biology (New York, John Wiley Sons), 22:676-740.

Bohara Chandan, and Arvind Kumar. (2004). Plankton Diversity in the Wetland of Tharkjhand. In: Arvind Kumar (eds.), Biodiversity and Environment. A.P.H. Publishing Crop, New Delhi, pp. 91-123.

Cairns J, P.V. McCormick and B.R. Niederlehner. (1993). A Proposed Framework for Developing Indicators of Ecosystem Health. *Hydrobiol.* 263:1-44.

Canfield T. J. and J.R. Jones. (1996). Zooplankton Abundance, Biomass, and Size Distribution in Selected Midwestern Waterbodies and Relation with Trophic State, *J. Freshwat. Ecol.* 11: 171-181.

Carter J. C. H., M.J. Dadswell, J.C. Roff and W.G. Sprules. (1980). Distribution and Zoogeography of Planktonic Crustaceans and Dipterans in Glaciated Eastern North America. *Can. J. Zool.* 58: 1355-1387.

Cavalli L.,A. Miqulies and R. Chappaz. (2001). Combined Effects of Environmental Factors and Predatory Prey Interactions on Zooplankton Assemblages in Five High Alpine Lakes. Hydrobiologia. 455(1-3): 127-135.

Chakrapani, B. K., M.B. Krishna and T.S. Srinivasa. (1996). A Report on the Water Quality, Plankton and Bird Populations of the Lakes in and Around Bangalore and Maddur, Karnataka, India. Department of Ecology and Environment, Government of Karnataka. http://wgbis.ces.iisc.ernet.in/energy/water/paper/Tr-115/ref.htm.

Chandrasekhar, S.V.A. (1996). Ecological Studies on Saroornagar Lake, Hyderabad. Thesis Submitted to Osmania University for the Degree of Doctor of Philosophy, October 1996.

Christou E.D. (1998). Interannual Variability of Copepods in a Mediterranean Coastal Area (Saronikos Gulf, Aegean Sea). *Journal of Marine Systems*. 15: 523-532.

Daday, E. (1911). Egg uj cladocera taj keletindiabol. Allattani kozlemenyek, 10:63-68;110-112.

Deshmukh, U.S. (2001). Ecological Studies of Chhatri Lake, Amravati; with Special Reference to Planktons and Productivity. Ph.D. thesis, Amravati University, Amravati.

Devi, Sarla, B. (1997). Present Status, Potentialities, Management and Economics of Fisheries of Two Minor Reservoirs of Hydrabad. Ph.D. thesis, Osmania University, Hyderabad.

Devika, R., A. Rajendran and P. Selvapathy. (2006). Variation Studies on the Physico-chemical and Biological Characteristics at Different Depths in Model Waste Stabilsation Tank. *Poll. Res.*, 24, 771-774.

Dhanapathi, M.V.S.S.S. (2000). Taxonomic Notes on the Rotifers from India (from 1889-2000). Indian Association of Aquatic Biologists, Publ. No. 10.

Dhavale, S.D., Lakde, H.M. and Lohare, S.D. (2009). Studies on Algal Flora and Physico-chemical Characteristics of Shikara Reservoir in Nanded District, Maharashtra. *Ecology and Fisheries*. 2 (2): 69-72.

Edmondson, W.T. (1959). Rotifera, pp. 420-494. In: Freshwater Biology (eds. H.B. Ward and G.C. Whipple). (2nd edition, W.T. Edmondson ed.) John Wiley and Sons. Inc. New York, 1248pp.

Elliott, J.A., Irish, A.E. and Reynolds, C.S. (2002). Predicting the Spatial Dominance of Phytoplankton in Light Limited and Incompletely Mixed eutrophic Water Column using the PROTECH Model. Fresh. Bio. 47: 433-440.

Escribano R and P. Hidalgo. (2000). Spatial Distribution of Copepods in the North of the Humboldt Current Region off Chile during Coastal Upwelling. *Journal of the Marine Biological Association of the United Kingdom*. 80:283-290.

Fuller D. R., R.S. Stemberger and J.E. Gannon. (1977). Limnetic Rotifers as Indicators of Trophic Change. *J. Elisha Mitchell. Sci. Soc.* 93:104-113.

Gannon J.E. and R.S. Stemberger. (1978). Zooplankton (Especially Crustaceans and Rotifers) as Indicators of Water Quality, *Trans. Am. Micros. Soc.* 97:16-35.

Goel P.K. and Autade, V.B. (1995). Ecological Studies on the River Panchganga at Kolhapur with Emphasis on Biological Components. In: Recent Researches in Aquatic Environment, (eds. Ashutosh Gautam and N.K. Agarwal), pp. 25-46, Daya Publishing House, New Delhi.

Gurney, R. (1934). The Development of Rhin-calunus. *Discovery Rcpt.*, 9: 207-214.

Harilal, C.C. (2005). Phytoplankton Diversity of Two Rivers of Kerala with Special Reference to Aquatic Nutrients. *Poll. Res.* 24 (4):773-776.

Harshey, D.K., Shrivastav, A.K. and Patil, S.G. (1987). Studies on the Ecology of Freshwater ostracoda. Part II. Population Ecology in Balsagar Tank, Jabalpur, M.P., India. *J. Curr. Biosci.* 4 (4):127-134.

Hellawell J.M. (1986). Biological Indicators of Freshwater Pollution and Environmental Management. In Pollution Monitoring Series. Elsevier Applied Science Publishers, London, UK (p 546).

Hosmani, S.P. and Bharthi, S.G. (1980). Limnological Studies in Ponds and Lakes of Dharwar. Comparative Phytoplankton Ecology of Four Water Bodies. Phycos. 19 (1): 27-43.

Hujare, M.S. (2005). Hydrobiological Studies on some Water Reservoirs of Hatkanangale Tahsil (Maharashtra). Ph.D. Thesis, Shivaji University, Kolhapur.

Hutchinson G.E. (1957). A Treatise on Limnology Vol. I Geography.

Jhingran, V.G. (1974). Fish and Fisheries of India, Hindustan Publishing Corpoaration, New Delhi.

Kalff, J. (2002). Limnology: Inland Water Ecosystems, Prentice Hall Publications. New Jersey, USA.

Kaushik, S. and Sharma, N. (1994). Physico-chemical Characteristics and Zooplankton Population of A Perennial Tank, Matsya Sarowar, Gwalior. *Environment and Ecology*. 12 (2): 429-434.

Khare, P.K. (1999). Phytoplankton as Indicators of Water Quality and Pollution Status of Jagat Sagar Pond, Chattarpur (M.P.). *Geobios New Reports*. 18(2):107-110.

Kiefer, F. (1939). Freilebende Ruderfusskrebse (Crustacea Copepoda) aus Nordwest und Sudindien (Pandschab, Kashmir, Ladak, Nilgirigebirge). Memoirs of the Indian Museum. 13 (2): 83-202.

Korovchinsky, N.M. (1996). How Many Species of Cladocera are there? *Hydrobiologia*. 321:191-204.

Kudari, V.A. Kadadevaru G.G. and Kanamadi R.D. (2005). Limnological Studies of Attriveri and Bachanki Reserviors of Uttar Kannada District, Karnataka (India) *Ecol. Environ and Conservation*.

Li M, A. Gargett and K. Denman. (2000). What Determines Seasonal and Interannual Variability of Phytoplankton and Zooplankton in Strongly Estuarine Systems? Application to the Semi-enclosed Estuary of Strait of Georgia and Juan de Fuca Strait. Estuarine, Coastal and Shelf Science 50: 467-488.

Mahajan, C.L.1981. Zooplankton as Indicators for Assessment of Water Pollution, Paper Presented at WHO Workshop on Biological Indicators and Indices of Environmental Pollution. Cent. Bd. Prev. Cont. Poll/Osm. Univ, Hyderabad, India.

Mathew, P.M. (1985). Seasonal Trends in the Fluctuations of Plankton and Physic-chemical Factors in a Tropical Lake (Govindgarh Lake, M.P.) and their Inter-relationship. *J. Inland Fish. Soc. India*. 17 (1&2):11-24.

Melack, I.M. (1979). Photosynthetic Rates in four Tropical Freshwaters. *Freshwater Biology*. 9:555-571.

Meshram, C.B. and Dhande. (2000). Algal Diversity with Respect to Pollution Status of Wadali Lake, Amravati, Maharashtra, India. *Jr. Aqua. Biol*. 15 (1&2): 1-5.

Michael R.G. (1973). A Guide to the Study of Freshwater Organisms, *Madurai Univ. J. Suppl.* (Ed.) 1:186 pp.

Mills, E.L., and A. Schiavone, Jr. (1982). Evaluation of Fish Communities through Assessment of Zooplankton Populations and Measures of Lake Productivity. *North American Journal of Fisheries Management* 2:14-27.

Mohite, J.S. and Joshi, P.K. (2009). Phytoplankton Diversity in Ramdara Reservoir Near Tuljapur, Maharashtra. *Ecology and Fisheries*. 2 (2): 67-68.

More, Y.S. and S.N. Nandan. (2000). Hydrbiological Study of Algae of Panzara River (Maharashtra). *Ecol. Env. and Cons*. 6 (1): 99-103.

Murugan, N., Murugavel, P. and Kodarkar, M.S. (1998). Cladocera (The Biology, Classification, Identification and Ecology), Publication No. 5, Indian Association of Aquatic Biologists, Hyderabad.

Nandan, S.N. and Ansari Ziya. (1999). Ecological Study of Algae from Mausam River Flowing through Malegaon City (Maharashtra). BRI'S JAST. 11 (1):31-38.

Nandan, S.N. and Jain, D.S. (2005). Study of Algae Tolering Organic Pollution of Sonvad dam and Devbhane dam of Maharashtra. In: *Advances in Limnology* (Ed.S.R. Mishra, Daya Publishing House, Delhi, pp. 214-222.

Nandan, S.N. and Patel, R.J. (1985). Seasonal Variations of Phytoplankton in the Vishwamitri River, Baroda. In: Advances in Applied Phycology (Eds. A.C. Shukla and S.N. Pandey), pp. 262-269.

Nasare, P.N., Wadhave, N.S., Harney, N.V. and Sitre, S.R. (2009). Studies on Phytoplankton Diversity of Vinjasan lake in Bhadrawati Town of Chandrapur District, Maharashtra. *Ecology and Fisheries*. 2 (1):95-100.

Neves, I.F. O Rocha K.F. roche and A. A. Pinto. (2003). Zooplankton Community Structure of Two Marginal Lakes of the River Cuiaba (Mato Grasso, Brazil) with Analysis of Rotifers and Cladocera diversity Braz. *J. Biol*. 63(3): 329-343.

Nogueira, M.G. (2001). Zooplankton Composition Dominance and Abundance as Indicators of Environmental Compartmentalization in Jurumirim Reservoir (Paranapanema River), Sao Paulo, Brazil, Hydrobiologia 455:1-18.

Pace, M.J. (1986). An Empirical Analysis of Zooplankton Community Size Structure Across Lake Trophic Gradients, *Limnol. Oceanogr*. 31: 45-55.

Pandit, S.V., Vaidya, V.V. and Joshi, P.P. (2007). Studies on Zooplankton Diversity of Pravara River, Near Sangamner Dist. Ahmednagar, M.S. *J. Aqua. Biol*. 22 (1):33-38.

Pathak, S.K. and Mudgal, L.K. (2004). Biodversity of Zooplankton of Virla Reservoir Khargone (M.P.), India, pp. 317-321. In: Arvind Kumar (ed.). Biodiversity and Environment, A.P.H. Publishing Corporation, New Delhi.

Patil, C.S. and Gaudar, Y.Y.M. (1982). Fresh Water Copepods of Dharwad (Karnataka State, India) *J. Karnataka Uni. Sci*. 27: 130-141.

Patil C.S. and Gouder B.Y.M. (1989). Freshwater Invertebrates of Dharwad, Prasaranga, Karnatak University, Dharwad 222 pp.

Peerapornpisal, Y., Sonthichai, W., Somdee, T., Mulsin, P. and Rott, E. (1999). Water Quality and Phytoplankton in the Mae Kuang Udomtara Reservoir, Chiang Mai, Thailand. *J. Sci. Fac. Cmu*. 26(1): 25-43.

Pendse, D.C., Yogesh Shastri and V.P. Barhate. (2000). Hydrobiological Study of Percolation Tank of Village Dasne. *Ecol. Env. and Cons*. 6 (1): 93-97.

Pennak R.W. (1953). Freshwater Invertebrates of the United States. The Ronald Press, New York, USA.

Pennak, R.W. (1978). Freshwater Invertebrates of the United States. 2nd Edition, John Willey Sons, New York, 803 pp.

Pulle, J.S. and Khan, A.M. (2003). Phytoplanktonic Study of Isapur dam Water. *Eco. Env. Conser*. 9: 4-3-406.

Rajashekar, M., Vijaykumar K. and Zebra Paerveen. (2010). Seasonal Variations of Zooplankton Community in Freshwater Reservoir of Gulbarga District, Karnataka, South India. *International Journal of Systems Biology*. 2 (1):6-11.

Ranjan, Goutam, Singh, N.P. and Singh, R.B. (2007). Physico-chemical Characteristics of Ghariyarwa Pond of Birganj, Nepal in Relation to Growth of Phytoplankton. *Nature Environment and Pollution Technology*. 6 (4): 629-632.

Rao, K.S. and Choubey, Usha. (1993). Systematic and Ecological Studies on Central Indian Lentic Cladocera. In Prof. K.S. Rao (ed.). *Recent Advances in Freshwater Biology*. Vol. I. pp. 264-276.

Rao, M.B and Muley, E.V. (1981). Seasonal and Species of Zooplankton Organism and their Succession in Two Fresh Water Ponds at Waghuli , Poona. Proc. Symp. *Ecol Anim. Pool. Zool Surv*. India 2:63-64.

Rawson, D.S. (1956). Algal Indicators of Trophic Lake Types. *Limnol. Oceanogr.* 1:18-25pp.

Renuga K. and Ramnibai R. (2010). Zooplankton Composition Present in Krishnagiri Reservoir, Tamil Nadu, India. *Current Biotica*. 3 (4):519-522.

Roff J C, K. Middlebrook and F. Evans. (1988). Long-term Variability in North Sea Zooplankton off Northumberland Coast: Productivity of Small Copepods and Analysis of Trophic Interactions, *Journal of the Marine Biological Association of the United Kingdom.* 68: 143-164.

Saha, L.C. and Pandit, B. (1990). Dynamics of Primary Productivity between Lentic and Lotic Systems in Relation to Abiotic Factors. *J. Indian Bot. Soc.* 69:213-217.

Sakhare, V.B. and Joshi, P.K. (2002). Ecology of Palas-Nilegaon Reservoir in Osmanabad district, Maharashtra. *J. Aqua. Biol.* 18(2):17-22.

Sakhare V.B. and Joshi P.K. (2006). Plankton Diversity in Yeldari Reservoir, Maharashtra. *Fishing Chimes*. 25(12): 23-25.

Sakhare, V.B. (2007). Reservoir Fisheries and Limnology, Narendra Publishing House, Delhi, pp. 187.

Sampaio, E.V., Rocha O., Matsumura-Tundisi, T. and Tundisi, J.G. (2002). Composition and Abundance of Zooplankton in the Limnetic Zone of Seven Reservoirs of the Pranapanema River, Brazil. *J. Biol.* 62(2): 525-545.

Sewell, R.B.S. (1919). A Pre-liminary Note on some New Species of Copepoda. *Rec. Indian Mus.*, 16: 1-18.

Sewell, R.B.S. (1934). A Study of the Fauna of the Salt Lakes, Calcutta. *Rec. Indian Mus.*, 36: 45-121.

Sharma, B.K. (1991). Cladocera, pp. 205-223. In: Animal Resources of India: Protozoa to Mammalia: State of the Art. *Zoological Survey of India*, Calcutta.

Sharma, B.K. (2009). Composition, Abundance and Ecology of Phytoplankton Communities of Loktak Lake, Manipur, India. *Journal of Threatened Taxa*. 1(8):401-410.

Sharma, B.K. and Lyngdoh. (2003). Abundance and Ecology of Net and Phytoplankton of a Subtropical Reservoir of Meghalaya (N.E. India), *Ecology, Environment and Conservation*. 9 (4):497-503.

Shukla, S.C., Kant Rajani and Tripathi, B.D. (1989). Ecological Investigation on Physico-chemical Characteristics and Phytoplankton Productivity of River Ganga at Varanasi. *Geobios*. 16: 20-27.

Shurin, J. B., Havel, J.E., Leibold, M.A. and Alloul, B.P. (2000). Local and Regional Zooplankton Species Richness: A Scale-Independent Test for Saturation. *Ecology*. 81:3062-3073.

Singh, (1979). Limnological Studies on Suraha Lake (Ballia) II. The Periodicity of Phytoplankton. *J. Indian Bot. Soc.* 58: 31-329.

Singh, A.K. and Ahmed, S.H. (1990). A Comparative Study of the Phytoplankton of the River Ganga and Pond of Patna (Bihar), India. *J. Indian Bot. Soc.*, 69:153-158.

Singh D.N. (2000). Evaluation of Physico-chemical Parameters in Oxbow Lake *Geobios* 27: 120-124.

Singh, V.P. (1960). Phytoplankton Ecology of the Inland Waters of Uttar Pradesh. Proc. Symposium on Algology, ICAR, New Delhi.

Sivakumar, K. and Karuppasamy, R. (2008). Factors Affecting Productivity of Phytoplankton in a Reservoir of Tamil Nadu, *India. American – Eurasian Journal of Botany.* 1 (3):99-103.

Sprules, W.G. (1977). Crustacean Zooplankton Communities as Indicators of Limnological Conditions: An Approach using Principal Component Analysis. *J. Fish. Res. Board Can.* 34: 962-975.

Sprules, W.G, Munawar, M. and Jin, E.H. (1988). Plankton Community Structure and size Spectra in the Georgian Bay and North Channel Ecosystems. *Hydrobiologia.* 163: 135-140.

Sreenivasan, A. (1964). The Limnology, Primary Production, and Fish Production on a Tropical Pond. Limnol. Oceanogr. 9(4): 391-396.

Sreenivasan, A. (1968). The Limnology and Fish Production in two Ponds in Chinglepat (Madras). *Hydrobiol.* 32: 131-144.

Sugunan, V.V. (1980). Seasonal Fluctuations of Plankton of Nagarjunasagar Reservoir, A.P., India. *J. Inland Fish. Soc. India.* 12 (1):79-91.

Sugunan, V.V. and Yadava, Y.S. (1991b). Feasibility Studies for Fisheries Development of Nongamahir Reservoir, CIFRI, Barrackpore, pp. 30.

Sunkad, B.N. and Patil, H.S. (2002). Biodiversity of Rotifers in Fort Lake of Belgaum city North Karnataka. Was Presented at a National Symposium on Conservation, Restoration and Management of Aquatic Ecosystem (Dec 9-13). Organised *by CES, IISc,* Bangalore.

Tiwari, Ashesh and Chauhan, S.V.S. (2006). Seasonal Phytoplanktonic Diversity of Kitham Lake, Agra. *J. Environ. Biol.* 27 (1):35-38.

Uttangi, J.C. (2001). Conservation and Management Strategy for the Water Fowls of Minor Irrigation Tank Habits and their Importance as Stopover site in Dharwad Dist. In: Hosetti, Venkatsehwarlu (Eds.). Trends in Wildlife and Management, Daya Publishing House, Delhi, pp. 179-221.

Welch, P.S. (1952). Limnology II edition McGraw Hill Book Co. New York.

Whitton, B.A. and Patts, M. (2000). The Ecology of cyanobacteria. Kluwer Academic Publishers, Netherlands.

Yazdandoost, M.Y. and Katdare, M.S. (2000). Study of the Population Density of Plankton with Respect to Physico-chemical Characteristics of Water in Pune Rivers-India. *Ecol. Env. and Cons.* 6(1): 127-135.

Index

****